Science and Religious Thought
A Darwinism Case Study

Studies in Religion, No. 3

Margaret R. Miles, Series Editor

Professor of Historical Theology
The Divinity School
Harvard University

Other Titles in This Series

Science and Religious Thought
A Darwinism Case Study

by
Walter J. Wilkins

U·M·I Research Press

Ann Arbor, Michigan

Produced and distributed by
UMI Research Press
an imprint of
University Microfilms, Inc.
Ann Arbor, Michigan 48106

Library of Congress Cataloging in Publication Data

Wilkins, Walter J., 1950-
Science and religious thought.

(Studies in religion ; no. 3)
Revision of the author's thesis (Ph.D.)—Florida State University, 1985.
Bibliography: p.
Includes index.
1. Religion and science—1946-   2. Evolution—Religious aspects.   3. Darwin, Charles, 1809-1882.
I. Title.   II. Series: Studies in religion (Ann Arbor, Mich.) ; no. 3.
BL263.W555   1987   213   86-24946
ISBN 0-8357-1778-X (alk. paper)

Contents

Preface

How can we discuss the presence and activity of God in a world whose processes are described by the sciences? That question has followed me around since my undergraduate days as a chemistry major and has been both the existential and the intellectual lure which has resulted in this study. After changing careers, studying theology in the Reformed tradition, and practicing ministry in several Presbyterian churches, I returned to graduate school to pursue that question in an interdisciplinary context where my understanding of the Christian tradition could be put in conversation with the culture in which it exists, especially the history and philosophy of modern science.

As I looked back on my experiences as a scientist, I became aware that religion could not be divorced from science since even scientists struggle with questions of the purpose and ultimate meaning of life. My training in theology, however, did little to engage the scientific side of me, or enable me to reflect on the interface between the two disciplines. That training did provide me with a perspective which recognized the historical continuity of much religious thought, and made me aware of the lack of such continuity in studies of the relationship between science and religious thought. As I further studied the secondary literature, I discovered a profusion of approaches to the relationship, but many seemed to miss the essential issues, create some strange juxtapositions of ideas, or not apply theoretical discussions to particular scientific theories. Very often, the problem seemed to be a lack of understanding of the scientific and philosophical issues at stake. This study reflects my desire to address those methodological issues in an interdisciplinary context, and suggest a possible way forward. I began my studies at the same time that my home state, Arkansas, was concluding a legal battle over the scientific and religious status of Darwinian evolution and creationism, and so Darwinism seemed an appropriate choice as a case study in science and religion.

Acknowledgments

Many people need to be thanked for their support and encouragement of this study. I express my thanks to Professor Margaret R. Miles of The Divinity School of Harvard University for "discovering" this work and inviting me to have it read for publication in a series which emphasizes works with current significance in their field and with methodological significance. Appreciation must also be expressed to the helpful comments which I received regarding the necessary revisions.

To Dean William M. Wilson and my colleagues and the students of Virginia Wesleyan College, many thanks for their support of my interdisciplinary teaching and willingness for me to further explore and share some of the ideas in this work in my courses.

To Professor Leo Sandon of Florida State University, many thanks for not only inspiring the structure of this work but also for the friendship and support I received from him and his family. Other faculty participants in the Graduate Program in Humanities are also to be thanked for the opportunity to study and teach in the program: John Carey, now President of Warren Wilson College; John Albright; David Gruender; David Darst; and Leon Golden, director of the program.

To my parents and sisters, I give thanks for the spiritual and financial support received at crucial times. I must also acknowledge and give thanks to an anonymous person in the Jacksonville area who surprised me beyond words with financial support for my graduate studies, and to those persons who founded the David Stitt Alumni Fellowship at Austin Seminary which provided both encouragement and support for graduate school.

To the Interlibrary Loan Office at Florida State University, many thanks for locating books and articles from the far corners of the country. Also, thanks must be given to the John Bulow Campbell Library of Columbia Theological Seminary, to the library of Union Theological Seminary, to Dr. Jon H. Roberts for access to his dissertation, and to the Widener Library and Archives of Harvard University for use of their resources.

Most of all, I give thanks to my wife, the Reverend Dr. Catherine Mason, a partner and critical reader. Our relationship has provided the depth and perspective from which this book has resulted.

1

Science and Religious Thought: Establishing a Method

The relationship between science and religious thought has been an enduring problem in modern Western intellectual history. The way this relationship is described has led to debates over the authority and interpretation of Scripture, how the realities described by science and religion are known, how divine power and wisdom relate to natural laws and processes, whether or not there is some purpose or direction at work in the natural world, and how the discoveries of science relate to our sense of morality and meaning in life. Even today, these issues are still debated, but with little sense of a historical perspective on the similarities between the historic and contemporary debates.

Underlying the complex debates are two different approaches to the relationship between science and religious thought. On the one hand, the relationship is often discussed as a theoretical issue in terms of epistemology and methodology: How do these fields of human knowledge relate to each other? What legitimate claims can they make upon each other? This theoretical approach has led to lists of different ways science and religious thought could relate to each other, such as being two different ways of knowing separate aspects of reality, or complementary approaches to one reality, or conflicting methods of knowing the same object. On the other hand, the relationship is analyzed through the issues raised by scientific discoveries. Specific scientific theories are usually discussed in terms of their impact on religious understandings of the world: How does our knowledge of physics relate to religious claims for a divine creator? How does our knowledge of geology relate to the biblical stories of creation? As a result, this content approach has dealt with most scientific theories and their impact on religious beliefs, such as evolution being God's way of doing things, or the laws of physics reflecting divine providence, or the stability of species pointing to divine order in the world. Seldom are the two approaches actually integrated into a coherent statement of how specific scientific theories function in terms of the possibilities for the theoretical relationship between science and religion. Even more seldom is an integrated approach offered which provides a historical perspective.

Such an integrated approach with a historical perspective is the goal of this study. By building on recent work in the history and philosophy of science, a consistent, historical method of analyzing religious responses to scientific theories will be developed which clarifies some of the epistemological and methodological issues of the relationship between science and religious thought. I will argue that a historical continuity can be discovered among a plurality of religious responses to any scientific theory, provided that a line of questioning, or hermeneutic, is chosen which grows out of the significant issues in the rise of modern science. This claim will be illustrated through an analysis of responses to Darwin's theory of evolution and its development into the twentieth century. Darwinism has been selected because it continues to be an issue which evokes a variety of religious responses, especially in the Anglo-American intellectual climate. Darwin's theory is an effective avenue into the problem of science and religion for it was the culmination of the modern scientific revolution begun in the sixteenth and seventeenth centuries and revealed the plurality of religious responses to modern science. The continual debates and refinements of the theory which have kept Darwin's work in the scientific and public consciousness provide a historical perspective which needs to be recognized by intellectual and religious historians.

The justification for a new study is usually found in the hermeneutical approach which is used. This study is no exception. The discussion of the relationship between science and religious thought, and Darwinism in particular, is well-travelled territory. Approaches to the relationship have included historical, philosophical, theological, topical, sociological, geographical, and linguistic perspectives, many of which have been employed to construct typologies or models. This study draws on its predecessors while attempting to move beyond them toward a more consistent, effective method of analysis. In order to lay the foundation for the method of analysis to be used in this study, a brief survey of the most important of these previous approaches will be presented: historical, epistemological and sociological, and models. The purpose of the survey is to provide a feel for analyses of the relationship between science and religious thought in general, and how each of those types of analysis has been applied to religious responses to Darwinism in particular. Along the way, we will discover what are perceived to be the strengths of the previous work which inform the particular approach to be used in the following chapters, and the weaknesses which are to be corrected.

Historical Approach

The standard historical approach to science and religion was established by John William Draper's *History of the Conflict between Religion and Science* (1874) and Andrew Dickson White's *History of the Warfare of Science with Theology in Christendom* (1896). Since their work, most analyses which employ a historical methodology have had to respond to the metaphors of conflict and warfare as descriptions of the relationship between science and religious thought. As a result, other nineteenth-century analyses used a historical approach to overcome a simple warfare image of the relationship by suggesting a series of historical periods in which science and religion were first in conflict but then moved toward reconciliation in some form. Though still revolving around the warfare metaphor, a revisionist historical perspective quickly developed.[1]

According to the revisionist theory, the rise of modern science was dependent on Western religious life and thought as it developed in the sixteenth and seventeenth centuries under the influence of Protestant doctrines and/or ethos.[2] These historical revisionists perceive science to be pursued out of charitable impulses and for the glory of God who established and works through natural laws. For them, the conflict which arises between science and religion reflects a confusion between the methods and goals of the two activities. The "two books of God," nature and the Bible, were created for different ends and should be studied with different methodologies.[3] Informed by both the warfare metaphor and the revisionist perspective, the standard historical approach has now become a chastened revisionism which recognizes the dependence of modern science on religious thought, but also acknowledges the genuine conflicts which have developed through the years.[4]

The example of Darwinism enables us to gain a perspective on this historical approach. The religious and scientific conflicts over Darwinism led to Draper's and White's work, and encouraged the spread of the warfare metaphor. The religious responses to Darwinism have, however, also undergone a revisionist historical analysis. In the mid-twentieth century, a popular approach was to suggest that a season of conflict in the 1860s and 1870s gave way to some form of reconciliation between Darwinism and religion in the 1880s, and then complete acceptance in the 1890s.[5] More recently, this periodization has been criticized for being too simplistic and failing to understand the critical issues of religion's so-called "acceptance" of Darwinism in the nineteenth century. Some have recognized that the form of evolution accepted was not Darwinism but variations on a theory of progressive development.[6] More significantly, a spectrum of responses has been recognized as rooted in positions held before Darwin's theory which revolved around the revisionist theme of a religious commitment to a belief in God working through natural law.[7] The recognition of a spectrum of religious responses has enabled the historical perspective to move beyond the warfare metaphor and its focus on Darwinism. The historical continuity of responses has been seen in a few cases where one particular type of response has been analyzed in terms of philosophical commitments which shape the religious stance to Darwinism. The most popular positions for analysis have been an opposition to Darwinism[8] or an attempt to synthesize Darwinian biology and religious thought.[9]

Epistemological and Sociological Approach

The efforts to move beyond the simplistic warfare metaphors and historical periodizations have been facilitated by the rise of epistemological and sociological studies of science and religion. In the nineteenth century, the role of analogies and metaphors was recognized as a significant issue in studying the ways science and religion come to knowledge, and that issue was incorporated into contemporary discussions of the role of models as ways of organizing experiences in both disciplines.[10] At the heart of the creative work of both disciplines is the process of moving from a limited frame of reference to more inclusive and broader frames of reference which provide greater insight into, and structure for, the understanding of reality. The genesis of the creative process is often the use of a metaphor which suggests analogies between known objects and the unknown which is being studied. Some of the familiar meanings of the word are transferred to the new context and become a "screen" or "lens" through which the subject is seen in a new perspective (e.g., God is my rock). Metaphors are not to be taken literally since there are always meanings which are not transferred to the new context (e.g., God is not inorganic matter).

The value of the metaphor is then tested in light of the information which is available, and the metaphor can become the basis of a model which elaborates and extends the new idea to interpret experiences and organize perceptions of the world.[11] In both science and religion, models correlate patterns of human experience and are taken seriously as representations of reality. Religious models tend to have more noncognitive functions than do models in science, and they elicit more personal responses. Where models in science change fairly easily, religious models resist change since they are essential for constructing a comprehensive conceptual scheme for understanding experiences and articulating basic beliefs.[12] The ever-present danger in religion is to take the metaphors and models too literally, turn them into idols, and thus misuse the language and exclude people whose experiences do not confirm the value of the metaphor or model.[13]

In recent years, Darwin's work has been analyzed for his use of metaphors in designing the theory of natural selection. Darwin's search for a mechanism of organic change led him to the analogy between the variety which pigeon breeders could produce and a similar process occurring in nature, and he found support for this analogy in his reading of Malthus on population pressures. The famous phrase usually identified with Darwin, "survival of the fittest," was also intended in "a large and metaphorical sense."[14] Darwin's use of such analogical and metaphorical language not only reflects the scientific process of discovery, but also points to the cultural influences which shaped his thought and language. This issue will be dealt with in greater detail in the next chapter, but it should be noted that Darwin's use of metaphorical language reflects the influence of William Paley's natural theology and the Scottish philosophy of Dugald Stewart.[15] The struggle to describe the operations of chance and population pressure led Darwin to follow in Paley's style of using metaphors both as a way of evoking faith in his theory when he did not have all the evidence necessary for explaining the laws of variation and as a way of avoiding mechanical explanations which would not be appropriate.

The metaphorical character of Darwin's thought provides an avenue into understanding the difficulties which his theory faced within the British scientific and religious communities. Bishop Wilberforce's review of the *Origin* focused on the paradox of anthropomorphic Nature being both uniform and yet selecting for change, implying that nature operates by uniform laws and only God can intervene to produce change. A. R. Wallace quickly recognized the difficulties which Darwin's metaphors produced because they were misunderstood by many who thought that some intelligence must be behind the selection process. On the other hand, others welcomed the metaphorical ambiguity of Darwin's theory because it seemed to allow for divine intelligence to be guiding the process.[16]

Sociological studies of science and religious thought have built on these analyses of the role of metaphors and models in an attempt to understand the role of the scientific and religious communities in the development and reception of new ideas and theories. Science and religion are seen to be similar in that both involve communities of persons searching for forms of reality in the world, and that search cannot be divorced from the personal, social, and philosophical climate in which the work is being done.[17] Both science and religion are social constructs which mediate between the person and the experience of the world, and demand a commitment and personal dedication to certain ways of learning, seeing the world, and standards of truth. These "paradigms" incorporate and organize a large amount of information, and are highly resistant to change.[18] Science and religion are to be understood as two similar methods of knowing, but with different objects in their search for knowledge. They are not necessarily in conflict, according to some, except when the distinctiveness of their objects is confused.[19] A warning, however, has been sounded that such sociological studies should not diminish the inherent conflict between a scientific will to control and dominate knowledge rooted in a Western, white male ruling class attitude, and a religious concern for human values and needs.[20]

Recent analyses of the religious responses to Darwinism have incorporated these epistemological and sociological perspectives, but this has led to two rather different positions. On the one hand, the sociology of knowledge has formed the foundation for a "nonviolent history." Darwinism presented a crisis of belief, not a revolution in paradigms, since there was no evolutionary paradigm in science over which a controversy could take place, and this crisis could be resolved by reinterpreting religious beliefs or reinterpreting Darwinism.[21] On the other hand, Darwin's work has been understood as presenting an epistemological revolution. From this perspective, the conflict is between two paradigms invoking different standards and methods of successful science, not simply a conflict between science and religion.[22] One scientific paradigm, claiming to be rooted in a Newtonian system of laws and Baconian induction, held that explanations of the natural world must include some reference to God in order to be complete. Darwin's work was the culmination of the other paradigm, based on the hypothetico-deductive method of Newton, which limited scientific knowledge to natural causes and the laws of nature and excluded supernatural forces from its sphere of inquiry since they were not open to scientific study and provided no new knowledge. The so-called conflict between religion and Darwinism was in essence a conflict between scientific epistemologies. The opponents of Darwin had committed themselves to a Baconian common sense model of science, assumed it normal for everyone, and saw Darwin's work as dangerous speculation.[23]

Models Approach

The reclamation of the reality of conflict through the deepened understanding provided by epistemological and sociological analysis has led many to rethink the relationship between science and religion in terms of a plurality of positions which coexist historically. The use of models has been recognized as important in both science and religion as a way of organizing experience, and the most popular method of analyzing both the general relationship between science and religion and the responses to particular theories has been to develop such models or typologies.

A benchmark in religious thought for general models was the work of H. Richard Niebuhr who dealt with the larger issue of the relationship between religion and culture. Niebuhr's approach is quite useful for studying the relationship between science and religion since, as we have seen, science is a social activity which reflects and shapes social values. Five "typical answers" to the question of religion and culture are suggested by Niebuhr: religion against culture, religion of culture, religion above culture, religion and culture in paradox, and religion transforming culture.[24] Niebuhr recognized that all the models for relating religion and culture are historical in nature. These models are not unique to any particular time frame, but they are based on significant figures throughout the history of Western thought who have understood the relationship between religion and culture in similar ways. A second strength of Niebuhr's work is the recognition that the situations described by the various models are present at the same time, rather than progressing from one to another. This sense of the historical perspective and the plurality of options is often missed in contemporary discussions of the relationship between science and religion.

Niebuhr's structure of models is seldom used to analyze science and religion. Ian Barbour made use of the typologies briefly in a discussion of technology, but his later work did not develop them.[25] Rather, Barbour has made a variety of efforts to develop his own models of the relationship between science and religion both in general and with reference to Darwinism. He has described the general relationship in terms of three types of responses. One type of response is categorized as "issues of earlier centuries." Here Barbour places three particular concerns: scriptural literalism, which is giving way to levels of interpretation; the God of the gaps who is giving way to secondary causality, existentialism, or immanentism; and evolutionary naturalism, which is recognized as a philosophical commitment rather than a science-and-religion issue. A second type of response is some variation on the theme of religion and science as separate and distinct disciplines, while the third, and most promising for future thought, includes theologies which incorporate evolutionary thinking.[26]

Barbour has made a significant contribution to the development of models of the relationship between science and religion by recognizing the similarity of what at first seem to be quite different religious responses to science. The separation made by some theologians of divine causality from secondary causality, existentialism's distinction between scientific objectivity and personal religious involvement, and linguistic analysis's claim that science and religion are unrelated languages are essentially variations on the model of science and religion being separate disciplines. However, Barbour dismisses the "earlier issues" of conflict and naturalism too quickly since they are still present with us.

An even more precise system of general models was attempted by the 1979 World Council of Churches' Conference on Faith, Science and the Future in its report on "The Nature of Science and the Nature of Faith," which included a brief historical overview and six ways of relating science and religion.[27] The report recognizes the plurality that is present by noting the strengths and weaknesses of each approach; the approaches are described as follows: science and religion (1)deal with separate realities, (2)are interacting approaches to the same reality such that they may modify each other, (3)are two distinct approaches to the same reality, (4)constitute two distinct language systems, (5)complement each other as "sciences" of their respective disciplines, and (6)can be integrated. While the report recognizes the plurality of models in the contemporary discussion, it would seem that only two models are actually presented when we take seriously Barbour's recognition that there are different nuances in the "two separate disciplines" approach: a model that sees a working relationship between science and religious thought (possibly comparable to Niebuhr's "transforming" type), and variations on the two disciplines model (comparable to Niebuhr's "above" or "in paradox" types).[28] Thus, neither Barbour nor the World Council of Churches' report takes seriously all the options which might be available.

When the focus shifts from the relationship in general to a specific scientific theory, Darwinism has been the most popular topic for analysis in terms of models of religious responses. Each of the proposed systems of models has its own particular hermeneutic that is used to analyze the writings of scientific and religious thinkers, and a variety of interpretive angles has been employed. One popular hermeneutic focuses on the philosophical traditions which religious thinkers choose as their basis for responding to Darwinism, for example, pragmatism, empiricism, Kantian dualism, Hegelian idealism, or process philosophy.[29] An even more popular approach focuses on some significant issues which Darwinism raised for religious thought and establishes types based on which issue becomes the focus of attention. The particular issues are usually biblical authority and interpretation, design and purpose in the universe, human nature and ethics. Debates rage in the literature as to which of these is "the" issue for the types of religious responses to Darwinism, but they are often used in conjuction with each other to demonstrate how various scientists and theologians have dealt with Darwinism.[30]

A comprehensive issues-oriented structure of religious responses to Darwinism has been provided by Barbour in his *Issues in Science and Religion*. In a section on "Religion and the History of Science," the nineteenth-century responses are organized around the challenges to the Bible, divine design in nature, human dignity, and ethics, which are discussed in terms of four religious types: traditionalism, modernism, liberalism, and naturalism.[31] The use of these categories creates some problems and inconsistencies since they include scientists and theologians who had widely divergent responses to Darwin's theory. For example, Charles Hodge and Asa Gray are suggested as representatives of the traditionalist response, which is characterized by maintaining traditional religious doctrines. But where Hodge rejected Darwinism as both bad science and atheism, Gray promoted Darwin's work and criticized Hodge's understanding of Darwinian science. When the focus moves to the twentieth-century responses to developments in Darwinian evolution, Barbour makes some attempt to relate the responses of the two centuries, but the categories do not correspond.[32] The traditionalist position is now represented by those who argue that science and religion represent two different levels of truth, which had been mentioned briefly as one position in nineteenth-century naturalism, while the concern for design is found in the liberalism typology. One strength of Barbour's analysis which must be mentioned, however, is that he does recognize the religious nature of evolutionary naturalism in the twentieth century.

This analysis of Barbour's models of religious responses to Darwinism reflects the shifting lines separating the types of responses when they are analyzed in terms of traditional religious issues such as biblical authority and design in nature. In order to resolve some of the dilemmas created by the use of such a hermeneutic, a more consistent approach has been sought which can construct typologies appropriate to Darwinism itself and which demonstrate historical continuities. This approach usually focuses on the epistemological and ontological issues raised by Darwin's method. One effort that met with some success focused on the issue of subjective and objective categories in nature and religious thought.[33] Richard Overman devised four categories of responses to Darwinism in terms of whether or not our convictions regarding nature's purposiveness are found as an objective reality in nature. This hermeneutic revealed some interesting continuities between nineteenth- and twentieth-century responses, but Overman failed to understand the opponents to Darwinism, such as Charles Hodge, in charging them with abandoning "the search for rational coherence in religion." Overman should have recognized the different epistemological commitments of the opponents who thought everyone could see the purposiveness of nature as an objective reality.

A more effective hermeneutic for revealing historical continuities and for recognizing the plurality of responses to Darwinism and the relationship between science and religion in general has been found in the epistemology and methodology which is at the heart of Darwin's work. Stephen Toulmin and Morse Peckham have argued that the most appropriate method for analyzing responses to Darwinism is based on whether or not the response maintains the distinction between science and religion for which Darwin argued. Toulmin suggests that any effort to cut loose the scientific theory from its observational foundation and to transform the "is" of evolution into an "ought" is to elevate evolution into a myth which provides "a cosmic sanction for ethics."[34] Such a move is inappropriate since Darwin attempted to remove religious implications and restraints from the inquiry of science, and resisted making the natural processes into a deity. This approach of discerning evolutionary mythology by looking for moral and religious conclusions drawn from scientific theories was developed further by Morse Peckham.[35] He argued that the responses to Darwinian evolution can be analyzed in terms of the distinction between "Darwinism" and "Darwinisticism." Darwinism refers to the scientific theory and its mechanism of natural selection which is observable in isolated instances, and the nonteleological world of chance and accident revealed by that theory. Darwinisticism can be any theory which constructs or makes claims for metaphysics, morality, economics, or human nature on the basis of what Darwin "really" meant in his theory. Darwin's theory has been wrongly extended to sanction an ethics of competition and capitalistic economies and a metaphysics of steady growth and complexity. Peckham argues that such implications of evolution are appropriate for Herbert Spencer's law of evolution but not for Darwin's scientific theory. Where Darwinistic metaphysics holds that reality lies in directed change which is introduced either from the outside or from the process itself, Darwin's accidental biological world has no such teleological direction and should have undermined metaphysical evolutionism.[36] The distinction between Darwinism and Darwinisticism forms an effective interpretive angle for analyzing the responses to Darwin's work, especially since it reflects the significant philosophical and methodological issues which will be examined in the next chapter.

This distinction forms the basis of the models of religious responses which James R. Moore has developed: Christian Anti-Darwinism, Christian Darwinisticism, and Christian Darwinism. The "Anti-Darwinism" position is rooted in two epistemological bases: Baconian induction, which led some to reject Darwin's speculations, and Platonic essentialism which opposed Darwin's undermining the belief in fixity of species. Moore is critical of this opposition since it was based on philosophical positions which are not necessarily Christian.[37] The "Christian Darwinisticism" response was supposedly free from the taint of philosophy because it focused more on the theological question of God as immanent in the forces of nature such that God's benevolent ethical plan for universal progress was worked out through the struggle of the fittest to survive. "Christian Darwinism" was able to accept

Darwin's theory and remain religiously orthodox, for this position recognizes Darwin as taking one more step in the direction of reclaiming the biblical view of God and nature, and of discerning God's will in the laws of nature. Though he does not accept the epistemological revolution as discussed in the previous section, Moore has recognized some of the important issues underlying the relationship between Darwinism and religious thought. His excellent study is, however, limited in its typologies since it does not include the response traditionally called naturalism.

This weakness has been corrected by Leo Sandon, who has sketched four models of religious responses to Darwinism.[38] Sandon incorporates Peckham's analysis into a system based on Niebuhr's analysis of the relationship between religion and culture. One strength of Sandon's approach is the suggestion of historical continuity between the nineteenth and twentieth centuries in each of the four models. "Theology *against* Darwinism" is represented by Charles Hodge and the contemporary creationists' objection to Darwin's treatment of design and teleology in nature. "Theology *of* Darwinism" claims that evolution is the point of departure for a naturalistic religion committed to Robert G. Ingersoll's Trinity of Science: observation, reason, and experience. The argument that Darwinism is an incomplete description of life, and that it does not provide answers to the questions of teleology and ethics, is the basic stance of the "Theology *above* Darwinism" response. Borden Parker Bowne is a representative of this search for meaning in life. John Fiske's cosmic theism was the classic representative of the fourth model, "Theology and Darwinisticism *in Concert*," while Henri Bergson and Teilhard de Chardin are the twentieth-century representatives of a religion in which evolution is the way an immanent God works. Sandon's models are a helpful correction to many of the efforts to construct a set of models, since the naturalistic response is not only included, but also moves beyond the ethical issues to reveal the epistemological commitment which is at the heart of that response to Darwinism.

In the search for a consistent, historical methodology for analyzing the relationship between science and religion and religious responses to Darwinism in particular, we have surveyed some of the most important approaches which have been used. The historical approach began with the metaphors of conflict and warfare, and attempted to move beyond them to recognize the religious sources for the rise of modern science and of Darwinism. The tendency toward simplistic historical periodization was corrected by the deepened understanding of both science and religion provided by sociological and epistemological studies which suggested a possible conflict over paradigms at the heart of religious responses to Darwinism. Models for the religious responses to Darwinism have been constructed in a variety of ways. The specific shape of the models depends on the hermeneutical approach which is taken and its ability to reveal the historical continuities in the responses. A recognition of the epistemological significance of Darwin's theory opens up one approach to the historical continuity of the religious responses to Darwinism. Toulmin and Peckham have provided an approach which focuses on how Darwin's theory was understood as a scientific theory, and how it was adulterated with other theories to turn evolution into a myth. As we shall see in the next chapter, these two issues are essential to an understanding of Darwinism itself, and thus are most appropriate for the hermeneutic used in establishing models.

2

Darwinism: Scientific and Philosophical Issues

On November 24, 1859, Charles Darwin published an abstract of his ongoing work under the title *On the Origin of Species by Means of Natural Selection; or, The Preservation of Favoured Races in the Struggle for Life*. Few scientific works from the nineteenth century have received the continued examination and critiquing from both scientists and humanists that Darwin's *Origin* has. The massive "Darwin industry" has examined all known documents written by this "genteel Victorian," yet there is still a great deal of confusion among nonscientists over what Darwin actually said. Most of the research and exposition of Darwin's work has been done by historians and philosophers of science, as well as by practicing scientists, and the results of their work have tended to remain within the circle of "believers." This fact has created problems for those whose expertise resides outside the natural sciences since they tend to be unaware of the significant scientific issues in Darwinism and how they relate to the broader philosophical, social, and religious issues often connected to Darwinism. Some arguments for the relationship between science and religious thought have revolved around misunderstandings of Darwin's work, particularly the epistemological and methodological issues. We will now examine some of the scientific and philosophical issues which were and are important in understanding the relationship between Darwinism and religious thought.

The division of this chapter into two sections, one dealing primarily with the scientific issues of Darwinism and its development into the twentieth century and another dealing with the epistemological and methodological issues involved in Darwinism as a model for modern biological science is artificial in that Darwin's scientific work was intimately tied to the philosophical issues with which he struggled, but this division will help focus on the types of issues actually involved in Darwin's theory and the impact which it had. It will be argued that the "Darwinian revolution" was an emphasis on natural selection involving a methodological, philosophical shift which Darwin established and which is at the core of the "conflict" between Darwinian science and religion. There is, thus, a need to clarify the issues in light of many popular misconceptions.

Scientific Issues

The concluding paragraph of the *Origin* is rich with metaphors which suggest the key concepts in Darwin's theory of evolution:

> It is interesting to contemplate a tangled bank, clothed with many plants of many kinds, with birds singing on the bushes, with various insects flitting about, and with worms crawling through the damp earth, and to reflect that these elaborately constructed forms, so different from each other, and dependent upon each other in so complex a manner, have all been produced by laws acting around us. These laws, taken in the largest sense, being Growth with Reproduction; Inheritance which is almost implied by reproduction; Variability from the indirect and direct action of the conditions of life, and from use and disuse; a Ratio of Increase so high as to lead to a Struggle for Life, and as a consequence to Natural Selection, entailing divergence of character and the Extinction of less-improved forms. Thus, from the war of nature, from famine and death, the most exalted object which we are capable of conceiving, namely, the production of the higher animals, directly follows. There is grandeur in this view of life, with its several powers, having been originally breathed by the Creator into a few forms or one; and that, whilst this planet has gone cycling on according to the fixed law of gravity, from so simple a beginning endless forms most beautiful and most wonderful have been, and are being evolved.[1]

All attempts at describing what is actually said in the *Origin* eliminate the beauty and carefulness of Darwin's argument, which can be appreciated only in the reading. Yet, for the sake of discussion and for those trained in the humanities, it is necessary to get at the essence of the scientific argument.[2] There are four elements in Darwin's argument. First, in any given area, there is more life produced than the area can support. This leads to a struggle for existence which involves food, protection, and the ability to procreate. Second, from the moment of birth, no two organisms are exactly alike. These small, random variations are transmitted by heredity, though the mechanism of that process was unknown. Third, in the struggle between these unlike individuals, those differences which are advantageous to the struggle will enable their possessors to win more often than those who lack the advantageous variations. Fourth, the winners of the struggle will transmit their characteristics by heredity more often (differential reproductive success). Over time, the modifications will give rise to new species. This whole process moves according to natural laws.

It is important to recognize that natural selection, as distinct from the more general concept of "evolution," is the key to Darwinism. Darwin's shorthand description of his theory was "descent with modification" and only in the metaphorical "tangled bank" passage did he use the word "evolve."

Evolution was already a widely used concept in the nineteenth century, but it had two different meanings, neither of which Darwin could accept. The technical use of the word referred to a theory in embryology in which embryos developed by "unrolling" their prepackaged form which originally had been created in Eve's ovaries and has been passed on from generation to generation. The more popular use of the word evolution referred to a concept of progressive development from lower to higher forms. Darwin did not use "evolution" because he could accept neither the technical meaning which eliminated variation and selection nor the popular meaning which implied progress. Darwin's theory refers to natural adaptation to an environment, not to progress as the concept is popularly understood. It was Herbert Spencer who started the process of identifying evolution and descent with modification, yet even he had reservations about the social progressiveness of evolution. Darwin's theory focused on the working of natural forces to explain the adaptation of organisms to their environment.[3]

Darwin claimed that he had two goals in writing the *Origin*: "I had two distinct objects in view, firstly to shew that species had not been separately created, and secondly, that natural selection had been the chief agent of change."[4] The first goal Darwin had established for himself set him apart from the scientific views of his contemporaries. These views can be classified into two groups: the minority evolutionist view, and the majority creationist view. Theories of evolution were well known over 100 years before Darwin published his theory, yet they were different from what Darwin had in mind. The most celebrated theory was developed by Jean Baptiste de Lamarck in the late eighteenth century, and it is still influential. Lamarck struggled to answer the question of whether species survived indefinitely or sometimes became extinct as the study of fossils was beginning to suggest in the eighteenth century. In other words, had God created organisms only to let them become extinct? Nature had come to be seen in terms of a highly structured "chain of being" or "scale of nature" which was rooted in Platonic and Aristotelian thought and had been designed by God.[5] In this "chain" the species could be organized in a hierarchy stretching from the perfection of humanity to the simplest forms of life, and this hierarchy was considered to be static: nature had been created in this way from the beginning, and it would always exist so. Yet fossils had been discovered of species no longer seen in nature, and this challenged the static view. In 1809, Lamarck presented his ideas in *Philosophie zoologique*. Lamarck followed the "chain of being" in presenting his theory, but his scale of nature was dynamic rather than static. Organisms moved up the scale toward higher and more perfect forms as they changed over the course of time, and new simple organisms continued to appear at the bottom of the scale. Lamarck's evolutionary process was a system of parallel lines progressing up the scale, rather than a theory of common ancestry such as Darwin developed.

Lamarck's continued impact is due also to the mechanism which he suggested for organisms moving up the scale. Lamarck was a student of the Enlightenment and tried to be a good materialist in his scientific explanation. He argued that organisms experience certain needs (*besoins*) which are brought about by the constantly changing environment. These needs involve new habits and act as catalysts for the movement of body fluids which create or change organs of the body. Through continued use or disuse these organs either continue or degenerate from lack of fluids. Lamarck believed that these new characteristics would be inherited and could have a cumulative effect. The popular simplistic picture of this process is that of the giraffe "growing" a long neck from its efforts to reach higher leaves, and this characteristic is then passed on to future generations. This process of inheriting acquired characteristics is Lamarck's great legacy which is still with us since people believe we can pass on to our children the intellectual and social advances our generation makes, and it is still an open question. Darwin was not completely free from Lamarckian elements of use and disuse, but he emphasized that natural selection was the primary mechanism for change. The continued popularity of Lamarckianism says more about our hopes for social progress than it does for our understanding of biology.

The evidence to support organic evolution, if not natural selection, had been available for many years before Darwin published his theory. Yet the large majority of scientists resisted any theory of evolution. The reasons have usually been described as "lack of evidence," but recently the more persuasive argument has been for "the power of retarding concepts."[6] The "silent assumptions" which opposed evolutionary science were religious in nature. Natural theology had a long tradition in England and America, and the issues of design in nature and the place of humanity were significant. Lamarck's theory explained what we see in terms of natural laws which were unguided and blind, and this left no room for a Designer. At the same time, Lamarck understood humanity as another organism, and this effectively denied the assumption that humanity had a special place in God's creation. These ideas came to be associated with all theories of evolution, and they were condemned as immoral materialism when Robert Chambers replaced direct divine intervention with the working of natural laws (secondary causes) in his *Vestiges of Natural History of Creation* (1844).[7]

The majority view of nineteenth-century scientists has been called "creationist" due to the close ties between the scientific work and natural theology. As we saw in the first chapter, the creationist discovered in nature evidence for the intervention and direction of the Creator. The resistance to evolutionary theories was based not only on a rejection of "immoral materialism," but also on a belief in the static world of the "chain of being." A commitment to idealism led to the belief in Platonic "essences" as the true reality. Louis Agassiz was a leading proponent of this view which held that reality, including species, is immutable. The variability which we see is neither permanent nor real, and the creation of species is a discontinuous process of divine intervention. Charles Lyell also argued for fixed types which have set limits of variability, and thus the changes we see occur only with nonessential characteristics. Natural theology and essentialism worked well together to support a static view of nature in which new creative acts were the result of divine intervention. This intervention could have been a discontinuous (catastrophic) progression through the work of such things as earthquakes and floods, followed by new creations of the organic world, or a steady-state system (uniformitarian) brought about by forces that are still present today. In either view, the Creator was responsible for the appearance of new species, especially humanity.

Against this background of evolutionary theories moving species toward perfection and creationist essentialism seeing divine intervention at every point, Charles Darwin presented his theory of descent with modification. Darwin rejected descriptive words such as "higher" and "lower" since he discovered change and adaptation, not an inevitable advance toward perfection. Rather than resort to divine intervention and design to explain the appearance of new species and their "fit" with their environment, Darwin argued for the continuous operation of natural laws to explain what we see in nature, including the place of humanity. By 1844, Darwin had written an essay which spelled out the essence of his theory, but he chose not to publish it. A great deal of debate has been occasioned by Darwin's "waiting period."[8] Some have argued that Darwin felt he needed more evidence, others that Darwin spent the time organizing a community of scientists who could support his theory, while some have taken Darwin's own words seriously: he felt that he was committing murder with his theory, the murder of the marriage between natural theology and science by his materialistic scientific explanation of nature. No doubt there is some truth in all these views, and, in light of the reaction to the publication of the *Origin*, Darwin's fears were well founded.

The structure and content of Darwin's theory make superfluous any reference to divine intervention as a creative force. Beginning with his experience in the breeding of pigeons, Darwin discusses the creative power of artificial selection to effect great changes. The breeder chooses as parents those pigeons with the characteristics which are desirable to pass on. Darwin recognizes the need for variation, and argues that it is surely as prevalent in nature as it it in the breeder's coop. With domestic variation established, Darwin uses it as an analogy to explain the mechanism at work in nature:

> I have called this principle by which each slight variation, if useful, is preserved by the term Natural Selection, in order to mark its relation to man's power of selection. But the expression often used by Mr. Herbert Spencer of the Survival of the Fittest is more accurate, and is sometimes equally convenient. We have seen that man by selection can certainly produce great results, and can adapt organic beings to his uses, through the

accumulation of slight but useful variations, given to him by the hand of Nature. But Natural Selection, as we shall hereafter see, is a power incessantly ready for action, and is immeasurably superior to man's feeble efforts, as the works of Nature are to those of Art.[9]

The essence of Darwinism is the *natural* process of selection, in contrast to the goal-oriented outside intervention of artificial selection. The lack of understanding of the role of the analogy and the personification of nature as "ready for action" led to a number of misinterpretations of his theory. Darwin argued that "struggle for existence" and "natural selection" should be understood as metaphors, rather than taken literally. In the sixth edition of the *Origin* Darwin argued that natural selection simply preserves the useful variations and is not "creative" in the sense of creating the variations. Neither is natural selection to be understood in Lamarckian terms as the organism modifying itself. Natural selection, no more than Newton's theory of gravity, was to be read with connotations of the divine:

> It has been said that I speak of natural selection as an active power or Deity; but who objects to an author speaking of the attraction of gravity as ruling the movements of the planets? Every one knows what is meant and is implied by such metaphorical expressions; and they are almost necessary for brevity. So again it is difficult to avoid personifying the word Nature; but I mean by Nature, only the aggregate action and product of many natural laws, and by laws the sequence of events as ascertained by us.[10]

Wallace and others suggested that Darwin could have made his theory more acceptable if he had reduced the role of analogy and metaphor. Yet that would have altered the structure of the argument and Darwin was establishing a method for biological science, as we shall see in the next section.

Darwin's goal was to establish a natural mechanism by which the adaptation we see in nature can be explained. These adaptations to the environment come through the work of "secondary causes" which build adaptation step by step. Natural selection is the primary directing force of the evolutionary process. Though Darwin included sexual selection and Lamarckian use/disuse as forces, natural selection is the creative force as it preserves from generation to generation the best adapted organisms from a pool of random variations. These variations must be *plentiful* since natural selection makes nothing directly, and they must be *small* in scope, otherwise the fit would result from the process of variation itself. Theories of "saltation" in which there are large "jumps" in the variations are excluded from Darwin's theory. Darwin was concerned with the question of the time involved for this step-by-step process, and he has been interpreted as having a fundamental commitment to a gradual, continuous, smooth process. Whether this gradualism is an essential element of Darwinism is still being debated, as we shall see below.

Most significantly for this study, these small variations are also *undirected*, and this was the most objectionable element for many people. Neither the environment (as in Lamarckian evolution) nor divine intervention (the creationist position) is responsible for the variations according to Darwin. Lamarckian evolution and creationist positions hold out for some form of directed process of variation. The creationist allowed for some variation within species, but this was a divinely ordained method of adapting to local environmental changes. After a discussion of variations in horses, Darwin strongly rejects the creationist argument:

> He who believes that each equine species was independently created, will, I presume, assert that each species has been created with a tendency to vary, both under nature and under domestication, in this particular manner, so as often to become striped like the other species of the genus... To admit this view is, as it seems to me, to reject a real for an unreal, or at least for an unknown, cause. It makes the works of God a mere mockery and deception; I would almost as soon believe that the old and ignorant cosmogonists, that fossils shells had never lived, but had been created in stone so as to mock the shells living on the sea shore.[11]

"Designed by God" could not be accepted as an explanation for what is observed, for it really explained nothing and was not open to investigation. Darwin recognizes that his own writings had led some to the conclusion that the only alternative was "chance." For many people "chance" meant without cause or law, but Darwin used "chance" to mean only "our ignorance of the cause" of random events. Darwin's world was based on uniform lawful causality which made more sense of nature than did divine contrivance.

Darwin both attacked the creationist position and established natural selection through the study of adaptations, especially in orchids. The creationist position emphasized the rationality, economy, consistency, order, purposefulness, and beneficence of the Creator. Darwin attacked these assumptions in his study of homologies (comparisons of body parts) as he wondered why a creator should use the same basic form to create the widely divergent mouths of insects, or the wing and leg of a bat, when they are used for quite different purposes:

> Nothing could be more hopeless than to attempt to explain this similarity of pattern in members of the same class, by utility or by the doctrine of final causes.... On the ordinary view of the independent creation of each being, we can only say that so it is;—that it so pleased the Creator to construct all the animals and plants in each great class on a uniformly regulated plan; but this is not a scientific explanation.
>
> The explanation is to a large extent simply on the theory of the selection of successive slight modifications,—each modification being profitable in some way to the modified form.... In changes of this nature, there will be little or no tendency to alter the original pattern, or to transpose the parts.[12]

When the creationist responded that this is evidence of God's economy, Darwin answered by pointing to the great diversity of structures in the orchid which all have the one goal of fertilization.

Darwin's argument in both the *Origin* and *Variation of Plants and Animals under Domestication* (1868) destroyed not only Paley's utilitarian argument for the existence of God but also the idealist argument for design. The purposeful design of Paley could be better explained through the random and gradual adaptation and selection pressures of nature. In other words, the apparent design in the fit of the organism to the environment is better explained by "secondary causes" (natural laws):

> To my mind it accords better with what we know of the laws impressed on matter by the Creator, that the production and extinction of the past and present inhabitants of the world should have been due to secondary causes, like those determining the death and birth of the individual. [13]

Darwin's position would seem to make room for an idealist form of design which argued that the natural processes were rationally ordered and that the existence of homologies is evidence of an ideal form that is the basis for organisms. Darwin's work on orchids destroyed this form of design since the similarities were better explained as a result of descent from a common ancestor. [14] If one wants a scientific explanation, the true Darwinian employs only secondary causes, otherwise known as *natural* laws, without recourse to divine intervention or planning. These sustained attacks on the creationist position were a "revolution" which transformed the scientific view of nature and left many in shock as their divinely designed world was shattered.

The Modern Syntheses

The major weakness in Darwin's theory was that element labelled "chance": Darwin had a very weak explanation for the source of the variations upon which natural selection worked and how the variations were transmitted from one generation to another. The lack of a strong explanation led to the decline of Darwinism among scientists before the turn of the century, while those with religious interests, such as Asa Gray, found a place for God in the natural process as the source of the variations. The widely recognized irony in the history of science was that an answer had indeed been discovered in Mendel's work with peas between the first (1859) and the last edition (1872) of the *Origin*, but neither Darwin nor his followers knew of the work. Even more ironically, the rediscoverers of Mendel's work emphasized large mutations as an alternative to Darwin's theory of the interaction between populations and the environment. Darwinism was not accepted as the basic theory of biology until the 1930s when more was known of the mechanism of heredity and genetics came into its own as a scientific field in the framework of Darwinian evolution.

The concept of a "modern synthesis" refers to the ability of Darwin's theory to form the core around which various aspects of biological science are integrated. Darwin himself began this process in the later chapters of the *Origin* as he brought the study of fossils, embryology, and morphology under the umbrella of his theory. With the developments in the study of genetics, Julian Huxley proclaimed that a "modern synthesis" had been achieved. This synthesis involved the incorporation of genetics into the Darwinian emphasis on small variations as the key to natural selection at work on populations in their environments. Gradual evolution came to be explained in terms of small, random genetic changes, often called mutations, and the effects of recombination of the genetic material of the parents in producing offspring. The organism which is produced is then subject to the pressures of fitness for the environment and natural selection. The large-scale effects on populations and species which can be observed only with difficulty in nature are thus also brought under the umbrella of the new genetic theory of Darwinism, which provides the working hypotheses for other fields such as paleontology, embryology, and morphology.

This triumph of Darwinism in the middle of the twentieth century led a number of the advocates of the new synthesis also to celebrate the triumph of secondary causes in the new scientific world view. In the introduction to his *Evolution: The Modern Synthesis*, Julian Huxley wrote:

> Darwin's original contention, that biological evolution is a natural process, effected primarily by natural selection, has thus become increasingly confirmed, and all other theories of evolution requiring a supernatural or vitalistic force or mechanism such as Bergson's creative evolution... together with all Lamarckian theories involving the inheritance of acquired characters, have become increasingly untenable.[15]

Since the work of Watson and Crick in 1953, the unit of heredity can now be identified with the molecules of deoxyribonucleic acid (DNA). The process of replication, transcription, and translation of the genetic code is essentially isolated from outside influences, except in the case of chemicals or radiation which can disrupt the process and cause "mistranslations" of the genetic code. The genetic basis for heredity and the new understanding of the role of DNA have made it extremely difficult to argue for the transmission of acquired characteristics or to locate the activity of God in the process.

There has been a great deal of debate about the reduction of biology to molecular studies due to the explanatory power of the genetic process. The incorporation of sociology into genetic Darwinian evolution has led E.O.

Wilson to argue for a "new synthesis" called sociobiology. Darwin himself had begun the process of incorporating the study of social behavior and emotions into biology in the *Descent* and *The Expression of Emotions in Man and Animals* (1872). In the conclusion to the *Descent*, Darwin attributed to natural selection the rise of social instincts which form the basis of morality, but suggested that the moral qualities themselves were shaped more by habit, education, and religion. Darwin noted the value of altruism for the survival of species, and, in 1902, Peter Kropotkin extended the discussion of "mutual aid" within the Darwinian structure of biology. On the other hand, in *On Aggression* (1963), Konrad Lorenz placed his study of aggression within the context of the Darwinian struggle for existence.

The process of incorporating sociology into the Darwinian theory of evolution reached a new level with E.O. Wilson's *Sociobiology: The New Synthesis* (1975) and *On Human Nature* (1978). Wilson argued that the organism's primary function is not to reproduce other organisms, but rather that the organism exists primarily to carry and reproduce genes.[16] The unit of selection is no longer to be understood as the organism in its relationship to the environment but rather the gene. All social behavior and morality can be explained in terms of the gene striving to reproduce itself. Altruism and religion can be explained in terms of kinship with genes of common ancestors working together to transmit these genes to the next generation. When Wilson argues in his conclusion to *Sociobiology* that it is time for ethics to be "biologicized," he is attempting to bring the humanities as well as the social sciences under the umbrella of the theory of Darwinian evolution updated by the study of genetics. In *On Human Nature*, Wilson extends his study of insects and primates to humans and offers a sociobiological study of human nature in which human sexual mores and roles, altruism, and religion are said to be determined by our genes and the need for biological survival. Wilson acknowledges that humans are governed less than other animals by genetically determined biological instincts, but he argues that the genetic basis for behavior is powerful enough to impose limits on human society.

A "new modern synthesis" has recently been proposed which would bring paleontology and the theory of human evolution under the umbrella of the genetic theory of Darwinian evolution. Darwin struggled both with the question of time for the slow step-by-step process and the evidence for this process in the fossil record. Darwin argued that the knowledge of the available fossils could fit with his theory, but he recognized that the record did not reveal the gradual transformations which his theory would suggest. Robley Light has argued for, and John Gribbin and Jeremy Cherfas have documented, a "new modern synthesis" which would offer a solution to the evolutionary time and ancestry of humans. These chemical, or molecular, anthropologists have demonstrated evolution by isolating proteins from different species in order to compare the differences in the DNA sequences.

They have found, for example, that the genetic difference between humans and chimpanzees is roughly 1 percent, as compared to a 12 percent difference between dogs and raccoons. These differences are attributed to random variations in the copying of the genetic material from one generation to another. Through a comparison between what the protein studies reveal and what the fossils have revealed, the argument is made that the "molecular clock" reveals humans are not nearly as old ("only" 5 million years old, versus the 20 million of fossil studies) or as unique as once thought.[17] The "new modern synthesis" of chemistry, genetics, and Darwinian evolution has so far focused only upon changes in existing structures, but the hope is that even formation of the human eye, which gave Darwin so much difficulty, will be decoded.

Contemporary Challenges

The modern syntheses represent an effort to broaden the application of the Darwinian theory in its updated genetic form. These efforts have not gone without challenge. The most public challenge has been the revitalization of the nineteenth-century creationist position under the banner of "scientific creationism." Since this challenge offers no new solutions and is at least implicitly inspired by religious concerns, scientific creationism will be discussed in detail later. There have been two other "in-house" scientific challenges to the "orthodox" synthesis of Darwinism and genetics: a new Lamarckianism, and "punctuated equilibrium."

Lamarck's theory that acquired characteristics are inherited has always been popular due to its social and educational implications. Recently there have been attempts to modify the modern synthesis of Darwinism and genetics by arguing for the influence of environmental forces on the genetic code. Arthur Koestler has long argued against the mechanistic determinism of Darwinism and in favor of a Lamarckian theory.[18] He felt that he had found some scientific support for his concerns in the work of Paul Kammerer, and, more recently, E.J. Steele, who argued that the environment may well effect DNA through a feedback mechanism, but neither work has been confirmed by others. More significantly, the work of two women, Barbara McClintock and Frances C. James, has slowly won acceptance among geneticists. They have argued for many years that changes in the environment can create changes in the genetic structure, thus enabling the organism to respond to new needs. Neither of these women wants to resurrect Lamarck, but they do argue for a relationship between genetic information, organisms, and the environment which is more complex than previously accepted.[19]

Darwin's concern with the fossil evidence has become the primary focus of another challenge to the accepted genetic theory of Darwinism which is popularly known as "punctuated equilibrium." Stephen Jay Gould and Niles

Eldredge have argued against the accepted theory that evolution moves in a smooth, continuous progression. Darwin was rightly concerned at the gaps in the fossil record, because there are gaps which represent periods of rapid evolution of forms. Gould has argued that the modern synthesis has broken down in its claims of gradualism and adaptive advantage for all changes:

> If most evolutionary changes, particularly large-scale trends, include major nonadaptive components as primary directing or channeling features, and if they proceed more in an episodic than a smoothly continuous fashion, then we inhabit a different world from the one Darwin envisaged.[20]

The issue is whether the world is in constant change, or whether stable structure is primary and change comes quickly when the structure is under too much stress. For Gould, Eldredge, and others, the latter position fits the fossil evidence better. Punctuated equilibrium is not only a critique of Darwin's world, but also of the tendency to reduce biology to genetics. Eldredge has been quite outspoken against the focus on the gene, but Gould and his followers have argued for a hierarchical approach to selection which would recognize genes, bodies, species, and other biological groupings as legitimate individuals for Darwinian selection.[21] With this hierarchical view of nature, interaction between the various levels can provide stability in the face of negative selection at one level and positive selection at another level. This "higher Darwinism" demands that each level be approached and appreciated on its own terms and for what it contributes to the stability and change of nature. "Darwin, at the centenary of his death, is more alive than ever. Let us continue to praise famous men."[22]

Philosophical Issues

Darwin's two goals, disproving creationism and establishing natural selection, represent not only the transformation of the scientific perception of nature but also the culmination of a revolution in scientific method. At his death, Darwin was proclaimed the Newton of biology by the London *Times*, and Loewenberg reiterated that claim at the centenary of the publication of the *Origin*.[23] While some have dismissed such claims on the basis that Darwin never discovered any new "information" and that some of his ideas have been proven wrong, Loewenberg rightly points out that Darwin's claim to greatness lies in his scientific method. Stephen Jay Gould also has suggested that Darwin's continued scientific relevance is due not to the two goals Darwin set for himself but rather to the principles he established for doing historical science as he worked toward his goals.[24]

Darwin can indeed be understood as the "Newton of biology" because his work provided a conceptual framework which opened up and influenced his own and other fields of study, and which provided a method for approaching old as well as new issues. Darwin's methodology can be understood in terms of four "rules" which reflect certain epistemological commitments. First, Darwin worked with the hypothetico-deductive method which was oriented toward specific hypotheses, and data were collected not simply to confirm the hypotheses but also to refute them where possible. Second, Darwin avoided typological thinking and focused on the small differences between individuals which allowed him to place a variety of present phenomena within a single historic process. Third, evidence from other fields was brought together such that the implications could be understood within a single framework. Fourth, Darwin used a model of selective retention rather than divine teleology and design. These four "rules" enabled him to link together studies from geology to behavioral psychology with the continuous thread of evolution by natural selection.[25]

The revolutionary character of Darwin's methodology is most apparent when placed in historical context. Bacon and Newton were the prominent spiritual leaders relied on for proper scientific method, and, during the 1830s and 1840s, several attempts were made to develop the methodology those two men symbolized. John Herschel's *Preliminary Discourse on the Study of Natural Philosophy* (1830), William Whewell's *The Philosophy of Inductive Science* (1840), and J.S. Mill's *System of Logic* (1843) were the most important works.[26] The key word in the rising self-consciousness was "induction," which usually referred to the Baconian method in contrast to Aristotle's "deductive" method. Herschel, Whewell, and Mill knew the limitations of Bacon's actual work, but Bacon remained the saint. The inductive method seemed to be the best method of gaining absolute certainty in knowledge since it was simplistically presented as moving from observable particulars to broader generalizations, in contrast to the deductive method of moving from general propositions to the particulars. The significant issue was *certainty*, not generality, since an inductive conclusion follows necessarily while a deductive conclusion is probably true.

All science was to be judged by the standards of the best kind of science, and the best kind of science was physics, as demonstrated by the results of Newtonian astronomy. Herschel called upon Bacon even as he developed the Newtonian method, which is called today the hypothetico-deductive system. This system sees scientific theories as being "axiom systems" in which a few laws are taken as the basic references to causes and from which all other laws are derived with reference to the observable world. Since the axioms refer to causes, they logically come first and are thus epistemologically more important. A hypothesis is formulated, then various consequences are deduced from it, and then the observable world is checked to see if the consequences are true. With this system, a hypothesis can never be completely verified or confirmed since it makes broad claims, all of whose consequences cannot be checked out. False consequences do not necessarily falsify a theory since a causal theory is made up of many hypotheses and any one of them may have been incorrect. The best kinds of hypotheses are those that demand quantitative results.

The heart of this system is the concept of *verae causae* (true causes). Herschel described two kinds of laws: empirical laws which point to regularities in nature without explaining why they occur, and causal laws which explain the reasons for the regularities. Herschel was quite vague about causes, but he seemed to be looking for a force that led from one phenomenon to another. This force can be discovered by arguing analogically from our own experiences: if we know the cause of one event from our experience, and we see another, very similar event, then we should assume a similar cause. Whewell also supported the search for "true causes," but his Kantian, rationalist position led him to reject Herschel's empiricist concept of analogically moving from the known to the unknown. Whewell thought that the empiricist position excluded the discovery of any new causes, and so he argued for a "consilience of inductions" in which the various areas of science are brought together and explained in terms of the same principle. This approach is an especially effective guarantee of truth when some areas are explained which once seemed to be in opposition to one's theory. These two approaches to "true causes" were not necessarily antagonistic, and they come to play an important role in understanding the argument Darwin set forth.

J.S. Mill's work is symbolic of the movement toward the acceptance of uniform lawful causality in the 1840s and 1850s. Mill was not the scientist Herschel and Whewell were, and so his work had less direct impact on the scientific community, but he made available the results of the new philosophy of science to a larger audience. Though he rejected Whewell's consilience as a guarantee of truth, Mill was quite willing to extend his concept of the lawfulness of all events into the study of human nature, and to undermine the religious concept of miracle. Mill dismissed the argument that events could be proven as miracles since there is always the possibility that there is an unknown natural cause for the event. To suspend the lawfulness of nature on the behalf of a miracle is not a question to be solved by empirical evidence, but reflects a different epistemological commitment. This different commitment was apparent in Whewell's position on the miraculous creation of organisms. Whewell believed that everything had to have a cause, that the cause must be sufficient to produce the effect, and that causes must refer only to what we can experience ourselves. The loophole in the third of these commitments is that there may have been events in the past to which there is nothing comparable today, and so we might have to refer to causes other than those presently at work. In this way Whewell allowed for the divine creation of life on earth:

It may be found, that such occurrences as these are quite inexplicable by the aid of any natural causes with which we are acquainted; and thus the result of our investigations, conducted with strict regard to scientific principles, may be, that we must either contemplate supernatural influences as part of the past series of events, or declare ourselves altogether unable to form this series into a connected chain.[27]

Where Mill argued for the explanation of all events in terms of natural laws, Whewell was one among many who could not see how natural laws could explain the creation of life on earth. Whewell believed that good scientists might well have to appeal to miraculous powers to explain the creation of life since there were no other laws which made sense of what we see in nature. After the act of creation, laws can explain what is happening. Whewell believed that he was offering a more consistent approach for scientists, yet he lost his argument to the empiricist position of those such as Mill who argued that science should consistently refer only to the working of laws throughout nature.

Darwin was quite aware of these debates over the methodology and philosophy of science. His notebooks from the 1830s and 1840s reveal his reflections on the movement away from the creationist position toward a more "positive" science. Darwin followed Herschel and Whewell's emphasis on the Newtonian scientific method and the universal lawfulness of nature. Even as Newton transformed the belief that God had ordered each planet to move in a certain way, Darwin was convinced that biology could also be transformed into a lawful process.[28] In this effort, Darwin believed that he was following the true spirit of Bacon who argued that "God's word" (the Bible) and "God's work" (nature) should not be confused or mixed since there are forms of knowledge appropriate to each.[29] The notebooks also reveal that Darwin found a "grand idea" in an 1838 review of Comte's *Positive Philosophy* (1830–35) which argued for the movement from a theological to a positive stage of science in which all events are explained in terms of invariable natural laws.

These various ideas encouraged Darwin farther down the road that the new scientific method was headed but had not yet reached: the intellectual freedom of science from religion which would allow new questions to be asked and new answers given for old questions. The move toward "positive" science, methodologically free from creationist presuppositions and recourse to divine causality, reached its culmination with the publication of Darwin's *Origin*. As David Hull has suggested, Darwin presented his theory before all the issues of deduction and induction, laws and experience, and the role of divine intervention in nature had been sorted out.[30] That Darwin's theory was rejected by most is an indication that Darwin was a "methodological revolutionary." Neal Gillespie has summarized this quite well:

> The old science was theologically grounded; the new was positive. The old had reached the limits of its development. The new was asking questions that the old could neither frame nor answer. The new had to break with theology, or render it a neutral factor in its understanding of the cosmos, in order to construct a science that could answer questions about nature in methodologically uniform terms. Uniformity of law, of operation, of method were its watchwords. The old science invoked divine will as an explanation of the unknown; the new postulated yet-to-be-discovered laws. The one inhibited growth because such mysteries were unlikely ever to be clarified; the other held open the hope that they would be.[31]

Darwin symbolized his commitment to this methodology by introducing the *Origin* with quotes from Bacon, Whewell, and, in later editions, Butler on the lawfulness of nature and the epistemological distinction between science and religion.

The *Origin* can be understood as the biological parallel to Newtonian astronomy with its hypothetico-deductive system.[32] Darwin set out his central arguments axiomatically, beginning with the insights he may have gained from reading Malthus's *An Essay on the Principle of Population* (1826) in 1838. The impact of Malthus has been widely debated. Malthus may have been responsible for Darwin's emphasis on thinking in terms of populations, but Darwin could have gained this insight from his experience with pigeon breeders. Or Malthus may have provided the insight into the struggle for existence resulting from the overproduction of life in a given environment and leading to the preservation of favorable variations, but Lyell had already written about the struggle for existence. Malthus could also have provided the methodological insight into analogical, deductive, and quantitative arguments. All three insights were at work in the axiomatic structure of Darwin's argument, which followed the philosophy of science set out by Herschel and Whewell.[33]

Following the method suggested by Herschel, Darwin argued from the analogy of the known to the unknown, from artificial selection to natural selection. This analogy provided the "logic of discovery" for the *vera causa* demanded by Herschel, and Darwin moved to demonstrate natural selection as the "true cause." This was done with the Malthusian hypothesis of the overproduction of organisms for the food in a given area which leads to a struggle for existence. Having established the struggle, Darwin then uses it and includes the variations which are observed from the initial analogy of artificial selection to imply the working of natural selection. In the first four chapters of the *Origin*, Darwin demonstrates the "new" philosophy of science and its methodology. Following further discussion of variation, Darwin faces the "difficulties of the theory" which could falsify natural selection, and answers them. The argument then shifts to incorporate Whewell's *vera causa*, the consilience of inductions, by explaining other areas of science (instincts, geographical distribution, embryology) in terms of the theory of natural selection. Darwin demonstrates a bold theory of natural selection by synthesizing three elements of the newly developing philosophy of science: the empiricist "true cause" of analogy from known to unknown, the deductive method based on Malthusian population thinking, and the rationalist "true cause" which unifies the various scientific disciplines under the theory of natural selection.[34]

Darwin's "new" method raised a number of methodological problems. The "Baconian" ideal of induction supposedly guaranteed the certainty of the conclusions which are reached. It became apparent that Darwin's metaphorical population thinking had replaced certainty with *probability*, and this led many to argue that Darwin had abandoned the Newtonian method and had proven nothing. William Hopkins quickly recognized this, and, though he supported the Newtonian hypothetico-deductive system, he argued that the fossil record could be deduced from Darwin's theory, but the proof was not conclusive. The argument was made that, since there was no certainty, only "maybe," there could be no predictions made from Darwin's theory, and predictions were taken as a strong point of Newtonian astronomy. In "The Fixation of Belief" (1877), C.S. Peirce noted the parallel in population thinking between Darwin's theory and the gas laws. Natural selection and gas laws are both statistical in nature, "predicting" what will happen to a population but unable to describe the future for specific individuals. Darwinian evolution includes a variety of factors, and is not as simple as Newton's two-body problems. For this reason Darwinian evolutionists are satisfied with "a high degree of probability" in their findings. Yet, for those impressed with the success of Newtonian astronomy, Darwin had "proven" nothing. The population thinking of Darwin and its statistical nature represented to some a radical change in viewing the world.[35]

A second methodological problem revolved around the concept of "species." As we saw earlier in this chapter, the creationist position argued for an "essentialist" definition of species which clearly separated one from another and erected a barrier between them. The argument for an unchanging essence could take either an Aristotelian form in which universals exist in nature, or a Platonic form in which categories exist in the mind of the creator. Whewell's rationalism depended upon a static, discrete essentialism in order for knowledge to be possible. The empiricism of Mill and Herschel depended upon an essentialism of discrete natural kinds in order to be able to discuss a chronological succession in terms of universal causal laws. Darwin's theory that species evolve seemed to destroy the possibility of the knowledge of causality in living systems since there was no finite number of discrete kinds which could be included in an inductive analysis of causation. Biological systems are more complex and more localized than Mill's concept of a universal theory of causality could accept. Even more difficult for some, Darwin's concept of evolving species rejected the religious essentialism of God having created distinct "kinds." Louis Agassiz and J.W. Dawson argued for this Platonic-Christian concept that species exist in the mind and the work of the Creator. There was little that Darwin could say in response to these opponents of his theory, except to demonstrate the complexity of the issue in the *Origin* and challenge others to see nature his way. Darwin's work accelerated the decline of essentialism in biological thought.[36]

These two methodological issues have led some to charge that Darwinism is not scientific.[37] In the nineteenth century, Darwin was charged with an irresponsible use of hypotheses which indicated that he had "deserted" the Baconian method. Obviously Darwin had abandoned the results which the Baconian method had produced in the past, and Darwin had used hypotheses to shape his argument. The primary problem was, and still is for some, the positive scientific method. More recently, Darwinism has been charged with being unscientific because the phrase "survival of the fittest" is supposedly a tautology which can not be scientifically tested. (In a tautology there is a logical redundancy between the two parts of a statement such that there is no new information given which can be tested; e.g., "my daughter is a female" is true by definition.) The critics ask how we know which organisms are fittest, and characterize the Darwinian response as being that the fittest are those who survive the longest and produce the most offspring. As Hull points out, there are some biologists who accept this definition, and this definition is a tautology since it simply means the "survival of those who survive." Yet Darwinian natural selection refers to a relationship between the organism and the environment in which variations give adaptive advantages. One organism is more fit than another because it can withstand changes in the environment (food availability, protection, challenges by other organisms). In this formulation, "survival of the fittest" is not tautological.

A third challenge to the scientific status of Darwinism came from Sir Karl Popper, who has made his mark in the philosophy of science by attempting to find a principle of demarcation between true and false science. Popper has argued for the "falsifiability" of a theory as evidence of true science: there must be some imaginable test of the theory whose negative results would disprove the theory. Pseudoscience, on the other hand, makes such vague claims that no such test is possible. Popper has claimed that Darwinism is not falsifiable since there could always be explanations which invoke some adaptation to explain the "negative" results, and the predictions that the Darwinian theory might make cannot be tested because they are not universal in nature. Popper's charges will be examined in more detail later since they form part of the contemporary creationist argument against Darwinism, but it should be noted here that Darwinians have been quick to respond. Ruse has argued that the scientific character of Darwinism is demonstrated in its "consilience," the ability to incorporate a variety of fields of study under its theory, and in its ability to "predict" the struggle for survival in terms of the variations which do occur in nature. Hull has noted that biologists are quite satisfied with a theory which "works," even if the theory is not universal because we can never know all the data. In spite of these various charges that Darwinism is not scientific, the theory has retained its central, organizing status in biological studies.

The question of teleology and design has continued to be a methodological problem for Darwinism. As we saw earlier in this chapter, Darwin argued in both the *Origin* and the "orchid book" for an undirected process of variation and natural selection. Natural selection may well lead to designlike appearances, but the adaptations are built up from a supply of random variations. Darwin's theory represented a clash between the Newtonian model of science and the appearances in nature. There is no discussion of final causes in Newtonian physics, yet biologists felt compelled to argue for a special status for organisms since their development appears to be teleological. The directing force could be either a Platonic external mind ordering everything, or an Aristotelian immanent force with the goal internal to the organism. In either case, Darwinian natural selection was offensive. Platonists could not like the mind Darwinism implied, and Aristotelians could not have their essences changing. Whewell was quite willing to exclude teleology from scientific inquiry and accept "accidental" events in the Newtonian system, but there had to be some explanation for those events, and so final causes were legitimate results of scientific inquiry. Teleology was a heuristic device necessary for understanding the life of an organism, and it was poor scientific method to exclude that necessary conclusion. The empiricists Herschel and Mill also rejected Darwinism since "chance variations" implied the absence of law. The more explicitly religious scientists argued that Darwin's "chance variations" were not worthy of a God whose character should be discernible from the order of the universe. If God is all-good and all-knowing and all-powerful, then all organisms should vary in a direction favorable to their continued survival. This was not what Darwin found. The efforts of Herschel, Whewell, and Mill to establish a natural, lawful explanation for events in nature culminated in Darwin's theory which demonstrated that the activity of God in nature was no longer a necessary conclusion. Hull has effectively summarized this:

> The architects of the demise of teleology were not atheistic materialists but pious men like Herschel, Whewell, and Mill, who thought they were doing religion good service by limiting the domain of the accidental and miraculous. To them the more the empirical world was shown to be governed by secondary causes acting according to God-given laws, the more powerful and omniscient God was shown to be.[38]

Darwin was quite aware of the philosophical and religious issues of teleology and design, and his personal struggle with design in nature has been extensively documented and debated. On the one hand, some argue that Darwin had abandoned all theological beliefs early in his career and the references to a creator in the *Origin* were there for public appeal. On the other hand, there is the argument that Darwin's *Autobiography* is to be taken seriously when Darwin says that it was only late in his life that he moved toward agnosticism. The more helpful perspective is to see Darwin struggling to relate his received religious views with his growing understanding of a proper scientific method.[39] The quotations which form the preface to the *Origin* represent Darwin's choice of seeing God governing nature through laws, rather than by intervention, and the discovery of those laws is not contrary to God's will. Darwin's theory was an effort to do precisely what other scientists were doing: expand the realm of natural law. Darwin simply extended secondary causes to explain the creation of species. God had instituted the laws, but left the details to "chance." Biologists can discover the laws which govern the activity of the world, but there is no more need to refer to God as intelligently directing the process. The spirit of the scientific method initiated by Bacon and Newton had reached its fruition with Darwin's theory.

Teleological language and concerns in biology, however, did not die with Darwin's theory. The religious presuppositions and conclusions about a divine directing force did die slowly as a factor in biological explanations, and this will be discussed in later chapters. Teleology as such is still a debated issue in scientific methodology.[40] Ruse has noted that "though his nontheological theory is often portrayed as taking the teleology out of biology, if anything Darwin was bringing it back in" by his emphasis on adaptation toward an end.[41] Biologists still use teleological language in describing structures and organisms as having "functions" and "purposes." The heart is described as having the purpose of pumping blood so that oxygen gets to the various regions of the body, or the organism has the function of passing on its genetic material. These questions of teleology and the mechanistic reduction of life need to be seen as qualitatively different from the nineteenth-century debates over the place and role of divine direction in biological systems. Yet, as we shall see in a later chapter, the contemporary scientific debate over the appropriateness and place of teleology has opened up again the question of an immanent, divine force.

These methodological issues raised by Darwin's theory have been incorporated into the modern syntheses and the challenges to Darwinism. The Darwinian transformation of biology into a science like Newtonian physics has been extended by the contemporary focus on the genetic and molecular levels of evolution. Some have argued that the molecular focus represents another methodological transformation in biological science: biology is not simply "like" physics, but it has become a part of physics and chemistry.[42] While this transformation may be the logical result of Darwin's work, many biologists resist the reduction of biology to physics and chemistry on the basis that there is something about the living organism (life) that cannot be reduced to chemical and physical descriptions. This objection to reduction is usually not an effort to reclaim a vitalism or a special life force (e.g., Bergson), but rather an attempt to recognize the various complex structures of an organism which enable it to relate to other organisms and the environment at different levels (genetic, molecular, specific characteristics of the organism, species kinship). Sociobiology can be understood methodologically as extending Darwin's original insight by discussing the organism at the genetic and kinship levels. The challenge of the "punctuated equilibrium" model can be understood methodologically as establishing the various levels at which selection takes place. Rather than a reduction of biology to physics and chemistry, we actually have various levels of the life of the organism which are involved in the process of Darwinian evolution. The understanding of these various levels is intended as a completely positive natural scientific explanation which recognizes the complexity of the living organism. Yet, as with the question of teleology, we shall see some who want to interpret the hierarchy in religious terms.

Since the publication of Kuhn's *The Structure of Scientific Revolutions* (1962), biologists and philosophers of science have been debating the evidence for a "Darwinian revolution." Kuhn himself briefly mentions Darwin's theory as an example of a scientific revolution and notes that the revolutionary character of Darwinism was not the idea of evolution or evidence for it, but rather the absence of a religious or philosophical teleology directing the natural processes. The debates over the validity of Kuhn's idea of a scientific revolution have essentially supported his perception of the Darwinian revolution: it was a revolution which offered a scientific method that neither wanted nor needed religious presuppositions and teleological explanations.[43] There are criticisms of Kuhn's approach to scientific revolutions when applied to biology, which help focus on the uniqueness of Darwin's work. For example, Kuhn argued that revolutions occur when there are significant problems with the standard scientific paradigm for explaining nature (e.g., the complexities of the Ptolemaic system before Copernicus). When a new paradigm is suggested that offers a better explanation, a shift is made in the understanding of nature and the new paradigm suggests the direction for future research.

This description of a scientific revolution does not fit biology in the nineteenth century. An evolutionary model of biology had long been in existence when Darwin wrote, and it was an equal counterparadigm to the static "chain of being" explanation of nature. It was no crisis in the ability of the static paradigm to explain nature that led Darwin to offer his theory, nor was there any new evidence for the evolutionary paradigm. Darwin's theory revolutionized both the static and evolutionary paradigms. Against the static world view, Darwin offered a vision of nature in which change is integral. More significantly, Darwin provided a completely natural explanation for the adaptations in nature in contrast to the partially supernatural, teleological explanation which was an accepted if not necessary part of the static world view. The creationist position attempted to hold together the experience of nature and the religious presuppositions, but Darwin demonstrated that a better scientific explanation was possible. Darwin offered the positive hypothetico-deductive system as the new set of rules for biological science, and those rules could not fit with the creationist presuppositions of a providential God at work in nature.

Darwin also revolutionized the evolutionist positions of the nineteenth century by arguing that there was no evidence for an ideal form toward which organisms move. Darwin's natural random variations removed the possibility of an immanent plan or creative urge which explained the evolutionary process. Darwin's hypothetico-deductive system established natural selection as the method of the change for which evolutionists had argued, and this effectively established a *Darwinian* theory of evolution as the new paradigm for biological studies. The revolution did not involve the production of a completely adequate theory of evolution, for Darwin did not have all the answers for the source of variations and inheritance. Darwin did revolutionize biological science, whether static creationist or evolutionist, by systematically disproving any religious or philosophical teleology as necessary to a scientific method, and by proving the power of a positive explanation to integrate many fields of scientific inquiry in terms of the relationship between an organism and its environment.

This methodological character of the Darwinian revolution is most significant for this study of the religious responses to Darwinism. The particular hermeneutic, interpretive angle, which is used to establish models for the relationship between the two should reflect the significant issues actually at work. As we have seen in this chapter, the general concept of evolution was not the key to Darwin's work. Darwin's goal was to dismantle the creationist explanation of nature, and offer a natural, nonteleological explanation for the adaptation we observe in nature. This explanation was established through a hypothetico-deductive system which had no need for divine intervention, in contrast to the received scientific tradition which accepted religiously orthodox presuppositions and conclusions as part of science. James R. Moore has argued that there was no evolutionary revolution, and in a sense he is correct, as we have seen. The revolution was methodological as it reflected the transformation in scientific epistemology which culminated in Darwin's work. An analysis of the religious responses to Darwinism must take this revolution as its hermeneutic key in order to remain faithful to the issues at stake in Darwin's work. The remainder of this book will establish models by focusing on how scientists and religious thinkers have responded to the epistemological and methodological Darwinian revolution in both the nineteenth and twentieth centuries.

3

Religion *against* Darwinism

The analysis of the relationship between science and religious thought has tended toward generalities without focusing on how the models of the relationship actually relate to specific issues. This book attempts to overcome that weakness by proposing four models of religious response to Darwinism. In the conclusion, I will suggest that these models are applicable to other areas of scientific thought. Based on the preceding two chapters, the hermeneutic used in this study focuses on the epistemological and methodological issues of the Darwinian revolution and incorporates a historical perspective. Scientists and religious thinkers of both the nineteenth and twentieth centuries will be examined for their response to the Darwinian method of excluding religious presuppositions and divine teleology from science, and for their tendencies toward Darwinisticism, the elevation of Darwinian evolution into an ethical and religious myth.

The first model I propose is "Religion *against* Darwinism." The "warfare" metaphor of the relationship between science and religion took this model to be the standard for nineteenth-century religious thinkers. The conflict was, and is, real, but we must examine the roots of this conflict in the epistemologies and methodologies at work. Charles Hodge, a nineteenth-century Presbyterian theologian, is usually portrayed as the leader of the conflict because of his conclusion that Darwinism is atheism. His thought will be examined in detail so that this claim is understood in its full significance. Hodge's position was rooted in Scottish common sense realism, the predominant American philosophical system in the nineteenth century, but there were other writers who took a different approach in rejecting Darwinism. Orestes Brownson will be discussed as a Roman Catholic "against" response, and Horace Bushnell will be examined briefly as offering a negative response but with some interesting possibilities for other models. When we shift our attention to the twentieth-century representatives of this model, we will focus on the contemporary scientific creationists, led by Henry M. Morris, and discover that they offer nothing new beyond their nineteenth-century forerunners. Variations on the basic theme will be discovered in the works of Jeremy Rifkin, a popular critic of recent scientific developments; Stanley Jaki, a Roman Catholic historian of science; and Huston Smith, who argues for a new epistemology. We will see a historical continuity in the responses which has not been generally recognized in most analyses of the religious response to Darwinism.

Nineteenth-Century Battle Lines

Charles Hodge

Charles Hodge (1797–1878) became the center of the religious storm that battered Darwinism, with the publication of *What is Darwinism?* in 1874. This small book and its argument should have come as no surprise to those who had read the first two volumes of his *Systematic Theology* (1871–73), or who understood the Princeton philosophical tradition. Massive systematics are seldom read outside of one's own religious circle, however, so Hodge's popular book on Darwinism became the focus of attention. The argument of *What is Darwinism?* cannot be appreciated without an understanding of both the Princeton tradition of philosophy in which Hodge was educated and the *Systematics*.

John Witherspoon brought the common sense realism of eighteenth-century Scottish universities to America and to Princeton. Witherspoon had learned his lessons well from such Scottish philosophers as Thomas Reid, Dugald Stewart, and James Beattie. Reid struggled with the epistemology of Locke and with Hume's attack on Locke. While Locke had correctly distinguished primary qualities from secondary qualities, Reid believed that Locke had not demonstrated that objects of our sense perceptions were only ideas in our minds. Locke had left a duality of an idea and a reality represented which trapped the mind within its own sensations and resulted in the immediate knowledge of nothing. A much better way was to define an idea as a mental act, not a mental object. The evidence for this is found in the way the mind works. Sensation and perception are different operations of the mind: "The natural furniture of the human understanding is of two kinds: First, the notions or simple apprehensions which we have of things; and, secondly, the judgments or beliefs we have of them."[1] Reid's realistic theory of perception has been summarized in terms of four major conclusions which shape Hodge's own epistemology. First, knowledge "depends on scientific observation" and the object is primarily self-consciousness, not other objects. Second, this observation establishes two kinds of principles "which are anterior to and independent of experience": necessary (such as cause-and-effect relations) and contingent (existence of things). Third, only an intelligent being can be an efficient cause, and thus matter "is only an instrument in the hands of a real cause." Fourth, self-evident intuition provides moral principles.[2]

This system gets its name of "common sense" from the fact that these operations of the mind cannot be demonstrated by reason, but only on the basis of our own consciousness, or common sense. It is "common" because this is the way the mind works in all people, and it is "sense" because the mind makes judgments about the sensations that are received. Examining how the mind works reveals that a "natural and original judgment" is an integral part of our perception of the world. These judgments are implicit in every experience and can be trusted to give accurate information. If some people lack this common sense, then others must guide them. Reid claims that

> all knowledge, and all science, must be built upon principles that are self-evident; and of such principles, every man who has common sense is a competent judge, when he receives them distinctly. Hence it is, that disputes very often terminate in an appeal to common sense.[3]

James Beattie's words summarize this meaning of common sense realism. It is

> that power of the mind which perceives truth, or commands belief, not by progressive argumentation, but by instantaneous and instinctive impulse; derived neither from education nor from habit, but from nature; acting independently on our will, whenever its object is presented, according to an intellectual law, and therefore not improperly called sense; and acting in a similar manner on all mankind, and therefore properly called common sense.[4]

This common sense approach to knowledge found support and a methodology in the Baconian scientific method. The empirical, inductive method was based on a confident trust in the senses and in a reality as supplied by our innate judgments. Common sense philosophy encouraged science to do its work of objective examination of the facts of nature and to discover the laws of nature. The role of science was to be taxonomical: to gather and classify the facts. In its work, science gives a causal explanation by assigning to an event its antecedents. Scientific knowledge of causality is restricted, according to the third principle of Reid's system, to the agency of ourselves or of God. In other words, science is excluded from talk about efficient causation, and its generalizations must be controlled by reference to the facts. When the question of efficient causation is raised, the answer must be God since the presence of intelligence in the world is self-evident.[5]

Common sense realism and Baconian science had a powerful impact on American Reformed theology and its use of Scripture. Since the common sense perceptions of the common person could be relied upon, all Christians could understand the basic information and message of the Bible. In 1812, Archibald Alexander of Princeton declared that "any sane and unbiased person of common sense could and must perceive the same things." The Bible does not represent the ideas of the authors about the past. It is an infallible presentation of the past itself. If anyone cannot see that, he is obviously in error and needs training in common sense. Since the Bible is a storehouse of facts, all persons should discover the same truths. Theology simply followed the Baconian method of classifying all the facts.[6] The objective, inductive investigation of nature by scientists would confirm what the biblical facts have revealed. Science thus becomes "doxological."

Charles Hodge was educated in this intellectual tradition at Princeton College and at Princeton Seminary. Following his graduation, Hodge was ordained in the Presbyterian Church in 1821, and began teaching at Princeton Seminary in 1822, where he remained for half a century. Hodge was not unfamiliar with the science of the times. In his early years on the faculty of Princeton Seminary, he attended lectures in anatomy and physiology. Hodge was founder and editor of the *Princeton Review*, and, in an 1851 editorial, he encouraged the work of science when the inductive method was used, but claimed that science was open to criticism when generalizations were made that conflicted with the Bible. Scripture was a valid and powerful piece of evidence that good Baconian scientists could not overlook. Hodge reiterated this Scottish common sense position in an article published in the year Darwin's *Origin* appeared:

> It is perfectly conceivable that a scientific sceptic may be led in his principles by a strictly logical process to decide a scientific question one way, when a scientific Christian, by an equally logical process would decide it another way. The reason is that the latter takes into view legitimate facts and considerations which the former ignores.[7]

In an article a year later, Hodge revealed his commitment to Reid's concept of efficient causation in nature as always due to mind, not matter:

> The development of a plant, and the growth of an animal body, are not to be referred to blind forces, inherent in matter, nor in any substance, material or immaterial, but to the omnipresent Spirit of God. The intelligence manifested in organic structures is clear evidence of mind guiding the operation of natural forces.[8]

The influence of Baconian science and common sense philosophy is evident in Hodge's theological methodology.[9] The *Systematic Theology* begins with a description of "Theology as Science." Since a science is more than simply facts but includes the "persuasion of what is true on adequate evidence," then theology "must include something more than a mere knowledge of facts. It must embrace an exhibition of the internal relation of those facts."[10] The inductive method of collecting, authenticating, arranging, and exhibiting the truths of the Bible is to govern the general truths that are inferred, and should protect against prejudices determining the conclusions. In this method, the scientist and theologian share certain methodological assumptions. They both trust their senses, their mental operations, and their common sense understanding of causality. They

> must rely on the certainty of those truths which are not learned from experience, but which are given in the constitution of our nature. That every effect must have a cause; that the same cause under like circumstances will produce the like effects; that a cause is not a mere uniform antecedent, but that which contains within itself the reason why the effect occurs.[11]

The theologian adds to these common sense assumptions the essential distinction between right and wrong, the punishment of sin, and the rewarding of good.

A final assumption in Hodge's methodology is that all truth comes from God, and thus truth must be consistent since God cannot contradict himself. We will not be put in a position of being commanded by the Bible to believe anything opposite of what we experience in nature. If there appears to be a conflict, Scripture and common sense are the superior guides since the Scriptures teach more authoritatively about God than does nature. To those who would claim that God is not revealed in nature, Hodge calls on the power of common sense to understand what is seen: "If a horse is born of a horse, the immortal spirit of man, instinct with its moral and religious convictions and aspirations, must be the offspring of the Father of Spirits." If we examine the natural world, common sense tells us "that it has not the cause of its existence within itself, and therefore must have had an extramundane cause; and that the infinitely numerous manifestations of design which it exhibits show that the cause must be intelligent, are arguments for the being of God."[12] Common sense tells us that "deistic rationalism" must be rejected because our "moral nature" assures us that God is quite present and constantly interferes in our lives. Any claim of science about nature and God must be tested by, and meet the requirements of, Scripture and common sense. Any conflict over truth can be resolved "easily" by appeal to these final judges.

Having rejected deism in the search for truth, Hodge presents two arguments for theism. A brief cosmological argument is presented first. The world is obviously an effect and is mutable, and, since the whole cannot be essentially different from its parts, a First Cause must be assumed as the efficient explanation for the existence of the universe. Since neither science nor common sense allows something to come from nothing, the explanation must be a creator rather than an infinite succession of contingent events.

The heart of Hodge's theology is the sovereignty of God, the conviction that the glory and purposes of God are the center of the Christian life. The fundamental belief that God actively rules all creation provides the background for the second argument for God's existence, and for Hodge's conflict with Darwinism:

Design supposes a designer. The world everywhere exhibits marks of design. Therefore the world owes its existence to an intelligent author. By design is intended, (1)The selection of an end to be attained, (2)The choice of suitable means for its attainment, (3)The actual application of those means for the accomplishment of the proposed end. Such being the nature of design, it is self-evident truth, or, even an identical proposition, that design is indicative of intelligence, will, and power. It is simply saying that intelligence in the effect implies intelligence in the cause. It is moreover true that the intelligence indicated by design is not in the thing designed. It must be an external agent. [13]

The evidence for this design in nature is as plain as a book having an author. According to Hodge, only if one can believe that a book is written by chance or blind force can one deny the argument of design as proof for the existence of a personal God. Common sense tells us that the eye, the ear, blood, lungs, digestive system, and the bone and muscle structure must have been designed, and thus must have had a designer. To deny an intelligent agency at work in nature is an "altogether irrational" act, and the denier must be trained in common sense in order to see the truth. Hodge employs an analogy from our own experience: "When we see such benevolent arrangements among men, we refer them instinctively and by a rational necessity to a benevolent and intelligent agent. No rational ground exists for refusing to ascribe like arrangements in nature to a similar source." [14] Any denial of teleology in nature is a denial of both God and common sense. There are obviously intelligent forces at work in nature choosing ends and the means to attain those ends. Logic demands a self-existing, eternal Cause with intelligence, will, power, and benevolence.

Hodge then moves to defend his common sense teleology against the claims of positivism, vitalism, and scientific materialism. The defense is based on common sense realism, as the words "intuitive," "every man," and "self-evident" form the keystones of the argument. Comte and the positivists are wrong because many people believe in God, and our intuition tells us that we are free agents, that every effect has a cause, and that there is a God to whom we are responsible. Scientific materialism comes under strong attack because it contradicts the "facts of consciousness" which "every man" has of the existence of mind. Sounding a note that is heard again and again from anti-Darwinians, Hodge asserts that materialism also contradicts the facts of moral and religious consciousness which attest to a sense of sin and the reality of a God to whom we are accountable. Hodge rejoices in the fact that we cannot free ourselves from this sense of moral accountability. Finally, materialism contradicts both reason and experience, which convince us of the need for an intelligent cause to produce intelligent effects. Matter alone cannot explain the appearance of life or the rational, moral, spiritual nature of humanity. According to Hodge, the assumption that matter itself is capable of such an explanation contradicts common experience.

Hodge plays the role of a Baconian scientist of religious thought and arrays the facts against the materialist world view. Materialism denies any teleology and design in the world, but it is wrong. The common sense facts of consciousness, of morality and religion, of reason, and of experience are overwhelmingly in favor of teleology and divine design. The fatal blow to materialism comes with the realization that it is atheism because it rejects theism. Hodge echoes the 1851 editorial with these words:

> If metaphysicians and theologians must be silent on matters of science, then scientific men devoted to the study of the sensuous, are not entitled to be dictatorial in what regards the supersensuous.... The senses have their rights, and so have reason and conscience; and the votaries of sense are not entitled to claim the whole domain of knowledge as exclusively their own.[15]

The leveling effect of common sense philosophy is brought into play when Hodge claims that everyone has the right to judge the scientific arguments, and to appeal to one scientist in favor of another. What do the many scientists, especially when that includes Louis Agassiz, and all the facts prove? The world moves with a purpose and with design. The normal mind always begins with God, whereas the materialists begin at the wrong end with blind, lifeless matter. The materialists are in error in both philosophy and science.

The results should be obvious when Hodge turns specifically to Darwinism in volume 2 of the *Systematic Theology* and in *What Is Darwinism?* The standards for evaluation continue to be common sense philosophy and the Baconian method in science. Darwinism is tested and fails on both accounts. The first thing to note is that Hodge had actually read and understood the writings of Darwin as well as those of Lamarck, Chambers, Spencer, Wallace, Huxley, Agassiz, Gray, and the German materialists. Hodge is capable of making the arguments he does only because he has taken the time to understand the arguments of the scientists. Hodge knew that he had to show he knew what he was talking about before he could answer the question: what is Darwinism? Evolutionary thought prior to Darwin is analyzed, and then the focus shifts to the distinctive elements of Darwin's theory. Darwin is recognized as a careful naturalist who does not speculate on the origins of the universe, and as one who shares many assumptions with Hodge, including the concept of a creator. Hodge correctly perceives the key elements of Darwin's work: Darwin assumes the efficiency of physical causes and claims that the diversity of life comes not from any "inward power of development" but from natural laws of heredity, variation, overproduction leading to a struggle for life, and the survival of the fittest by natural selection over a long period of time. *Systematics* quotes Darwin's "tangled bank" metaphor and *What Is Darwinism?* has four pages of Darwin quotations.[16] Hodge concludes his analysis with "man (body, soul, and spirit) is descended from a hairy quadruped, furnished with tail and pointed ears" and in amazement quotes Darwin's question as to why descent by natural selection should be any more irreligious than normal laws of reproduction.[17]

Hodge may be guilty of exaggerating Darwin's stance, as some critics claim, but Hodge does this to sharpen Darwin's major point that many had missed or ignored: *natural* selection. In contrast to some of his contemporaries, Hodge does understand Darwin's use of natural selection: natural laws working without design or final causes. As we have seen, natural selection without divine teleology is the key to Darwin's theory, and Hodge focused on this issue in the origin of species. It

> is owed not to the original intention of the divine mind; not to the special acts of creation calling new forms into existence at certain epochs; not to the constant and everywhere operating efficiency of God, guiding physical causes in the production of intended effects; but to the gradual accumulation of unintended variations of structure and instinct, securing some advantage to their subjects.[18]

Evolution and selection, as the means of evolution, could be reconciled with theism by claiming that God planned it all, but Hodge argues that that position is *not* a Darwinian position. A true Darwinian denies any divine design or telos in the selection process. Hodge is astounded at the thought that the eye and the orchid could be explained without a designer. Darwinism is like a person explaining the Bible by pointing to a typesetting machine working at random.

In spite of the rhetoric, which is all some critics have heard, Hodge did focus on the primary epistemological and methodological issues of Darwinism. The epistemological issue for Hodge and common sense realism is that anyone can see the workings of mind in nature:

> It shocks the common sense of men to be told that the whale and the hummingbird, man and the mosquito, are derived from the same source.... It cannot be true, because it is founded on the assumption of an impossibility. It assumes that matter does the work of mind. This is an impossibility and an absurdity in the judgment of all men except the materialists.... God, says Darwin, created the unintelligent living cell [and] after that first step, all else follows by natural law, without purpose and without design. No man can believe this, who cannot also believe that all works of art, literature, and science in the world are the products of carbonic acid, water, and ammonia.[19]

Hodge is claiming that the moral and religious convictions of many people simply cannot be ignored, and anyone who denies the presence of intelligent design in nature is blind, irrational, or immoral. Intelligence and teleology are present in nature since we can see adaptations toward an end. The epistemological denial of teleology by Darwinism is wrong because it conflicts with "the intuitive and irresistable convictions of all mankind."[20]

Darwinism is also in error because it breaks the canons of scientific methodology. Hodge claims at this point that he wants to be "irenic" with regard to the conflict between science and religion. First, Hodge acknowledges that the scientist and the religious thinker work with different rules of evidence since one studies matter and the other studies phenomena of the mind. The conflict comes when scientists claim that the senses are the only source of knowledge. By falling into this error, Darwin has excluded other kinds of evidence necessary for true knowledge. Second, Hodge claims that Darwin has failed to make the proper distinction between facts, explanations of those facts, and the theories deduced from them. The issue is that the facts of biology have not changed, but only the explanation of those facts in terms of natural selection as the means of evolution has changed: "All the facts relied upon by evolutionists have long been familiar to scientific men. The whole change is a subjective one."[21] Any new explanations must be held lightly and their holders must respect the testimony of the conscience of others. Hodge raises the question: what has changed between Chambers's *Vestiges* in 1844 and Darwinism in 1864? The evidence has not changed. Darwin has offered a theory with no pretenses that it can be proven, and with no valid explanation for such things as the eye, the sterility of hybrids, or slave ants. Darwinism has failed to take seriously Baconian scientific methodology, and it offers only a hypothesis that cannot be proven when all the facts are taken into consideration.

What is Darwinism? According to Hodge, it is bad epistemology and bad scientific methodology. These two errors have led it into atheism. The origins of life can be known for certain only by divine revelation, and anything else is conjecture. Darwin abandoned scientific facts and Baconian certainty for probabilities, and "Christians have a right to protest against the arraying of *probabilities* against the clear teachings of Scripture."[22] The clear teachings of Scripture rest on the infallible authority of the Word of God. They do not conflict in any way with the truths of reason or the truths of experience. They account for the spiritual nature of humanity which our very nature confirms. Scripture is a vital piece of evidence that accounts for the obvious design in nature. Darwinism, by excluding teleology from nature, conflicts with common sense, with all the facts that science should consider, and with religious beliefs. Hodge was convinced that the ateleological, atheistic Darwinism would go the way of "cobwebs in the track of a tornado."

The epistemology, methodology, and conclusions of Darwinism stand in fundamental opposition to the philosophy and world view of Hodge. Darwin had revolutionized scientific method and destroyed the doxological role of "Baconian" science. This revolution undermined the confidence of common sense philosophy, and left the common sense realists with an anachronistic view of epistemology, nature, science, and religion. Yet this perspective is still with us, and the same arguments are being made today, as we shall see in the next section of this chapter.

Orestes Brownson

Orestes Brownson(1803–76) was the most outspoken and most listened to American Roman Catholic on Darwinism and evolution from 1863 to 1873. The attention that Brownson received was due to his well-known shifting allegiances. In 1828, he was the leader of New York's Workingmen's Party, and joined the Roman Catholic Church in 1844 after experiences as a Congregationalist, Methodist, Presbyterian, Universalist, Unitarian, socialist, and transcendentalist. Following the path of many converts, Brownson became an ardent conservative supporter of his chosen church, and his stance was supported by Pope Pius IX's condemnation of liberalism in the 1864 Syllabus of Errors.[23] Writing in his own *Brownson's Quarterly Review* and in *Catholic World*, Brownson attacked modern civilization and its evils of materialism, progress, and Darwinism.

As Hodge was viewed as representing *the* Calvinist response to Darwinism, so too Brownson was viewed as presenting *the* Roman Catholic response. The difference between the two was that Hodge was much more interested in, and knowledgeable about, the modern sciences and Darwin's theory. Brownson displays the influence of Baconian and common sense realism as he presents some of the same arguments against Darwinism as are found in Hodge: the confusion of the authority of facts and theories, the lack of new evidence to support Darwin's theory, and Darwin's ignoring the Bible and failure to prove that his theory is better than the creation stories as an explanation for the appearance and organization of life. Although Hodge respected Darwin's personal religious beliefs and skills as a scientific observer, Brownson described Darwin's intellectual skills as feeble and concluded a discussion of Darwin's work by describing him as one of "Satan's most efficient ministers."[24]

None of this would make Brownson particularly interesting for this study except insofar as his conflict with Darwinism represents a Roman Catholic epistemology and presupposition as to how science and religious thought relate. Brownson is quite consistent in his method of attack. In an 1863 article, "Science and the Sciences," Brownson attacks Roman Catholics who dismiss any need for confronting the results of science on the basis that, since all truth comes from God, there can be no conflict between science and religion. Roman Catholics do have a duty to protect society and aid its true progress. To this end, Brownson distinguishes between science and the sciences, and attacks those who claim that the Baconian method of classification and induction is science. Kant had demonstrated that noumena cannot be concluded from phenomena, and thus God cannot be concluded from the universe. The true scientific method must synthesize the *a priori* and *a posteriori* methods since there are both contingent and ideal elements in the sciences:

> The fault of modern science is in separating,—not simply distinguishing, but separating,— in its method the contingent from the necessary, the empirical from the ideal, or the mimetic from the methexic, and hence its inductions and generalizations are nothing but unscientific and arbitrary classifications of phenomena or particulars.[25]

The offense of modern science, of which Darwin is a classic representative, is its exclusion of the ideal from its explanations, and thus its methodological exclusion of God from any explanation of the universe.

Brownson argues that any true science begins at the beginning, the creative act of God, and then moves from that whole to the parts. Reason must be free, but reason is never free to do its normal work without the aid of divine revelation. Descartes and Bacon led science astray when they separated science from the aid of religion: "Faith does not restrain reason in matters of science; does not say to it, Thus far, but no further; but bids it use all the light it has, and aids it to go further than by its own light it could go."[26] Faith is necessary for it provides us with the understanding of the laws of nature necessary for science. Brownson asks where the laws come from, and whether they are superior or inferior to nature. He concludes that, since the laws must be superior to govern the operations of nature, the laws must originate in the supernatural, and thus have an existence contingent upon the creative act of God. If we methodologically deny the creative activity of God, then there can be no understanding or explanation of the laws of nature. Brownson presents the Roman Catholic position that faith complements and completes human knowledge:

> There is no philosophy or science, if God and his creative act are excluded or ignored, because there is no cosmos left, and neither a subject to know nor an object to be known.... Religion and science are indeed parts of one whole; but religion, while it includes science, supplements it by the analogical knowledge called faith. The truths of faith and of science are always in dialectic harmony, and between the Christian faith and real science there is no quarrel, and can be none; for religion only supplies the defect of science, and puts the mind in possession of the solution of the problem of man and the universe, not attainable by science.[27]

As mentioned earlier, Brownson had little respect for Darwin or any philosopher or theologian who supported an evolutionary theory. Brownson's focus on the creative act of God initially led to a conflict over scientific methodology, but Brownson turned Darwinism into an emotional, moral issue by conflating Darwin's theory and the progressive evolutionary theories of Spencer and Fiske. Brownson led an ongoing attack against any theory which suggested that humanity was progressing rather than deteriorating as the biblical stories might suggest, and he could not see the difference between Darwinism and theories of progress:

> If Sir John [Lubbock]'s theory of the origin of civilization is untenable, or if Herbert Spencer's theory of evolution is evidently false, unproved, and unprovable, Darwin's theory of the origin of species is an untenable hypothesis, and his theory of the descent of man falls to the ground. [28]

All theories which can be labeled progress or evolution are lumped together and then dismissed for suggesting a movement from imperfect to perfect humanity. Darwin, Spencer, Lyell, Huxley, and others are attacked when they present their theories and conjectures in the name of science, and thus "unsettle men's minds, bewilder the half-learned, mislead the ignorant, undermine the very bases of society, and assail the whole moral order of the universe." [29] Why such a strong attack? Brownson surveys world history and discovers material growth, but to suggest a purely natural progress of humanity undermines the role of the Christian religion, particularly Roman Catholicism in its medieval glory, in aiding human reason and correcting our natural immoral tendencies. [30] Though his position was extreme even among Roman Catholics, Brownson's attack on Darwinisticism, rather than dealing with Darwinism, contributed to the confusion between science and moral theories associated with it, and set the tone for many religious attacks against Darwin's theory in both the nineteenth and twentieth centuries, according to which all social ills are placed at the feet of Darwin, his method, and his theory.

Horace Bushnell

Horace Bushnell (1802–76) was also deeply concerned with the moral symbolism of nature, but he offered a more subtle analysis which moved away from mechanical models to organic images of nature. [31] Bushnell was not a major figure in the American debate over Darwinism, but his understanding of language, metaphor, and symbolism in nature suggested a response to Darwinism that we will meet in a later chapter. The intellectual context which shaped Bushnell's thought had three focal points: the tradition of Jonathan Edwards's typological view of nature, common sense realism and its theory of aesthetics, and Coleridge's *Aids to Reflection*. These came together to shape a theory of language which is reflected in Bushnell's view of nature. The central question was how one mind influences another mind through communication. Bushnell rejected Emerson's naive realism regarding language and human nature, and argued that there are two dimensions of communication:

the literal sounds for the name of an object, and the figurative meaning which stimulates thought. Any form of language is inexact, and so communication must be understood in analogical and metaphorical terms. Words symbolically express intentions whose goal is to shape the human mind and moral character. Communication is possible because, according to the Scottish tradition, we all share an intuitive capacity for imaginatively understanding the meanings contained in the expressions of others. As we understand the character being expressed by the other, our own character is being shaped. The character of God is expressed not only in the Scriptures, but also through nature understood imaginatively, metaphorically. We do not have to ascend the "scale of being" or look behind nature to find God because God is expressed in nature even as a person is known through physical expressions.

Bushnell was quite open to the discoveries of science and its ability to further religious understanding:

> As the science of nature goes toward completion, religion, having all the while been watching for it in close company, will have gotten immense breadth and solidity, from the ideas and facts unfolded in its discoveries, and will be as much enlarged in its confidence and the sentiment of worship, as beholding God's deep system in the world signifies more than looking on its surfaces.[32]

Yet Bushnell rejected naturalism and Darwinism because they undermined his epistemological system. Bushnell argued for "nature and the supernatural as together constituting the one system of God," the title of his 1858 book. The influence of Coleridge is evident in the definitions of nature and supernatural. Nature is "that created realm of being or substance which has an acting, a going on or process from within itself, under and by its own laws."[33] These laws may well be the power of God at work, but they seem to be inherent in the substances themselves. The supernatural is defined as "whatever is not in the chain of natural cause and effect, or what acts on the chain of cause and effect, in nature, from without the chain."[34] In this hierarchical system of inorganic, organic, and living forms, God provides the final causes for which nature exists, and acts to correct the damage done by the natural laws, and by human disruption of those laws. Not only is God supernatural, but humanity is also supernatural since we have the power of will to effect changes in the natural system and are not constrained by the chain of cause and effect.

In contrast to Hodge and the tradition of Paley's design in nature, Bushnell argues that nature is not perfectly designed. He could see no value whatsoever for the harsh winters of New England, and, like Edwards, discovered in insects analogies for God's relationship with humanity. Bushnell concludes that nature is not a complete system, but must allow for both disorder, strife, and conflict which are not part of the natural laws as well as a power to correct them. Human power to act and affect the system of cause and effect is evident in the growing number of deformities found in nature, even though geology discovers movement toward higher forms of perfection. The one complete system needs a power to correct the "unnature" which is a result of human sin, and so the power of God is necessary:

> We may regard the Almighty Ruler of the world as the sensorium and active brain of the world; having an immediate power of action through every member and every line of causes in it; able, in that manner, to maintain a constant living agency in its events, without really infringing its order, or obstructing and suspending its laws in any instance.[35]

Even though Bushnell had this immanent view of God in nature and an organic, metaphorical understanding of communication, he could not accept Darwinism and the naturalism movement. Naturalism was rejected because Bushnell accurately saw that it allowed no supernatural reference and it attempted to establish a religion within the terms of nature. The scientific method as it was developing in the nineteenth century was claiming to be the only source of truth, and Bushnell refused to believe that humanity was to be subject to the laws of nature and thus unable to act upon nature. Some aspects of science were welcomed, including those which had attacked past religious presuppositions about the cosmos and creation. Bushnell categorized scientific theories into five classes of acceptance, and he put Darwinism in the fourth class, where the new discovery had not been demonstrated and there was no reason to think that it ever would be. The problem with Darwinism was once again the epistemological question and the desire for certainty:

> What is science, anyhow, but the knowledge of species? And if species do not keep their places, but go a masking or really becoming one another, in strange transmutations, what is there to know, and where is the possibility of science?... If there is no stability or fixity in species, then, for aught that appears, even science itself may be transmuted into successions of music, and moonshine, and auroral fires. If a single kind is all kinds, then all are one, and, since that is the same as none, there is knowledge no longer. The theory may be true, but it never can be proved, for that reason if no other. And when it is proved, if that must be the fact, we may well enough agree to live without religion.[36]

The closing line reflects the fear of anti-Darwinians: their religious faith is intimately tied to an epistemology and view of the natural world which was being undermined by Darwinism. Bushnell's fear of the new understanding of human nature and Darwin's epistemological and methodological revolution captures the essence of the religious response against Darwinism. Bushnell's biographer, Theodore Munger, lamented Bushnell's inability to extend his organic, metaphorical understanding of God's communication to include Darwinism, but such a move would have to wait for others. Yet even those efforts have not diminished the fears of common sense realists who are still carrying on the battle.

Twentieth Century: The Battle Continues

The American scientific and religious communities have witnessed continued attacks on Darwinism and evolution in this century. The best-known period of strife came in the 1920s with William Jennings Bryan as the most visible leader and culminated in the 1925 Scopes trial in Dayton, Tennessee. While some declared that the battle against Darwin was over, contemporary revitalizations of legal efforts to gain "equal time" in schools for the creationist paradigm indicate that the common sense realist tradition and fears of Darwinism are still very much alive.[37] The contemporary "scientific creationist" movement reached a high point in the trial of *McLean versus the Arkansas Board of Education* in 1981–82. Although Judge Overton's decision was a conclusive case against the establishment of scientific creationism in public education, the issue is still with us as demonstrated by activities in Louisiana, Texas, and Florida. The extensive media coverage of these legal battles reflects the ongoing American interest in how nature is to be understood, since, as we have observed, our understanding of nature and human life becomes a rallying point for the social and ethical issues in American life. We Americans have an interesting dependency on science to confirm our self-understanding and well-being, and, when our sense of stability is felt to be shaken, the "monkey theory" becomes an easy scapegoat for the complexities of modern life.

The contemporary creationist movement raises a number of social, legal, and philosophical issues: the separation of church and state, who decides what will be taught in our public schools, and what actually constitutes science. This section will examine the work of the scientific creationists in terms of their understanding of science, scientific methodology, and their use of scientific theories to make their case that the creationist paradigm is at least equal, as a scientific theory, to the modern synthetic theory of evolution.[38] We will discover that their arguments are quite similar to the common sense realist arguments used by Hodge and others in the nineteenth century, and that they are also afraid of Darwinistic implications of evolutionary theories. There is, however, a fundamental difference between the creationists of the nineteenth and twentieth centuries. As we saw in chapter 2, nineteenth-century scientists struggled with a transformation in the understanding of how science should be done. This struggle helps us understand the rejection of Darwinism by scientists and religious thinkers since the epistemology and methodology were still being developed. The creationists of the nineteenth century were not reactionaries; they engaged in the scientific debates, took part in the scientific community, and offered viable alternatives to the proposals being set forth. Adam Sedgwick, a catastrophic creationist, had moved beyond a simplistic explanation based on a great flood such as Cuvier had suggested earlier.

The spirit of the contemporary creationists is quite different; they do not offer new and viable options, and they wish to revert to the epistemology of Whewell and the common sense realists. The contemporary creationists do parallel their nineteenth-century forerunners, but they are hardly the true heirs of the nineteenth-century spirit of scientific discourse. The one exception to this is Huston Smith, who offers a new epistemological structure for relating science and religious thought.

"Scientific Creationists": Morris and Gish

The leader of the contemporary incarnation of creationism is Henry Morris, trained as a hydraulic engineer, whose *Scientific Creationism* (1974) is the standard work in the field. Morris and Duane Gish, trained as a biochemist, are the intellectual leaders of the Institute for Creation Research which provides the inspiration and much material for establishing creationism as an equal to Darwinian evolution.[39] Morris's leadership began in 1961 with the publication of *The Genesis Flood*, with biblical scholar John Whitcomb, in which Morris used his expertise in hydraulics to offer an explanation of the geological record in terms of the biblical flood. Over the past 20 years, the creationists have shifted away from the explicit religious concern of defending the Genesis 1 story of creation to presenting the "scientific argument" against Darwinism; thus the name "scientific creationism."

The goal of *Scientific Creationism* is to attack Darwinian evolution and offer a scientific alternative. The first two chapters in the book provide the philosophical underpinnings for the argument. The first move is to focus on the question of origins, not the evolution of species, and then to deny the possibility of scientific proofs of origins. The argument is made that the heart of the scientific method is observation and repeatability, but no scientist can ever observe or repeat the origins of life.[40] A philosophy of origins thus can be held only by faith, not sight, even as we must believe in invisible atoms. The second move is to deny scientific status to both creation and evolution since neither of them can be proven. Creation is supposedly not happening now, and so it is not available for scientific study. Evolution, even if it is taking place, is much too slow to be measurable, and is thus outside science since we cannot experiment on something that takes millions of years. The variations to which evolutionists point do not prove variation in "kinds" (the creationist's substitute for "species"). Slight variations are expected by the creationist model since they are necessary for adjustment to changes in local conditions. The efforts to artificially create life in the lab do not *prove* that such events happened in the past. The third move is to take out of context quotations from leading scientists on the slowness, irrefutability, and dogmatism of evolutionary theory. These three steps lead to the conclusion that natural selection is a tautology because it attempts to explain everything by saying simply that the fittest are the ones who survive.

Following this introductory refutation, Morris expands on the nonscientific character of evolution and creationism, and then offers a model by which they can be compared. Neither evolution nor creationism can be called a theory since neither can be tested, confirmed, or falsified. This does not mean that the two cannot be discussed scientifically and objectively. The basis of comparison is to look at evolution and creationism as "models," as systems of thought which correlate and predict observable data. The criteria for comparison are the ability of each model to correlate data, and the discussion of which model needs the fewest "secondary assumptions" to fit the model with the data. Evolution is then presented as a model for a self-contained, uniformitarian universe in which the innate laws develop everything into higher levels of complexity.[41] The creationism model is explicitly "supernaturalistic" and understands the universe as "running down" from the original perfection toward lower levels of complexity. The originally perfect world could come only from a special act of creation:

> All the basic laws and categories of nature, including the major kinds of plants and animals, as well as man, were brought into existence by special creative and integrative processes which are no longer in operation. Once the creation was finished, these processes of *creation* were replaced by processes of *conservation*, which were designed by the Creator to sustain and maintain the basic systems He had created.[42]

The world of creationism is disintegrating and catastrophic, in contrast to evolution's supposed view of the world as moving uniformly toward integration and complexity.

Morris then moves to draw up a chart of "predictions" which each of the "primary models" should predict without "secondary assumptions" which are not natural predictions of the models. An examination of the chart reveals a curious understanding of the theory of evolution. For example, according to Morris the evolution model predicts a constantly changing structure of natural law and an array of organisms which forms a continuum. It also predicts that all mutations are beneficial to organisms and that humanity is quantitatively superior to animals, while the creation model predicts an invariable structure of laws, distinct kinds of organisms, harmful mutations, and humanity as qualitatively distinct from animals. The question then becomes which of these basic predictions are actually observed today. Morris claims that the creationist model and predictions fit the observed facts better than the evolution model since creationism "predicts" the data while evolution must "explain" the data.[43]

The last move by Morris follows in the long tradition discussed by

Lovejoy in *The Great Chain of Being* and that forms the key to the common sense realist position. The creationist model, it is argued, follows the law of cause and effect: "No effect is ever quantitatively 'greater' nor qualitatively 'superior' to its causes." A God or a First Cause must exist in order to make sense of limitless space, time, and moral values:

> Can random motion or primeval particles produce intelligent thought or inert molecules generate spiritual worship? To say that Matter and its innate properties constitute the ultimate explanation of the universe and its inhabitants is equivalent to saying that the Law of Cause-and-Effect is valid only under present circumstances, not in the past.[44]

What are the elements of the argument that Morris has set forth? The fundamental move is to regard creationism and evolution as equivalent, logically comparable, and thus mutually exclusive theories. A curious inconsistency appears when both models are argued to be equally nonscientific and religious, yet both are considered equally scientific since predictions can be made and tested. The creationists and the evolutionists, the fundamentalist religious community and the scientific community, have debated these "models" as logically equal, and that is the basic error.

The creationists continue to rebel against "naturalistic explanations" since they are inherently atheistic. As we have seen, this was an essential aspect of the Darwinian revolution. If any explanation leaves out reference to God or a creator, the creationists argue that the explanation is clearly false and cannot be good science. The assumption is that science defines what is true for all areas of human life, and so the science of the evolutionists cannot be true science because it leaves out reference to God who is a necessary part of a complete explanation of nature. Science is still expected to be "doxological" rather than a tentative hypothesis with some "holes" on which scientists are working. Darwinian evolutionary theory remains atheistic from the creationist perspective.

The echoes of Hodge's argument are clear, and the contemporary creationist roots in common sense realism and Baconian science are again the source of the conflict with Darwinism. Creationists talk of scientific facts and scientific evidence, and not of scientific theories except in a derogatory manner. They assume that if enough evidence can be organized to "prove" the facts we see, then we have science, even if appeals are made to supernatural agents and purposes. Such an approach to scientific explanation was acceptable in the mid-nineteenth century, but not in contemporary scientific discourse. The creationists define science much too narrowly. A scientific "fact" must be observable, and, since the "facts" of neither creation nor evolution can be "observed," neither can be scientific. The contrast between the creationist "fact" and "theory" arises from the search for Baconian certainty which has carried over into our ordinary discourse.[45] In contemporary scientific discourse, the better contrast is between theory and data where data are used to support the search for a well-established theory which can be defined as "a systematically related set of regularities that allegedly explain numerous and diverse phenomena" by offering "a family of problem-solving strategies."[46] The essence of a successful modern scientific theory is its power to solve more problems than it raises, but creationism adds another demand: that science be supportive of religious presuppositions.

The creationist demand that events be *universally* observable and repeatable in order to qualify as scientific also runs into difficulties. Morris has argued the point as follows:

> True science thus is necessarily limited to the measurement and study of present phenomena and processes. There is obviously no way of knowing that these processes and laws that describe them have always been the same in the past or that they will always be the same in the future.[47]

Since evolution and creationism cannot be universally observed, there are no universal laws, and neither qualifies as science. Morris rejects both the nineteenth-century concept of uniformitarianism and the hypothetico-deductive method of predicting a process and discovering data that support the theory.

Morris has followed many others in failing to understand the accepted validity of laws with temporal and geographic locations. The power of a hypothetico-deductive theory is its ability to deduce certain observable consequences and auxiliary assumptions from an event in a given environment.[48] The creationists' demand for universal laws leads them to reject any law tied to a given environment, especially in the lab:

> The standards of evidence to be applied to evolutionary biology have suddenly been raised. In this area of inquiry, it is not sufficient that a theory yield observational consequences whose truth or falsity can be decided in the laboratory. Creationists demand special kinds of predictions, and will dismiss as irrelevant any laboratory evidence that evolutionary theorists produce.[49]

Having denied evolution any validity as a scientific theory, according to their definition of science, creationists claim a leading contemporary philosopher of science, Karl Popper, in support of their decisive blow against evolution: it is not falsifiable. Creationists rely quite heavily upon Popper's criterion of true science, falsifiability, but Popper cannot support them since they neither defend falsifiability within their system nor accept Popper's understanding of evolution. Popper did say "Darwinism is not a testable scientific theory, but a metaphysical *research programme*—a possible framework for testable scientific theories."[50] The creationists also fail to acknowledge that Popper has recanted twice the implication that Darwinian evolution is unfalsifiable: "It appears that some people think that the historical sciences are untestable because they describe unique events. However, the description of unique events can very often be tested by deriving from them testable predictions or retrodictions."[51] The proper way to test a theory is to evaluate it as a whole in its ability to solve problems, rather than pull out a few claims and see if they can be falsified. Such was the case with Newtonian physics, and some counterevidence could be accepted since many parts of the theory worked quite well.[52] The complexity of biological theories and the role of unknown factors should not count against the power of the theory.

Even though they have sought to destroy the validity of evolution as science because it is not falsifiable, the creationists move to falsify evolution. It would not seem to be sound strategy to claim that evolution is not falsifiable and then move to marshal evidence against it. Given the claim that creationism is equal to evolution on the theoretical level, one or the other must be demonstrably true. Creationism, however, is not falsifiable under the same rules. As the creationists' paleontologist, Duane Gish, states:

> We do not know how the Creator created, what processes He used, *for He used processes which are not now operating anywhere in the universe.* That is why we refer to creation as special creation. We cannot discover by scientific investigation anything about the creative processes used by the Creator.[53]

Since creationism cannot accept any data which will falsify it, it is inconsistent for creationists to claim to be engaged in contemporary scientific debate when evolution is to be tested by a criterion that its rival will not accept. It should be pointed out that the creationists never actually claim that they set out to falsify evolution, since they would then admit that it is falsifiable. According to the canons of modern science, creationism is not falsifiable because it invokes agents and causes which are outside the scope of natural laws. Since no law exists for creationism, it would seem that neither explanation nor prediction should be possible, for there is no basis for them. Contemporary creationists have established a double standard for evaluating creationism and evolution, and have thus abandoned their nineteenth-century counterparts' commitment to scientific inquiry.

The creationist theoretical and empirical arguments against Darwinian evolution echo those of the nineteenth century and offer little that is new. Very often the arguments reflect little understanding of the present state of scientific dialogue. For example, the argument that natural selection is a tautology appears early in the literature. The theory of natural selection can be written in the popular, shorthand version which is tautological, but this does not have to be the case, as we observed in chapter 2. The issue is not simply survival, but survival as means to reproduction, and this survival is not random, but is related to the characteristics of the organism in a specific environment. The creationist method is to pull out one element of the theory and attack it without going deeper into the fuller meaning and complexity of natural selection. Another example of lack of understanding is evident in Morris's predictions from the two "models" of creation and evolution. The predictions come from Morris's own projections of what metaphysical evolutionism should mean. The claim that evolution "predicts" that laws are evolving has not been part of the Darwinian methodology or theory.

On a more substantive level, one of the more popular pieces of creationist evidence against Darwinism is the second law of thermodynamics. Evolution is characterized as an "upward trend" toward greater complexity, and the characterization is then described as blatantly contradicting entropy. Morris has learned from earlier debates by attempting to thwart the evolutionists' claim that the second law works only in closed systems.[54] Morris asserts that there is no significant difference between open and closed systems in the availability of energy necessary to explain evolution. Next in the theoretical arena comes the "randomness ploy" which appears in several forms, but with one basic question: how could chance produce the order we see in the world? Probability and statistical computations appear in discussions of variation, mutation, and the dating of the age of the earth. In overwhelming the reader with figures such as 1 chance for order to appear in 10^{53} random variations, creationists do not distinguish between "apparently random" events which have a deterministic basis with "irreducibly random" events which are governed by the probability laws of quantum mechanics.[55] In spite of the discussion of entropy, creationists seem to deny any role for laws in "chance" events. Beneficial mutations cannot be preserved, according to the argument, since mutations can only be harmful. Even if beneficial mutations occur, they are overwhelmed by the statistics. Natural selection cannot possibly provide the design to preserve and pass on the beneficial variations. An intelligent creator is the only "common sense" explanation for beneficence in nature.

The primary empirical evidence against Darwinian evolution is supplied by the fossil record. First, the creationists point to gaps in the fossil record and then claim that creationism "predicts" them while evolution must "explain" them. The argument is that fossils should correspond to the theory of evolution's "prediction" of increasingly complex forms in a continuum. The creationists dictate what forms should be expected, and then point out that they do not exist. The forms that we do have (*Archeoptyrex*, for example) are not true transition forms, but one form or another.[56] Second, creationists exploit the details over which evolutionists are arguing. The "punctuated equilibria" model of Eldredge and Gould is popular because it supposedly supports the creationist prediction of gaps in the fossil record. A valid criticism is raised here in that the evolutionists need to agree on the details of speciation and evolution, but creationists have taken a debate within the Darwinian paradigm outside the paradigm for their own use and with their own scientific language ("kinds," which is never defined).

The creationists do offer a mechanism for how the fossils came to be the way they are. A catastrophic flood is suggested as the mechanism, but there is offered no detailed study of the fossil record, no effort to broaden the range of investigation, and nothing new is offered. Even the creationists of the nineteenth century were able to move beyond the biblical flood. Contemporary creationists have challenged the evolutionists to take the details of the fossil record seriously, but they fail to do so themselves. The contemporary double standard of scientific discourse appears again as a form of religious opposition to Darwin's methodology and theory.

Most responses to contemporary creationism attack the creationists' misunderstanding of the role of scientific theories in contemporary science, the distortion of Darwinian evolution, and the misuse of the scientific data. Following the work of Marsden and others, the epistemological and methodological roots of creationism are being recognized, but few works have moved toward an understanding of why creationism continues to thrive in America, or demonstrate an appreciation of the "substructure" of creationism.[57] Morris has offered an explanation for the value of and need for creationism, and his argument reflects the deep influence of Scottish common sense realism:

> Creationism is consistent with the innate thoughts and daily experiences of the child and thus is conducive to his mental health. He knows, as part of of his own experience of reality, that a house implies a builder and a watch a watchmaker. As he studies the still more intricately complex nature of, say, the human body, or the ecology of a forest, it is highly unnatural for him to be told to think of these systems as chance products of irrational processes.[58]

Evolution contradicts this innate sense of reality and creates intellectual and emotional conflicts. Morris echoes the words of Brownson and others from the nineteenth century who experience their epistemology and world view being shattered.

Morris turns from attacking the epistemology and methodology of Darwinism to attacking various aspects of Darwinisticism. Where creationism encourages hard work and ethical behavior, evolution removes all restraints and eliminates any reason to rise above the amoral behavior of animals. Darwinian evolution has once again become the scapegoat for the social ills which the creationists perceive to be undermining American society. Morris has claimed that "*all* of the anti-Christian systems of modern times have found their quasi-scientific basis in the supposed fact of evolution," and so Darwin is blamed for selfishness, anarchism, collectivism, communism, facism, racism, militarism, Dewey's educational philosophy, and liberal religion.[59] The insecurity and complexity of modern society is traced back to Darwinian evolution and the moral, ethical dictates which some have derived from the theory. Darwinism is a much easier and more emotional target in the popular mind than higher biblical criticism and the study of the history of religions which have also been felt to have undermined the religious faith of many since the nineteenth century. The contemporary creationists will not distinguish between the scientific theory and the myths which can be derived from it since their religious faith is based upon an epistemology which demands the close connection between science and religion that was prevalent in the first half of the nineteenth century.

Variations on the Theme: Rifkin, Jaki, Smith

The contemporary creationist fear of Darwinism has been articulated even more forcefully by Jeremy Rifkin. Rifkin is the director of the Foundation on Economic Trends, and has written on the popular implications of scientific theories and technological developments in books such as *Who Should Play God?*, *The Emerging Order*, and *Entropy*. Most recently, Darwinism and Darwinisticism have been attacked in *Algeny* (1983), which focuses on the developments in recombinant DNA research. It should be noted that the creationists' efforts to achieve "equal time" in the schools have been matched by Rifkin's efforts to coordinate a legal and congressional ban on genetic research. *Algeny* presents the intellectual and moral argument for his efforts. The word "algeny" was coined by the biologist Joshua Lederberg to describe some of the activities of contemporary science. Even as the medieval alchemists attempted to transform base metals into gold, today's biochemical engineer attempts to change the fixed essence of living species to make them perfect. The bioengineer is not simply a scientist, but, more significantly, he attempts to give "metaphysical meaning" to the new relationship with nature:

> Life is seen as a process in which every organism is seeking to complete itself. In this regard, the algenist doesn't think of an organism as a discrete entity but rather as a temporary set of relationships existing in a temporary condition, on the way to becoming something else. For the algenist, species boundaries are just convenient labels for identifying a familiar biological condition or relationship, but are in no way regarded as impenetrable walls separating various plants and animals.[60]

The goal of the algenist is seen to be perfection defined in terms of "optimal efficiency," and thus the algenist is "the ultimate engineer" who will enable us to overcome our fears of mortality.

The core of Rifkin's argument against recombinant DNA research is a discussion of Darwin's theory which has supposedly supplied the cosmology for Western thought the past century. Even though Darwin's world view is being left behind with the advent of algeny, Rifkin is compelled to offer his critique of what led us to where we are now. The heart of the critique is that Darwin did not discover a scientific theory, but rather projected the assumptions of industrial England onto nature. Rifkin's initial analysis of "Darwin's Vision" is a discussion of the rise of social and economic theory in nineteenth-century England, and he claims that "any disinterested observer comes to an unmistakable conclusion: Darwin dressed up nature with an English personality, ascribed to nature English motivations and drives, and even provided nature with the English marketplace and the English form of government."[61] Darwin himself is described as a "modest—if not slow—learner," and his own personal life and health are contrasted with his theory. The concepts of natural selection and survival of the fittest are to be understood solely in terms of the economic and social theories of Thomas Malthus and Adam Smith and the rising industrialism of British cities. Darwin's theory is simply a scientific justification of industrialism and an unconscious desire to enthrone efficiency as the secular god which legitimizes the way we treat our environment and each other. Having established the context in which Darwinism is to be understood, Rifkin turns to the "Darwinian Sunset" in which he offers what have become the traditional scientific creationist arguments against Darwin's theory (not verifiable or falsifiable, fossil record, natural selection as a tautology, mathematical improbability). Darwinism is thus shown to be dying as a cosmology.

Rifkin's fear is that Darwinism is being replaced by something even worse. Drawing on field theory, biological clocks, process philosophy, the role of the computer, and information theory, Rifkin sees a new paradigm forming which again projects upon nature our social developments. As our complex society now seems to revolve around the processing of information, biologists have projected these forces onto nature. Darwin's survival of the fittest has been transformed into the survival of the best informed, and the competition for life has been transformed into the creation of life through DNA research. Humanity has abandoned the concept of life existing outside itself, under natural restraints, and we have become convinced that we control and design the world. Rifkin then challenges us to choose whether we will "engineer the life of the planet, creating a second nature in our image" or whether we will "participate with the rest of the living kingdom" in an ecological approach to life.[62]

The contemporary scientific creationists have found and attacked their enemy. Darwinism did revolutionize the epistemology and methodology of science, and the creationists rightfully feel challenged at that point. Rifkin is correct to devote so much energy to Darwinism in his attack on recent developments in genetic research since the understanding of heredity was one of the problems with Darwin's theory, and the solution of that problem has strengthened the Darwinian theory. There is a great deal of irony in Rifkin's plea to "choose," which he misses. The plea to take an ecological approach to human life and the rest of life on this planet is very much in debt to Darwin's theory. Darwin's theory initiated population thinking in biology, and genetic research has confirmed humanity's close relationship to all other life forms. In spite of Rifkin's attack on Darwin and Darwinisticism, Darwin's "cosmology" leads Rifkin to plead for an ecological approach to life.

The epistemological issue of religious opposition to Darwinism has been approached from a variety of directions. Stanley Jaki and Huston Smith do not belong in the same category as Morris, Gish, and Rifkin, but they do offer a creationist reaction against Darwinism in that they reject the epistemology and methodology of Darwinism. Jaki, a Roman Catholic historian and philosopher of science, is the Distinguished University Professor at Seton Hall University. His 1975 and 1976 Gifford Lectures at the University of Edinburgh establish an epistemology which provides "a single intellectual avenue forming both the road of science and the ways to God." Jaki is convinced that science is creative when it discovers its true and solid foundation in "the mind's ability to find in the realm of things and persons a pointer to their Creator."[63] Darwinism is properly perceived to be a fundamental threat to this view as Jaki provides a history of the philosophy of science from the Greeks through contemporary physics before addressing Darwin and evolution in two concluding lectures, "Pointers of Purpose" and "The Ethos of Science." Darwin's failure, according to Jaki, was not so much the theory of natural selection itself as the way Darwin presented it. It is possible to accept both natural selection and some sense of design and purpose in nature, but Darwin argued for a mechanical, purposeless nature. Even worse, Darwin failed to understand Baconian principles of scientific method, and thus did not follow the method properly as he abandoned deduction for induction. Jaki's common sense realist epistemology is quite evident when he argues that Darwin failed in his efforts to eliminate purpose in nature, since to account for mimicry, parasitism, and organ adaptations by natural selection "amounts to explaining miracles by magic." Darwin's primary failure was his lack of the metaphysical perspective to see and understand the wholeness of organisms and their organs: "It is that perspective of wholeness which reveals purpose and ultimately permits a genuine reference to the Creator, a reference which was wholly out of place in the *Origin*."[64] This lack of perspective did not allow Darwin to recognize the natural and philosophical boundaries which form a hierarchical structure contingent upon a Creator who is responsible for it. This sense of structure and design is the foundation of modern science and its discovery is the goal of all science: "What Darwin and the Darwinians failed to see—and this is why Darwin's theory, though not his vision of evolution, failed—was that time needed a womb, a purpose, if it was to issue ultimately in the most purposeful activity of science and not merely in its stillbirths."[65] Darwin's failure led to the rise of "scientism" which claimed that science is ethically neutral. Jaki will not accept the epistemological and methodological revolution which Darwin caused by removing divine teleology and ethics from the presuppositions of science. This opposition to Darwin and the need to reclaim the old methods places Jaki within the creationist paradigm.

While Jaki thinks that Darwin did not follow the proper scientific method by excluding the obvious design in nature, Huston Smith accepts the epistemological distinction between science and religion. Smith, however, believes that scientism has triumphed, and that the contemporary creationists are doing us all a favor by exposing the expansion of evolution into evolutionism. Where Jaki criticizes Darwinism from a realist perspective, Smith has taken up the critique of the Romantic tradition that modern science has reduced understanding to control and excluded a concern for value and meaning in life. Science itself is a useful and powerful source of knowledge, but its concerns are objectivity, control, prediction, and number. Those concerns cannot give us a complete view of the world since they do not include values, ultimate and existential meanings, purposes, and qualities. Scientism results when other approaches to knowledge of the world are denied any validity and this has led to the "modern Western mind-set" of a Promethean naturalistic epistemology "that aims relentlessly at control [and] rules out the possibility of transcendence in principle."[66] The decline of religious belief in the West can be blamed on the triumph of evolutionism as an epistemological system, and so Smith seeks to separate evolution from evolutionism.[67] Evolutionists claim that they have both a *description* of the advance of life on earth, and an *explanation* for the advance. Smith allows that evolution is correct as a description of the fossil record, and contemporary creationists are mistaken. On the other hand, as an explanation, evolutionism is a failure since natural selection is a tautology, "chance" mutations refer to events that cannot be explained, and the statistical improbabilities are too great. Smith is willing to grant that the fossil record demonstrates that life has advanced, and he thinks that is the heart of evolution as science. In the rush to deny any metaphysical implications to evolution, Smith has failed to distinguish accurately between evolution and evolutionism and to understand the arguments he has used against evolutionism.

The religious arguments against Darwinism have been rooted in the epistemological and methodological revolution Darwinism represents and the ethical implications which some have drawn from Darwin's theory. The nineteenth-century creationists tended to remain within the intellectual mainstream until it became apparent that their Scottish common sense realism and the doxological role of science had become anachronisms. The contemporary scientific creationists attempt to maintain the epistemological and methodological position of their forerunners, but they have abandoned dialogue within the scientific community. The fears of rapid social change and instability have found a scapegoat in Darwinistic implications of natural selection and survival of the fittest. Smith's effort to shape a "post-modern mind" with an epistemology that recognizes other forms of knowledge and is open to transcendent dimensions is valid and needed, but his tactic of praising the creationists has failed to win him the audience needed. He would have been wiser to take a more constructive approach, such as will be seen in chapter 5, or to tackle those in the following chapter who present a "religion *of* Darwinism."

4

Religion *of* Darwinism

The second model for the relationship between Darwinism and religious thought welcomes and explicitly builds upon the scientific developments of its age, and thus can be called "religion *of* Darwinism." This "of" typology is considered following the "against" typology because both models share a high commitment to the epistemology and methodology of science, and both depend on the scientific enterprise to support their religious faith. "Religion of Darwinism" represents a significant and intentional break from the content of the traditional Judeo-Christian doctrines, and offers in its place a rational, monistic, evolutionary religious faith. The nineteenth-century advocates of this position explicitly offered a "religion of humanity" to replace Christian orthodoxy. Some twentieth-century leaders have worked to formulate a naturalistic religion in terms of contemporary understandings of Darwinian evolution. Others have been more hesitant to claim their position as religious, yet they do offer a religion when examined from the point of view of the functionalist approach of Berger and Luckman since they offer a "canopy" of meaning and purpose.[1] The "religion of Darwinism" takes as its starting point the epistemological and methodological concerns of science, and then elevates scientific knowledge into a Darwinistic myth with metaphysical and ethical implications for the purpose and meaning of human life and society.

In the nineteenth century, the members of the Free Religious Association were the primary American representatives of this model. Octavius Brooks Frothingham and Francis Ellingwood Abbot were the leaders of a movement which took the scientific method and evolution as the starting points for their faith. Very often this approach is portrayed as reducing religion to ethics, but, as we shall see, the essence of their faith was the scientific method. Frothingham is usually mentioned as the leader of free religion, but his approach was more Romantic and Hegelian. Abbot was the intellectual leader as he developed a "scientific theism" based on a careful study of epistemology and scientific method. Robert G. Ingersoll was on the fringes of the F.R.A., but he was by far the most well known as he raised up the "Trinity of Science" to attack the intellectual and ethical perversions which Christianity supposedly inflicted upon modern culture.

Naturalism and the commitment to the scientific method continued into the twentieth century. Two of its early leaders were Henry Nelson Wieman and Julian Huxley. Wieman, the American theologian, struggled to maintain some form of transcendence, yet he claimed naturalism as his perspective. Julian Huxley, the British scientist, argued for a vision of evolution that would function much in the same manner as the Kingdom of God in the Christian tradition. The kinship of these two men and their ideas is reflected in their signing of the *Humanist Manifesto II*. More recently, Ralph Wendell Burhoe, founding editor of the journal *Zygon*, has continued this model by attempting to translate the new developments in Darwinian evolution into a religious language. One of these new developments, sociobiology, has become the center of much discussion regarding the relationship between science and religion, and we will examine the thought of Edward O. Wilson as a representative of the "religion of Darwinism."

The Free Religion Movement

The analysis of the nineteenth-century "religion of Darwinism" has tended to focus almost exclusively on British and German figures. Thomas Huxley, Herbert Spencer, and Ernst Haeckel are the usual representatives of a response to Darwinism that significantly rethinks traditional epistemological, religious, and ethical perspectives in light of evolutionary theory.[2] The American scene did incorporate reactions to those men, but the roots of American "religion of Darwinism" extend further back to the Unitarian movement as it moved from Enlightenment rationalism through transcendentalism to the scientific arguments of Frothingham and Abbot.[3] Thomas Paine was often recognized as an early leader in the movement since his rationalism attempted to reclaim a true religion with a God immanent in nature and culture. In 1824, William Ellery Channing argued for a religion in step with the spirit of its age, engaged with the culture in which it finds itself, and in dialogue with philosophy. The transcendentalism of Emerson was critical of the past and the present in favor of the reality behind contemporary culture and what might be in the future. Emerson's 1838 Harvard Divinity School address was significant for the disturbance it created at Harvard, and students who were not "converted" to transcendentalism at first, e.g., Frothingham, were caught up in the social reform movements of the time. Orestes Brownson was one of the first to articulate this Romantic "religion of humanity" which incorporated some philosophical discipline and concern for social reform in arguing for a God immanent in humanity. The growing field of the comparative study of religion seemed to support this "religion of humanity" by providing evidence for a common human religious sense. The move was being made toward an epistemology which could incorporate a variety of sources of knowledge, especially scientific:

> The religion-of-humanity formula, from Brownson's time to Frothingham's, provided a convenient way of erecting a bridge between epistemological principles. Religion could be seen as fundamentally a matter of intuition, of a universal "religious sentiment"; yet the proof of this assertion could be made to depend more or less heavily upon scientific demonstration. Just what one should do if intuition and scientific demonstration pointed to opposite conclusions was a question that the enthusiasts of this faith rarely confronted.[4]

This question of epistemological dualism is one of the distinguishing factors between Frothingham's "religion of humanity," Abbot's "scientific theism," and twentieth-century naturalism.

Octavius Brooks Frothingham

Octavius Brooks Frothingham (1822–95) was the most prominent leader of the Free Religious Association. The son of a leading Boston minister and related to the Adams family, Frothingham was educated at the Boston Latin School, graduated from Harvard in 1843, and went on to the Divinity School. Frothingham maintained his Unitarian orthodoxy until he came under the influence of Theodore Parker's transcendentalism in Salem, Massachusetts. Frothingham's Unitarian parish in Salem became alienated over his antislavery stance, so he moved first to Jersey City and finally to New York in 1859 where he reorganized his Unitarian society into an independent Liberal Church based on a "faith of reason." After its first meeting in 1866, the Boston Radical Club invited Frothingham to preside at further meetings and to take part in drafting the constitution of the Free Religious Association, which had its first "convention" in 1867.[5]

In *Creed and Conduct*, Frothingham declared that all religious thought must begin with the fact of evolution as its strongest credential, yet his concept of science and evolution was more in debt to Hegel and Romanticism than to the Darwinian scientific paradigm. Frothingham's basic commitment is made clear in the opening lines of *The Religion of Humanity* (1872): "The spirit of any age is the spirit of God."[6] The core of Frothingham's religion is not Darwinian evolution, but rather the challenge to adapt to the spirit of the culture. While chemistry is used as the symbol for the powers of reason and the spirit of the age, Frothingham's prophetic science is quite Romantic:

> It is a Natural Science, taking Nature in its largest sense. For while in the lower material sphere it pulverizes the solid substances of the earth—reduces adamant to vapor, and behind the vapor touches the imponderable creative and regenerating forces—in the upper intellectual sphere it grinds to powder the mountainous institutions of man, resolves establishments into ideas, and behind the bodiless thought feels the movement of that Universal Mind whose action men call the Holy Spirit.[7]

Frothingham proclaimed his faith in naturalism and natural powers, but his naturalism was more closely related to Enlightenment optimism regarding humanity and Emerson's nature than to nineteenth-century science. Frothingham sees a divine power at work in and through human nature. The natural powers are quite effective in maintaining order in the natural world, and so, if they are allowed to work freely and not restrained, they will work also in the spiritual world to create a free humanity more harmonious, orderly, balanced, and beautiful.

The epistemological dualism of science and religion is important for Frothingham's religion of humanity because he must separate his religion from Comte's religion of humanity. Where Comte reduced religion to a mechanical world view, Frothingham maintains a more organic view in which religion is based on ideas that science and philosophy dismiss, i.e., God, revelation, incarnation, atonement, providence, immortality. These basic concepts are not to be restricted to the traditional Christian interpretation, but must be understood in terms of what modern science and the comparative study of religion discover. The major portion of *The Religion of Humanity* is Frothingham's reinterpretation of these ideas in terms of his naturalism. In many ways, Frothingham's work is a forerunner of Wieman, who also reinterpreted traditional concepts in a naturalistic fashion.

The reinterpretations of God and revelation serve as good examples of how the classical doctrines can adapt to the spirit of the age. Frothingham rejects Comte's idea of law by asking, "What is *law* but steady, continuous, persistent, consistent power; cumulative, urgent, regulated power; power moving along even tracks and pressing toward distinct aims; power with a past behind it and a future before it; power that is harmonious, rhythmical, as he calls it himself, *orderly*?"[8] To talk of power and force demands association with will and mind, and will and mind are associated with wisdom and goodness. Therefore natural laws are to be understood as the "footprints" of a God who is hidden in order to not interfere with the will and work of humanity. This hidden God must be revealed, and revelation comes to the sensitive minds of scientists such as Darwin who no longer see nature as a hard, dull, and stubborn substance for divine manipulation: " The man of science needs nothing more, for he lives among the living laws; he is conscious every moment of the intimate relation between himself and the subtile forces that weave the investiture of God. His finger is laid on the very pulse of creation."[9] Those of us who do not have a sensitive mind require bibles, the best thoughts of all ages, spoken and written to communicate moral power for the average mind.

The theory of evolution comes into play when Frothingham turns to the "power of moral inspiration" in society. The theory which is used includes Darwinian elements in the sense of recognizing the interconnectedness of all life and the work of natural selection, but Frothingham's Romantic vision of nature overpowers Darwin's argument against teleology and purpose. Evolution displays the working of divine power to bring higher forms out of lower, and society is conceived as an organically developing creature. The law of social development is the law of evolution which has been fully demonstrated and illustrated:

> This law simply rivets the members of the human family together, making links of gold of the airy sentiments that were supposed to be ephemeral. In view of this law of evolution which makes of society an increasing organically developed creature, the significance of the moral element becomes very impressive. This significance lies in its rendering society self-developing, self-organizing, self- evolving. It compresses all power within the compass of human attributes, makes the race its own providence, its own reformer and saviour.[10]

Frothingham does note that the theory of evolution includes humanity as a "passive" agent in the process, but this is of relatively little importance compared to the active role which humanity can have. God is no longer responsible for human progress; humanity is now in control of its fate through the use of its rational faculties.

Natural selection is indeed recognized, but its role is the aesthetic preparation of humanity to assume the role of directing society's evolutionary process. Frothingham does not overlook the reality of pain and suffering in nature and society, and he dismisses traditional ideas of providence because they do not fit reality. Science comes to the aid of faith at this point and rescues a concept of the "order of providence" in which the universe is shown to be a living, symmetrical, evolving organism with all of its parts interconnected, as in a rose or tree. Everything has its place in this organism, and, following Darwin's views, there is no room for pure chance or luck since these simply represent laws that have not been discovered. One such law which has been discovered is natural selection, and Frothingham turns it to his providential use:

> If the law of self-preservation will give to the butterfly its brilliancy and to the lily its whiteness, why should not the same law, working out the safety and felicity of man, bestow the dazzling qualities of the hero, the sweet fragrance of the philanthropist and the transparent purity of the saint? . . . The natural method is the beautiful method.[11]

The workings of such natural laws should educate the conscience with regard to social relations, and thus humanity itself takes over the roles traditionally ascribed to God of foresight and forethought. Beyond us, there is nothing to be known. We are the willing and loving God. Through the power of wealth and human providential activity, evolution works to accumulate resources and apply them to satisfy the needs of everyone.

Frothingham attempted to reach a balance between theism and humanism, but his "religion of humanity" established a fully developed humanity as a religious goal and eliminated any traditional concept of a transcendent deity in the name of scientific law and evolutionary theory. The work of Darwin is accepted in the sense of eliminating any divine intervention in scientific explanations of natural processes and recognizing the role of natural selection. Frothingham could not free himself from his transcendentalism, and his vision of discovering truth in the order of nature is more Romantic idealism, or Darwinistic, than Darwinian. No doubt those transcendental influences made Frothingham's vision more acceptable and more popular than the more rigorous philosophical vision of Abbot.

Francis Ellingwood Abbot

Francis Ellingwood Abbot (1836–1903) was the organizer and philosopher of the Free Religious Association. Abbot was also from an old New England family, and also attended the Boston Latin School and graduated from Harvard in 1859. Following a religious experience while in college, Abbot enrolled in Meadville Theological Seminary, graduated in 1863, and became the minister of the Unitarian society in Dover, New Hampshire. Abbot moved beyond the transcendentalism he encountered at Meadville and alienated his congregation by claiming that all truth is equally divine and that the traditional fall and restoration of humanity should be replaced with a progressive law of history in which God is revealed. He played an important role in drafting the constitution of the Free Religious Association, but his argument for a "scientific study of theology" eventually lost out to Lucretia Mott's argument that the F.R.A. should "encourage the scientific study of man's religious nature and history." *The Index* became the primary organ for Abbot's "scientific theism," which formed one branch of the free religion movement.[12]

Abbot's primary concern was a rigorous analysis of epistemology, the role of scientific methodology, and how they shape our religious understanding. His basic work, *Scientific Theism* (1885), was preceded by a series of articles which established the foundation for his argument. In "The Philosophy of Space and Time," Kant, Spencer, and William Hamilton are analyzed and critiqued for their understanding of the relationship between subjective and objective knowledge. Abbot contrasts the subjectivity of idealism with the objectivity of realism, empiricism's knowledge from experience with transcendentalism's nonempirical elements of knowledge, materialism's identification of matter and mind with immaterialism's distinction between physical and mental processes. By focusing on the ideas of space and time, Abbot demonstrates the truth and falsity of each absolute position, and argues that there are both *a priori* and *a posteriori*, nonsensuous and sensuous, aspects to complete knowledge since the focus of knowledge is *relations* between the two aspects.[13] In his next article, "The Conditioned and the Unconditioned," Abbot attacks all forms of epistemological dualism, especially the arguments of Kant and Hamilton, for their distinction between faith and knowledge, since they are based upon contradictions which faith and human reason should not be forced to accept:

> The "Faith" which cannot stand unless buttressed by contradictions, is built upon the sand. The profoundest possible faith is faith in the integrity of human nature and in the unity of truth. If there is found to be any want of concord in the normal interaction of human faculties, any conflict in the results of a right reason, any inevitable treachery to truth on the part of her sole interpreter, no appeal to practical interests, or traditionary authority, or intuitional or theological faith, can stay the flood of scepticism.[14]

Abbot abandoned his transcendental roots, the belief in an intuitional religious knowledge, by asserting that there can be no true knowledge, whether religious or otherwise, which is not rational.

In the preface to his *Scientific Theism*, Abbot claims that the epistemological position worked out in his early articles is the only way to solve the issues of phenomenism and noumenism, of idealistic and realistic evolution, of mechanical and organic evolution. He calls his basic principles "the Objectivity of Relations" and "Perceptive Understanding." Modern science and the scientific method have confirmed that "we do know the objective relations of things," and this is to be affirmed in spite of claims to the contrary by philosophical idealism.[15] The long introduction is a reprinted article which establishes Abbot's two principles through a historical study of the various forms of realism and nominalism. Kant's "Copernican revolution" is rejected in favor of a scientific realism which argues that knowledge does conform to things, and that things can be known, if incompletely, as they are in themselves. Otherwise, verification of knowledge would be impossible. Abbot's scientific realism, or relationism, is formed from a blend of classical nominalism and realism, and argues that knowledge is a "dynamic correlation of object and subject" which has its source in both the experience of the world *and* the action of the mind upon the world. Experience is thus the source of knowledge so long as it is understood that there is both an objective (world) and subjective (mind) aspect to that experience. Abbot then asserts that:

> this extended conception of experience destroys the distinction of noumena and phenomena, as merely verbal and not real; that "things-in-themselves" are partly known and partly unknown; that, just so far as things are known in their relations, they are known both phenomenally and noumenally, and that the possibility of experimentally verifying at any time their discovered relations is the practical proof of a known noumenal cosmos, meeting every demand of scientific certitude and furnishing the true criterion and definition of objective knowledge.[16]

Abbot moves toward a monistic world in which Kant's noumena is that which appears, and thus the noumena and phenomena cannot be separated. Science demonstrates the unity and intelligibility of the world through its propositions, which describe the objective relations in the universe, and relationism is the only philosophical system which allows science to provide knowledge of the world.

This analysis of epistemology and scientific methodology lays the foundation for Abbot's scientific theism. Abbot is aware of the claims that science has nothing to say about God, and he agrees with this claim, if there is no God but the one he hears about from the American churches. There can be, however, a higher view of God, and science has both the method and the results which are valuable for religion, and which suggest "that the present tendencies of science are in the direction, not of atheism, but of an enlightened theism."[17]

Abbot's optimism focuses on the scientific method of observation and experiment, hypothesis, and verification rather than the specific results of scientific research. This method has led to the growing sense that what is unknown can indeed be known, that the universe is infinitely intelligible, in contrast to the claims of Spencer who builds his religious agnosticism on the unknown. The only unintelligible aspects of the world are disorder and chaos since they are destructive of intelligible relationships, but they can exist only in relationship to a larger system which is itself intelligible. The religious implications of the scientific method are based on a very detailed argument which moves from the intelligibility of the universe to an intelligent universe. The key move in the argument is based on an understanding of intelligence as being teleological: it either discovers or creates ends (ideal system of relations to be realized in the future) and means (ideal systems of relations in the present by which the ends are realized). Abbot concludes that:

> intelligibility, as an attribute of the thing, consists in the possession of an immanent relational construction, and that the infinite intelligibility of the universe, as the infinite, eternal, and self-existent All-Thing, consists in its possession of an immanent and infinite relational constitution . . . [and that] intelligence itself is that which either discovers or creates relational systems or constitutions, and that the nature of intelligence, as such, is identical in all possible forms and degrees. What is the unavoidable inference or conclusion from these principles, as premises?
>
> This—that *the infinitely intelligible universe must be likewise infinitely intelligent.*[18]

In other words, the intelligibility of the universe must be the effect of an intelligent cause. From the perspective of this infinite intelligence, science is divine revelation; from the perspective of finite intellect, science is human discovery. A fully developed philosophy of science will be the highest wisdom of humanity, and the word of God.

Having established the universe as an infinitely intelligent system of relations, Abbot draws on evolutionary theory and Darwin to explicate the meaning of such a universe. The concepts of organism and machine are contrasted as ways of imagining this system. The most perfect relational system is an organism because it lives and grows: it projects itself out and subjects external forces to its own ends, and thus fulfills its own existence. Where a finite organism lives, reproduces, and dies, an infinite organism lives by transforming itself from force into form. While a finite organism changes because of interaction with the environment, an infinite organism's environment is immanent to itself and does not affect its identity.

The concept of the universe as an organism is based on "the fact of evolution," even though there is a battle being waged over how evolution is to be understood philosophically. Abbot satirizes the idealistic view of evolution which holds that evolution is simply a phenomenal event, and argues for a "realistic evolution" as both a phenomenal and noumenal fact. While Darwin is proclaimed as "spotless and immortal," Abbot takes issue with Darwin's mechanical view of evolution.[19] The work of Darwin established an objective, intelligible system of relationships in nature, and almost eliminated supernatural interventions in natural processes. Darwin's failure was to allow for a miraculous initial creative act to explain the origins of life. If he had had a consistent organic view of nature, Darwin would have needed no such event, but Darwin's mechanical view of nature allowed no room for such creativity. Abbot draws upon the French vitalist tradition of Claude Bernard to argue for a system which does allow for internal, rather than external and mechanical, forces of creativity. The universe is either organic or inorganic, not both. If the dualist position is taken, then there must be a "Great Mechanic" who runs the universe for his own glory. If a mechanical monistic position is taken, there is no end for which the universe is a means. All mechanical views of nature fail for they eliminate an immanent teleology, and thus reinstate an external creator.

An organic understanding of evolution, however, demands a teleological view: "It is *as if* there had been in the whole process a regular march of thought—the development of a universal idea."[20] The organism exists in relationship to itself as its own end, and yet also as a means to the end of the universal organism which created it. An organism thus exists both to fulfill itself and to fulfill the life of the "cosmical organism": there is "both an *Indwelling or Immanent End* and an *Outgoing or Exient End.*" The immanent end explains the drive toward self-preservation, while the exient end is the basis for altruism and self-sacrifice. Abbot claims that this teleological understanding of life and evolution is the only way to make philosophical sense of Darwinism.[21] Darwinian natural selection did eliminate design in the sense of special adaptation, but Darwin did not explain why the system as a whole should develop the way it did:

There is a large teleology, not mousing about in petty details nor aiming to prove God piece-meal, but sweeping over the whole field of thought, which finds an answer to those queries in the idea of an Infinite Mind. The teleology I would urge is the *unity of plan* which must result from *unity of force* and *unity of law*, if these two are made one in *mind*; and this unity of plan I hold to be a far truer explanation of the evolution of an orderly universe out of chaotic nebulae than the arbitrary *must* of the pure mechanist.[22]

Abbot's "scientific theism" emerges explicitly at this point. If God is real, God can not be understood as outside or above nature since science understands "nature" to be all that is real. The teleological process described above thus becomes "the Infinite Creative Life of God." Nature itself is the self-revelation of the noumenal reality in the phenomenal world. The "exient principle" of altruism and self-sacrifice "manifests itself as that Natural Providence of Law and Love in One which is the support of every instructed, steadfast religious mind," and this principle of love is nothing but "the All-Embracing Fatherhood and Motherhood of God."[23] Abbot rejects the label of pantheism for two reasons. First, pantheism denies all personality, but scientific theism is founded upon teleology, and teleology presupposes the essential elements of personality (thought, feeling, will). Teleology wedded to a monistic view of reality produces an infinite, purely spiritual personality in God. Second, pantheism eliminates any transcendent element in God, but the God of scientific theism is transcendent in the world that lies beyond human experience, though this is included in the infinite universe. This transcendent personality in God supposedly overcomes the sterility of philosophy and engages the religious emotions in a rational understanding of the universe:

Scientific theism is more than a philosophy: it is a religion, it is a gospel, it is the Faith of the Future, founded on knowledge rather than on blind belief,—a faith in which head and heart will be no more arrayed against each other in irreconcilable feud, as the world beholds them now, but will kneel in worship, side by side at the same altar, dedicated, not to the "Unknown God," still less to the "Unknowable God," but to the KNOWN GOD whose revealing prophet is SCIENCE.[24]

Robert G. Ingersoll

The role of science as a revealing prophet was popularized by Robert G. Ingersoll (1833–99). Ingersoll's father was a Presbyterian minister, and his traveling from parish to parish in the midwest meant that Robert's education came from his father. Edwards, Milton, and Bunyan formed Ingersoll's core reading, but Shakespeare, Burns, and Paine provided the world view that Ingersoll would come to prefer. In 1854, Ingersoll was admitted to practice law in Illinois, and he immediately began his crusade against social injustices. The rationalism of Paine merged with the Romantic faith in humanity to shape Ingersoll's vision of social progress and his critique of all that held back such progress.[25] The institution of slavery was Ingersoll's first target, and he saw it as a parallel to organized religion: the one enslaved the body out of physical fear; the other enslaved the mind out of fear for spiritual punishment. Reason demonstrated that all forms of slavery were evil, and that truth could be discovered only through free rational inquiry into the only world we know. Ingersoll viewed himself as the emancipator of the intellect, and every form of slavery had to be destroyed first.

The spirit of Ingersoll's argument is captured in an early, and his most carefully argued, article called "The Gods" (1872). All gods have been created by, and resemble, the nations that believe in them. Ingersoll suggests that these gods have always depended on the priests for their knowledge, and so it is no wonder that the gods are ignorant:

> These gods did not even know the shape of the worlds they had created, but supposed them perfectly flat.... None of these gods could give a true account of the creation of this little earth. All were woefully deficient in geology and astronomy. As a rule, they were most miserable legislators, and as executives, they were far inferior to the average of American presidents.[26]

Even worse, these ignorant gods demand degrading obedience, but there are some who refuse to bow: "Let the people hate, let the god threaten—we will educate them, and we will despise and defy him."[27] The story of the Garden of Eden demonstrates that the god fears such education, and so religion is destined to hate science.

Ingersoll focuses on the arguments that design and order in nature prove the existence of a divine power. Against those who argue for design, Ingersoll asks why cancer is not as beautiful in its design as a rose. Against those who point to lawful order in nature as evidence of a power superior to nature, Ingersoll popularizes Abbot's argument: "A deity outside of nature exists in nothing, and is nothing. Nature embraces with infinite arms all matter and all force. That which is beyond her grasp is destitute of both, and can hardly be worthy of worship and adoration even of a man."[28] Evolution has corrected the errors of Paley and others who would have to accept a deity who began life with the simplest and crudest organisms and allowed immeasurable periods of time before humanity appeared, only to live with snakes and earthquakes. Science led the exodus from slavery to the useless gods with the discovery of order and regularity in the universe. This liberation was led by Darwin and has allowed humanity to correctly perceive nature: "Nature, without passion and without intention, forms, transforms, retransforms forever. She produces man without purpose and obliterates him without regret. She knows no distinction between the beneficial and the hurtful."[29] Darwinian evolution was the culmination of Newtonian rational science which eliminates the supernatural from natural processes, yet Ingersoll would not accept a deterministic view of humanity.

The conflict between religion and science was essentially a battle for the freedom of the mind to do its work and reform society without restraint from the church. Ingersoll categorizes this war as a battle between the few who appeal to reason, honor, law, freedom, and happiness and the many who appeal to prejudice, fear, miracle, slavery and misery:

> Reason, Observation and Experience—the Holy Trinity of Science—have taught us that happiness is the only good; that the time to be happy is now, and the way to be happy is to make others so. This is enough for us. In this belief we are content to live and die. If by any possibility the existence of a power superior to, and independent of, nature shall be demonstrated, there will then be time enough to kneel. Until then, let us stand erect.[30]

In *Some Mistakes of Moses* (1880), Ingersoll satirizes the Judeo-Christian ethic as slavery, polygamy, war, and religious persecution. The only salvation humans can possibly know will come from science and the control that it gives us over our own destiny. One ethical issue which Ingersoll and other free religionists championed was women's rights, and his last essay hails the power of science to liberate the world from ignorance and to liberate the woman to control her own destiny: "Science, the only possible savior of mankind, must put it in the power of woman to decide for herself whether she will or will not become a mother."[31] No doubt that with such uses of science, many did believe Ingersoll to be the "Great Infidel."

The free religion movement could have developed without Darwin's theory since its foundation was essentially a blend of Enlightenment rationalism and Romantic optimism regarding human progress. Darwin provided a scientific justification for an evolving universe without divine interference. In that sense, these men do offer a "religion of Darwinism." Frothingham's religion of humanity was the least Darwinian, and Ingersoll's acceptance of a nature without regard for human values is probably the most Darwinian. The highly philosophical monistic teleology of Abbot's scientific theism did not win him many followers, even though his God was more personal than the Spencerian unknowable force of Frothingham. Abbot viewed the late nineteenth century as the age of agnosticism, since there was no valid substitute for a spiritual life except for free religion and his scientific theism. As Persons has suggested, this was the age of the "cult of science" with Darwin and other scientists as the saints and religious dogma as the enemy of a rational understanding of life.[32] While evolution was regarded as having finally disproven the creationist paradigm, the content of Darwin's theory was seldom addressed directly except to "improve" upon it. Science was viewed as the means of revealing the possibilities for human meaning and salvation. Abbot's claim that the key is epistemology and the scientific method rather than the content of any specific theories accurately describes the focus of a "religion of Darwinism" in the nineteenth century.

From Epistemological to Ontological Commitments

The "religion *of* Darwinism" model has continued into the twentieth century along the lines of the arguments set forth by Frothingham, Abbot, and Ingersoll. The nineteenth-century advocates of a "religion of humanity" drew upon the epistemological revolution of Darwin, but they were hesitant to adopt the ontological implications of Darwin's theory. Acceptance of the Darwinian theory of evolution reached a low point in the early twentieth century with the debate over how Mendel's genetic theory of inheritance fit with Darwin's theory. The growth of the comparative study of religion, the psychology of religion, and pragmatism in philosophy led to definitions of religion which were broader than the orthodox Christian tradition. The epistemological concerns of Darwinism were incorporated into these new understandings of religion, and naturalism became a religious as well as philosophical starting point. Few attempts were made to incorporate the debatable content of Darwinism into a religious world view until the rise of the "modern synthesis" and the writings of Julian Huxley.

With the increasing confidence in the content of neo-Darwinism, efforts have been made to rethink traditional religious concepts in the light of Darwinian evolution. The argument is now made that religion does indeed have a place in a naturalistic evolutionary world view, and that place is to enable us to adjust to the world around us and to survive in the Darwinian selection process. In this section we will examine the movement from an epistemological theological naturalism to an evolutionary naturalism with its "religion *of* Darwinism."

Henry Nelson Wieman

Henry Nelson Wieman (1884–1975) was a leading spokesman in the first half of the twentieth century for a theological naturalism which was founded on an empirical "scientific" method of religious thought. Wieman was born into the Missouri home of a Presbyterian minister and followed in his father's footsteps by attending San Francisco Theological Seminary after graduating from Park College. After a year of study in Germany with Troeltsch, Wieman returned to Davis, California, for four years of parish ministry, during which time he read Henri Bergson's *Creative Evolution*, which shaped his thinking for the rest of his life. In 1915, Wieman went to Boston to study in Harvard's

Philosophy Department, and earned the Ph.D. degree in 1917 with a dissertation on "The Organization of Interests." The idealism of Josiah Royce and William Ernest Hocking was tempered with the pragmatism of William James and John Dewey which reflected the Darwinian epistemological and methodological paradigm. Wieman taught at several small colleges following his graduation from Harvard, and carved out his place in the philosophy of religion with his *Religious Experience and Scientific Method* in 1926. Because of his incorporation of Whitehead's thought in that book, Wieman was invited to the University of Chicago to lecture on Whitehead's *Religion in the Making* (1926) which had just been published. Wieman's skill at interpreting Whitehead led to an invitation to join the faculty of the Divinity School as professor of philosophy of religion.

The relationship between science and religious thought was a continual concern for Wieman, and, as the title of his first book suggests, he believed that religion and science were to be brought together through epistemology and methodology. William James's study of the psychology of religion was an early influence on Wieman's method as they both sought to blend an empirical method with a cosmological "more." James argued that things are knowable and definable from our experience of them. The mind is an instrument with the Darwinian teleological goal of adapting to the environment, to survive. There is nothing beyond our experience, and truth is measured by the correspondence of experimental results and the ongoing consequences of an idea. If the idea cannot be tested and shown to make some difference for the future, then it is useless. John Dewey's influence is also apparent in Wieman's thought since Dewey gave the name "creativity" to a concept similar to James' instrumental use of the mind. Dewey claimed that our response to an experience is more than a reflex action, and that intelligence is instrumental in shaping a unity of action which incorporates the present conditions and the end desired. Our creativity is our ability to respond to meanings and to use them in a social context. Under the influence of Darwin, Dewey understood the human being as an organism within an environment, and meaning is experienced in the functional quality of an act in its context. Creativity and meaning are dependent upon a twofold commitment: a commitment to the belief that creativity is at work in nature, and a commitment to our human capacity to participate in the process of meeting ideal ends. The naturalist epistemology and methodology is relevant here since we must focus on what is actually observable in human life.[33]

This background in American pragmatism led Wieman to the question which he claimed was the focus of his life's work: "What operates in human life with such character and power that it will transform man as he cannot transform himself, saving him from evil and leading him to the best that human life can ever reach, provided that he meet the required conditions?"[34]

Wieman was convinced that the traditional affirmations of Christianity were bankrupt, and that the solution to the human religious question is to discover empirically and designate concretely what religious people mean when they talk about their experiences and faith. The only way to know what actually operates in human life is the empirical method, and this method demands that religious thought abandon its speculation on transcendent being. Wieman welcomed the label of "naturalism" for his religious thought since he explicitly rejected any transcendent as having any value:

> We cannot know anything, and nothing can make the slightest difference in our lives unless it be an event or some possibility carried by an event. Transcendental realities literally have nothing to do after we have discovered that all value, all meaning, and all causal efficacy are to be found in the world of events and their possibilities.[35]

Modern science provides the method for discerning what operates in the natural world, and thus what operates in human life. Wieman claims that all knowledge ultimately depends on science since science is "nothing else than the refined process of knowing, . . . a method of discriminating accurately between false and true."[36] The scientific method is described as a process of sensory observation, experimental behavior, and rational inference which will correct sentimentality in religion, which tends to focus on words which refer only to other words rather than words as a medium for interpreting experience.

Wieman's epistemology had been shaped by Bergson and Whitehead at this point. Bergson rejected a mechanistic, deterministic view of evolution, and claimed that an *élan vital*, a creative impulse, is at work in nature overcoming subject-object dualism through an experience of quality in an object. The uniqueness of the human being in nature is the expansion of consciousness, which integrates a greater and greater variety of experiences to form new meanings. Whitehead's organic epistemology of creativity, developed in *The Concept of Nature* (1920), argued for "events" as the locus where mind and purpose work to create "novelty." The mind has an active role in focusing on that something which gets our attention out of the mass of data which come to us in experience. A "principle of concretion" is at work in an event to bring meaning to an object which "prehends" (integrates in different levels) the world. Though Wieman rejected Whitehead's concept of God since it contained a transcendent element, Wieman draws on Whitehead to argue that we experience the world as events, rather than as separate entities, which consist of many objects and experiences that come together in a perceiving and feeling event. We do not exist alone, but always in interaction with our environment as a qualitative flow.[37] In later writings, Wieman was more critical of Whitehead, and his epistemology is more closely tied to the human being as a "biological organism capable of using symbols" whose meanings can expand as we come to know more of the universe through creative interaction, in which the human mind selects data according to the interests of the organism, which are shaped by what the organism requires for survival and by its culture.[38]

The concepts of creativity and interests form the core of Wieman's argument. His Harvard dissertation established the relationship between these:

> Our problem will be to discover that organization of human interests which is most conducive to their maximum fulfillment. The object of our quest is the greatest good. The principle of organization, which we propose, we shall call creativity. Our thesis is that all interests should be so organized as to function as one; and that one should be creative interest.[39]

Wieman assumes that satisfaction is the guiding principle for making choices. The human being is an organism that desires food, housing, sex, and these are "good" because they satisfy our desires. Something is good if it fulfills any interests of an organism, where "interests" are understood as all the activities of the organism, and the greatest good is "that system which gives us the most constant and ample fulfillment of purpose." The value of something does not reside in itself, but in the total event in which the organism desires something.[40] Life is not simply one entity seeking another entity, but a Bergsonian structure which provides for maximum fulfillment by organizing past activities as they connect with present and future interests. Maximum fulfillment is reached through a creative conflict of interests—rather than through harmony—in which we disrupt our partial selves in order that we may grow further.

To understand the idea of creativity, we need to understand the kinds of interests we have. There are three types of actions that lead to satisfactions: an adaptation to the environment, unconscious of future situations; an instrumental action, done to consciously gain something; and a creative action, a coordination of interests to reach maximum satisfaction.[41] Creative action is the highest good since it sustains the "qualitative meaning," the relationships between different enjoyments, and broadens the amount of enjoyments we can experience in other events. Qualitative meaning is created in a "creative event" in which the "creative good" is at work. This event is a process of generating new meanings through communication with others and integrating them with the old to give a wider range of reference, which results in a more unified life. As evidence of this process at work, Wieman points to the evolutionary "triumphs" of the cell, the organism, and humanity in which the interests were so organized at each level to produce greater perspective, quality, and meaning.[42] To satisfy our value yearnings, we must adapt ourselves to this creative process, and be willing to suffer for lesser interests to fulfill greater ones.

Religion and science work together when we recognize the need to shape our conduct and the conditions around us so that the creative event can be released to produce the maximum good. True religion consists of the concepts which correctly define the supreme good and enable us to make adjustments to it. Religion is not to identify itself with any given form of knowledge since all forms of knowledge are subject to change. "God" and the Christian message are not the true focus for religion since they are proposed answers to the basic religious question of human existence. Wieman follows in the pragmatist tradition of "right religious adjustment" by defining the function of religion as follows:

> Religion is the most comprehensive, over-all, ruling commitment accepted on the belief that this commitment will direct human striving in such a way that human existence will be saved from its self-destructive and degenerative propensities and transformed to contain the fullest content of value that human life can ever embody.[43]

The symbols, rituals, and beliefs of religion must present creativity in such a way that commitment to creativity is always the goal, and much of *The Source of Human Good* was an effort to make this commitment intelligible in terms of the Christian tradition. Religion must constantly reform itself in order to make this commitment meaningful in times of cultural change, and Wieman draws on the thought of Kenneth Boulding to assert that the second half of the twentieth century is such a time of change as life comes to be dominated by scientific research and technology. A religion appropriate to this "postcivilization" must work in close cooperation with the sciences to symbolize creativity in a fresh way:

> This is so because only the sciences can search out the conditions at all levels of human existence which must be shaped in such a way that creativity can operate most effectively to expand the valuing consciousness of each individual in community with others. The responsibility of science is to provide this knowledge along with the technology required to use the knowledge effectively. The responsibility of religion is to maintain throughout society a ruling commitment to this *creativity* ... which creates, sustains, and magnifies the values of human existence.[44]

The emphasis on the cooperation of religion and the content of the sciences reflects a lifelong commitment on Wieman's part. In articles from 1929 and 1968, Wieman argues that religion makes a mistake if it tries to establish faith on science, or make a religion out of science, since science itself separates the disciplines and theories become obsolete.[45] Cosmic evolution is not to be confused with the process of creativity operating in human existence since we cannot commit ourselves to evolution operating at the prehuman level. The influence of Bergson is still evident in Wieman's thought:

Biochemical processes may have led to human existence, but with the development of symbolized meanings we have something radically and incomparably different. Only as biochemical processes are integrated into the creativity that expands the valuing consciousness, or can otherwise be made to serve this creativity, are they involved in our ruling commitment.[46]

Wieman's epistemological naturalism makes a religion out of the method of modern science as understood through the pragmatist and process philosophies rather than out of the content of any scientific theory. Though he rejects humanism since it elevates human purpose, Wieman also rejects theism since it tends to distinguish religious and scientific methods of knowing while holding onto a transcendent order which is unknowable by the one, scientific method of knowing. Whitehead, Hartshorne, and their followers are not sufficiently committed to naturalism, and they maintain that something transcends creativity. The danger of their position, as well as that of all all theists, is that they abandon the power of science to those who are not committed to creativity.[47] Science and religion must cooperate in a naturalistic epistemological and methodological framework in order for humanity to adjust itself to the creative process at work to save it.

Julian S. Huxley

At the same time that Wieman was arguing against making a religion out of the content of Darwinism, Julian S. Huxley was seeking to do just that. Huxley had a double career in the first half of the twentieth century. On the one hand, as a British scientist, Huxley is recognized as a leading participant in the formation of the "modern synthesis" of Darwinian evolution and genetics. His *Evolution: The Modern Synthesis* (1942) is often referred to as a major text for the revival of Darwinism in the twentieth century.[48] On the other hand, the great majority of Huxley's writings comprises a sustained effort to interpret religion in terms of an evolutionary ontology. His expertise in biology allowed him to carry his gospel of evolution across the world, by means of visiting professorships in American universities among other things. Throughout his writings, Huxley argues that religion is an effort to come to terms with the powers outside of our control, and the best way to understand those powers today is the theory of evolution. By discerning the trends and direction of the evolutionary process, humanity discovers its purpose and destiny as the "business manager for the process of cosmic evolution."[49]

Huxley consistently articulates a position which parallels the earlier work of Herbert Spencer, in which cosmic evolution is seen as a progressive development in understanding and dealing with the environment. In "Progress, Biological and Other," the greatest need of humanity is to discover something, some being or power, some force or tendency, which was moulding the destinies of the world—something not himself, greater than himself, with which he yet felt that he could harmonize his nature, in which he could repose his doubts, through faith in which he could achieve confidence and hope.[50]

Huxley recognizes that "God" has traditionally met this need, but evolutionary biology "in the shape of a verifiable doctrine of progress" now meets this need more effectively. While some would argue that there has been no progress in adaptation, Huxley suggests that the objective method of science, drawing conclusions *a posteriori*, can demonstrate biological progress. After tracing the increasing aggregation of minds from termites and ants to humanity, Huxley claims to have found the general direction of evolution under the pressure of natural selection as the increasing intensity of qualities which humanity has traditionally called valuable: power, knowledge, purpose, emotion, harmony, and independence. Huxley is aware of his circular reasoning with regard to values in evolution, but he somewhat naively dismisses this concern:

It is immaterial whether the human mind comes to have these values *because* they make for progress in evolution, or whether things which make for evolutionary progress become significant *because* they happened to be considered as valuable by human mind, for both are in their degree true.... What is important is that the human idea of *value* finds its external counterpart in an actual historical *direction* in phenomena, and that each becomes more important because of the relationship.[51]

Drawing upon the work of James and Freud, Huxley argues that religion has an important role to play in the progressive movement of evolution. The concept of God is to be understood as a product of evolution, but God can still be used, if necessary, to describe certain processes outside human control. In humanity, the evolutionary process produced the ability to generalize, to frame concepts, and to communicate them to others through traditions. Religion is simply one way of framing concepts which generalize about powers that underlie the operations of the world and human emotions. The raw material for these concepts has always been found in natural forces which are perceived to operate in a consistent way. The Christian tradition framed these powers in terms of a personal ruler of the world, and Paley found this personal God in the adaptations in nature. Following Darwin, this option was no longer possible, and so many took refuge in Bergson's concept of progress. For Huxley, the goal of religion is always to resolve conflicts between our experiences and our soul or inner being, and thus to seek a harmony between ourselves and the world around us. When this harmony is attained, we have "found religion" and have "communion with God" in which we reach a serene conviction that our experiences are of significant value.

Given this basic human need for organizing our experiences of the universe, religion will always have a place in human life. Huxley's *Religion without Revelation* (1927) was an effort to articulate that place in the light of psychology, comparative religion, and the discoveries of modern science. Huxley gave a sigh of relief when he was able to jettison the concept of a personal divine figure since he was now able to get on with the business of taking care of human affairs. The Christian doctrine of the Trinity is given a naturalistic, monistic interpretation that celebrates the incarnation of spirit in matter in the evolutionary process.[52] Huxley has called his religion "scientific" and "evolutionary" humanism because they provide the proper perspective on human nature and our relationship with the world. In contrast to Wieman, Huxley welcomes humanism because it recognizes that the only source of values is the "commerce between mind and matter that we call human life."[53] This humanism is scientific since it understands humanity as an experiment of the universe in rational self-consciousness by which we are "endowed with infinite powers of control should [we] care to exercise them." Scientific humanism is a protest against dualistic supernaturalism and religious dogma in the name of human nature as the source of all value: "It insists on human values as the norms for our aims, but insists equally that they cannot adjust themselves in right perspective and emphasis except as part of the picture of the world provided by science."[54]

The "evolutionary vision" provides the proper perspective for understanding the role of humanity and the values for which we are to strive. Huxley moves beyond the epistemological commitments of those such as Wieman and looks to Darwinian evolution for an ontological understanding of the world. Evolution provides a unified world view in which there is a single process of self-transformation and progress from one level to another, characterized by increasing and improving patterns of organization.[55] Humanity must understand itself not as the final stage of evolution but rather look for future possibilities in which we are the "sole agent" of further evolution. Natural selection has reached its limits in humanity, but evolution will continue at a psychosocial level operating through cultural traditions. Echoing the language of Teilhard's *The Phenomenon of Man*, for which Huxley wrote the English introduction, we must strive for a noosystem, the unity of knowledge and culture, in which all humanity comes together and shares its wisdom. The scientific method is the only adequate, universal method of discerning truth from error, and thus it must form the basis of the noosystem. From this description of the trends of the evolutionary process, Huxley moves to prescribe what humanity must do to further it: enhance global thinking, rather than ideological and nation conflict; develop individual personality, talents, and possibilities; foster diversity of excellence through a "free but unequal" approach to education; control the growth of the world's population and provide hope for a higher quality of life through genetic improvement. The ultimate aim of evolutionary humanism is the fulfillment of humanity through a restoration of its unity with nature in which the beauty and diversity of the natural world are enjoyed and humanity has the experience of participating in an enduring project, the cosmic project of evolution.[56]

Julian Huxley carried on a running debate with his grandfather, Thomas H. Huxley, and the character of this debate is an effective summary of the younger Huxley's evolutionary religion. In his 1893 Romanes lecture, T.H. Huxley followed Darwin in denying any moral ends in the evolutionary process of the struggle to survive, and so argued that "the ethical progress of society depends, not on imitating the cosmic process, still less in running away from it, but in combating it."[57] Fifty years later, Julian Huxley's Romanes lecture argued that his grandfather's contradiction could be resolved by a broader understanding of evolution as a developmental process and by understanding ethics as part of that process. Only at the point when the process unintentionally produced humanity by natural selection is it possible to begin to talk of ethics since at that point the process became conscious. Humanity can discern the trends in which evolution was moving without purpose, and now inject aim and purpose into the evolutionary process, aiming toward higher levels of organization. The grandson attempted to alleviate the paradox of the grandfather, but the grandson failed to resolve his own paradox: How can nature, without aim or purpose, move toward higher levels of value and order? How can an amoral process produce a level of organization which will then ethically direct the process? If the process is moving in the direction indicated, what difference, other than simple survival, will it make if humanity makes a religious commitment to further the process? These are some fundamental questions that must be asked of those who build a religious commitment on the content of Darwinian evolution.

The nineteenth-century advocates of the "religion *of* Darwinism" had the Free Religious Association and *The Index* as institutional and literary organs to debate and popularize their position. Although these have not continued into the present, there are contemporary parallels to be found in groups that have been loosely organized to write two "manifestos," establish the Institute on Religion in an Age of Science, and publish the journal *Zygon*. Although Huxley and Wieman differed on the relationship between religion and the ontological significance of scientific theories, they came together publicly as signers of the *Humanist Manifesto II* (1973). The manifesto argues for a naturalistic epistemology based on the scientific method as the sole determiner of truth. This method discovers no transcendent divine purpose for humanity, and discredits a dualistic view of human nature: "Science affirms that the human species is an emergence from natural evolutionary forces. As far as we know, the total personality is a function of the biological organism transacting in a social and cultural context."[58] Religion is valued as a way of "inspiring dedication to the highest ethical ideals," while the discoveries of science provide the sense of wonder in life. The ability to create and develop our future is the source of human meaning within this naturalist epistemology and ethical religion. Reason and intelligence are to be harnessed to foster the dignity and freedom of the individual through a democratic method of policymaking which should transcend nationalism and thus form a world community.[59]

Ralph Wendell Burhoe

While the many signers of the *Manifesto* may disagree on the ontological significance of scientific theories, they do agree on a naturalistic, monistic epistemology and methodology for integrating science and religious thought. The issues raised by Darwinian evolution, as well as by other theories, have been the focus of the Institute on Religion in an Age of Science and the journal *Zygon* which it copublishes. The I.R.A.S. was founded in 1954 when two groups of scientists and religious thinkers came together out of their common concern for the meaning of life and religion in the light of new scientific developments. According to its statement of purpose, the I.R.A.S. "aims to understand, interpret, and advance in the light of the sciences and critical scholarship the continuing functions of evolving religion that guide humanity's relation to the ultimate conditions of its destiny." In 1966, a journal was established as a communications channel for those people concerned with linking religion with the issues raised by science. The perspective of *Zygon* was stated as follows:

> We respond to the growing fears that the widening chasm in twentieth-century culture between values and knowledge, or good and truth, or religion and science, is disruptive if not lethal for human destiny. In this split, the traditional faiths and philosophies, which once informed men of what is of most sacred concern for them, have lost their credibility and hence their power. Yet human fulfillment or salvation in the age of science requires not less but more insight and conviction concerning life's basic values and moral requirements.[60]

The name of the journal is taken from both the biological term "zygote" and the Greek word for "yoke" in order to convey the need to yoke together the religious and scientific "blueprints for life" in order for humanity to reach a union with ultimate reality. The particular way that this yoking occurs can best be seen in the writings of the founding editor, Ralph Wendell Burhoe. The present editor, Karl Peters, has articulated positions very similar to those of Burhoe, and has attempted to make this position more acceptable to those with more personalistic religious views.[61]

Ralph Wendell Burhoe was an active participant in the early days of the I.R.A.S. Burhoe's early education was in the sciences, but he turned to religious studies as a profession. His career has taken him from being an officer in the American Academy of Science to a position as professor of theology and the sciences at Meadville Theological School of Lombard School in Chicago, where he is now Research Professor Emeritus. Having once acknowledged that he continues in the tradition of Abbot, Burhoe has continually argued for a scientific religion.[62] He has followed in the tradition of Wieman and Huxley by beginning with a "generic definition" of the function of religion in culture. Religions are

> the organs or institutions whose function it is to engender attitudes and behavior that tend to adapt man to the conditions of his total environment in such a way as to optimize his prime values. I submit further that these prime values will probably be found to be essentially a continuation of the long-established values of all living creatures: the continuation and advancement of life.[63]

Humanity's need for religion is rooted in the fact that we need a "constructive and co-operative" interpretation of reality in order for us to respond to threats and live in harmony with the underlying forces of the world.

Burhoe claims that there have been five steps in the process of discerning these values toward which life is directed. At the most fundamental level, genetic information provides us with billions of "commands" for living. When multicellular organisms developed a specialized nervous system, the brain formed the next step as it integrated the genetic information with what was learned in the process of development. As the nervous system became complex enough to transmit information to other organisms, culturally transmitted knowledge became the third factor in the shaping of values. Burhoe argues that the knowledge which has been selected for its capacity to promote survival becomes embedded in a "culturetype" which is a product of the genotype and the environment. The myths, language, technology, and social behavior that make up the culturetype are fed back to each new generation, and thus become a form of knowledge independent from the genotype. Culturetypes are also under pressure from natural selection, as seen in the rise and fall of civilizations. The fourth step in the evolution of knowledge of values is reached with rational knowledge, symbolized in language, in which events and relationships can be predicted, tested, and proven based on logic. Developing out of reason, the rise of scientific knowledge in the seventeenth century is seen as the fifth step in knowledge. Modern science recognized that our models of the world are not necessarily true, and that we needed a way to test their validity and then to reconceive the symbolic system to fit the facts of experience. Humanity has now reached the stage of being able to consciously adapt to reality as best we know it using the information we have of the values intrinsic to living systems.[64]

Given the functional definition of religion and the evolution of epistemology, religion and science function together to motivate human behavior toward the values and goals which science reveals. Drawing upon the work of Norbert Wiener in cybernetics, Burhoe argues that values are facts when values are defined as goals of a system. In a goal-directed system, the scientist can talk of "norms" and "oughts," and can state the facts which explain the "ought" of a system and how that condition can be reached. Science has, according to Burhoe, discovered that "life" is the supreme value for living systems, and all other values are instrumental in achieving that supreme value. Given that life is the supreme value, all instrumental values can then be understood as information or knowledge necessary to promote life. Science thus has the role of both revealing the supreme value for humanity and supplying all other information necessary for the realization of that value.[65] In this cybernetic view of life, religious thought becomes an "applied science" which organizes scientific information at the top of a hierarchy of integrated cybernetic mechanisms shaping human behavior.[66] In its myths, texts, and theologies, religion applies the genetic, cultural, and scientific information to questions of human hopes and fears, the meaning of life, relationships with others, and the relationship with ultimate realities. In its rituals and behavioral patterns, religion provides the mechanisms and motivations for attaining humanity's goals. The culturetype discussed above is now held up as the primary unit of selection in human evolution. While individuals and species have been selected in terms of genetic information, humanity has created a new unit of selection which transcends individuals since the cultural information can be transmitted much more quickly than genetic information, and religion has the function of integrating this information in order to successfully adapt behavior. Religion is thus "cultural evolution's agent for transforming apes into men":

> Religions are the agency of coadaptation or synthesis of the individual's unique, genotypically programmed system of values and his values as structured by his symbiont sociocultural organism, so that he becomes indeed a suitably coadapted product of the interaction of two separate species—ape-man and sociocultural organism.[67]

When Burhoe applies this conceptual system to specific religious issues, some interesting juxtapositions occur. Modern science and traditional Christian religion share a commitment to recognizing the reality of laws and boundary conditions external to humanity. Humanity is not the master of its destiny since there is a reality that has created and sustains us and which prohibits many things. Burhoe criticizes Julian Huxley for suggesting that science puts humanity in control of its own evolution since Huxley knew that we owe our life to something beyond our control to which we must adapt ourselves.[68] This process of discovering the external, ultimate reality and adapting to its laws is necessary for living a good life, or, in other words, being "saved." Religions have named "God" as that external, ultimate reality upon whom we are dependent for living. Modern science calls that reality natural selection: "From the view of god meaning the ultimate constellation of forces outside of and prior to life (including man) that did in fact create and sustain life, nature or natural selection is in reality a modern statement or revelation of such a god's nature."[69] One of the traditional attributes of God has been the judgment of evil in the world, and natural selection fulfills that function in our contemporary understanding of life: "The wicked do in fact perish, and the righteous are rewarded, if we take reward to mean that their 'good' or 'fit' patterns of life will survive. If you trust in the Lord of natural selection, you need not fear that the wicked will triumph."[70]

Although Darwin rejected the accusation that he renamed God, Burhoe juxtaposes Darwin's description of natural selection as "daily and hourly scrutinizing throughout the world" with the God of Psalm 139 who "hast searched me, and known me," and declares them equivalent in many respects.[71] When we have integrated ourselves not only with the immediate sociocultural situation but also with the species and the ultimate reality system called nature, we have attained the Kingdom of God. The core of our being, the pattern of our genetic and cultural information in relationship to boundary conditions established by the Lord of natural selection, forms the "soul" which will survive (be transmitted) as we successfully meet the challenges of living.[72]

Edward O. Wilson

Burhoe's argument that religion plays the role of integrating information and adapting humanity to the culturetype reflects the recent development of the discipline known as sociobiology. As we saw in chapter 2, sociobiology is the scientific study of the biological basis of social behavior. Edward O. Wilson, Professor of Science and Curator of Entomology at the Museum of Comparative Zoology, Harvard University, argued in *Sociobiology: The Modern Synthesis* (1975) that it was time for all disciplines of study, including the humanities, to be incorporated into the modern synthesis, and for ethics to be biologicized. *On Human Nature* (1978) won the Pulitzer Prize for taking up the challenge of closing the gap between the two cultures. Wilson opens this hotly debated work by describing the effect of Darwinism:

> If humankind evolved by Darwinian natural selection, genetic chance and environmental necessity, not God, made the species. Deity can still be sought in the origin of the ultimate units of matter, in quarks and electron shells (Hans Küng was right to ask atheists why there is something instead of nothing) but not in the origin of species. However much we embellish that stark conclusion with metaphor and imagery, it remains the philosophical legacy of the last century of scientific research.[73]

Wilson recognizes that this new naturalism raises "two great spiritual dilemmas." The first is that there is no purpose "beyond the imperatives created by [our] genetic history." This undermining of transcendental goals demands that we "search for a new morality based upon a more truthful definition of man," and that search makes it "necessary to look inward, to dissect the machinery of the mind and to retrace its evolutionary history." This leads to the second dilemma: we must choose between the emotional guides which we have inherited, and this choice must be based upon biological knowledge.[74] This necessary knowledge is then described through an engaging study of hereditary mechanisms and the evolutionary process, leading up to the human behavioral patterns of aggression, sex, altruism, and religion.

Wilson focuses on the interrelationship between genes and culture, and his more recent writings, with C.J. Lumsden, argue for a pattern of coevolution.[75] Where Burhoe located the role of religion at the level of the culturetype, Wilson has a more individualistic point of view. He rejects the concept of cultures as organisms under the pressure of natural selection and claims that cultural change is the product of separate behavioral responses of large numbers of individuals coping as best they can with existence. The choices we make are a combination of the behavioral rules encoded by genetic information and cognitive process with the behavior patterns of other members of the society. The behavior patterns produced determine the genetic fitness of individuals, and the transmission of those coping patterns influences the evolution of the epigenetic rules. Genetic and cultural information evolve as a coupled system.

One element of the behavioral coping process is religion, which undergoes "a kind of cultural Darwinism" in which the "more advanced religions" are selected. While sociobiology may explain religion in terms of genes and culture, Wilson believes that science can never eliminate religion. Religion is a uniquely human behavior and is the process of persuading individuals to subordinate their immediate self-interest to the interests of the group.

This process can be analyzed in terms of three structural levels at which natural selection works. At the level of cultural inheritance, there is an ecclesiastic selection process in which rituals and conventions are chosen, and those that are successful in gaining adherents are culturally transmitted. These practices are then tested at the ecological level by the demands of the environment. If a religion weakens the people during warfare, encourages destruction of the environment, or interferes with procreation, it will lead to its own decline. At the third level, the frequency of genes changes. These three levels coevolve, and the selection at the ecclesiastic level can indeed affect the genetic level if the practices enhance survival and procreation: "When the gods are served, the Darwinian fitness of the members of the tribe is the ultimate if unrecognized beneficiary."[76] Religion provides individuals with a sense of group identity and purpose which is compatible with the individual's self-interest and fosters altruistic acts to enhance the survival of the group since the group is the source of strength and guidance in life.

There is a place for myth in this view of religion if myth is understood as narratives which rationally explain our place in the world in terms of our understanding of the physical world. With the advance of science, traditional theology has been forced to retreat to the idea of God as first cause of the universe. Wilson offers a different myth to explain our place in the universe and direct our actions—scientific materialism:

> It presents the human mind with an alternative mythology that until now has always, point for point in zones of conflict, defeated traditional religion. Its narrative form is the epic: the evolution of the universe from the big bang of fifteen billion years ago through the origin of the elements and celestial bodies to the beginnings of life on earth. The evolutionary epic is mythology in the sense that the laws it adduces here and now are believed but can never be definitely proved to form a cause - and - effect continuum from physics to the social sciences, from this world to all other worlds in the visible universe, and backward through time to the beginning of the universe.[77]

Wilson argues that we can solve the dilemma of moral choice by believing in the myth of scientific materialism since it explains religion as a product of the brain's evolution.[78] Moral choices can now be made on the basis of scientific knowledge rather than religious dogma. Science can provide the information which the humanities need to take the synthetic step of arguing for the primary values of survival, a diverse gene pool, and universal human rights.

We have examined a "religion of Darwinism" model in which the epistemological and methodological issues at the core of Darwin's work are first taken over for religious thought. The nineteenth-century advocates of this position looked upon the methodology of science as the way to discover truth in any field, including religion. Wieman drew upon pragmatism, Whitehead, and Bergsonian evolution to create an empirical, naturalistic method for religious thought. The epistemological monism of these men resulted in a world with nothing of significance transcending it. Huxley, Burhoe, and Wilson assumed that world view and sought to create a religious vision out of some of the ontological implications of contemporary Darwinian evolution. Huxley rejected Darwin's reticence to use the words higher and lower, and Burhoe explicitly made the move to do what Darwin never would do: equate natural selection and God. Wilson took this one step further by raising the description of evolutionary processes to the level of myth. In this process we have made a 180 degree turn. Darwin established a methodology which liberated science from the dictates of religious orthodoxy and which sought to eliminate value judgments from the results of science. In other words, Darwin removed the religious "ought" of the previous chapter and replaced it with the "is" which science discovered. With Huxley, Burhoe, and Wilson, we have moved in the direction of the scientific "is" becoming the religious "ought."

The relationship between "is" and "ought" has been the focus of much discussion surrounding the "religion of Darwinism" model.[79] As we saw in the first chapter, Toulmin and Peckham have taken this issue as the key question for dealing with Darwinism and those who would develop philosophical and ethical precepts from Darwin's theory. With the development of sociobiology, the "is/ought" issue has arisen again. While Hume and G.E. Moore attacked the idea of deriving ethical "oughts" from descriptions of the way life "is," Huxley, Burhoe, and Wilson decided that science demonstrates that the evolutionary facts are values that should determine how we live. This is not the place to resolve that issue, but many have argued that this move does little for establishing a religious commitment.

At the conclusion of the discussion of Julian Huxley's "quarrel" with his grandfather, several questions were raised which must confront those who would argue for a religious commitment based on the content as well as epistemology of Darwinian evolution. Those who follow the model of "religion of Darwinism" must face the paradox: how can nature, without aim or purpose, move toward higher levels of value and order? How can an amoral process produce a level of organization which then will ethically direct the process? If the process is moving in the direction indicated, what difference, other than simple survival, will it make if humanity makes a religious commitment to further the process? Those who follow the direction described in this chapter are left with reading their own values back into the evolutionary process. Others claim that there is something which transcends the process that answers those questions. We shall now turn to them as they synthesize religion and Darwinisticism.

5

Religion and Darwinisticism in Concert

A third model for the religious responses to Darwinism makes use of the content of scientific theories of evolution to develop religious concepts. This is a Darwinistic approach since some aspects of Darwin's theory are given metaphysical and ethical implications while true Darwinian evolution is often revised or disregarded to fit philosophical and religious commitments. This "in concert" model is considered following the "religion of Darwinism" model because both models are deeply interested in reconciling religious thought with contemporary scientific world views.

The two models differ in several ways. The "in concert" model strives to remain in contact with traditional religious thought, but is committed to a revision of religious thought in light of scientific theory. Where the "of" model claims to work with the epistemological and methodological perspective of Darwin's revolution, the "in concert" model uses other philosophical positions as the basis for synthesizing scientific and religious thought. The "in concert" model does not completely identify God and nature, as does the "of" model, but maintains an immanent divine presence with nature and/or an idealist view of God's design and purpose in nature. Where the "of" model takes the scientific epistemology and methodology as the starting point for religious thought, the "in concert" model usually begins with religious experience and attempts to interpret that experience in terms of the scientific world view.

John Fiske is often suggested as the key representative of this model in nineteenth-century American thought. Fiske's "Cosmic Philosophy" is founded upon Herbert Spencer's philosophical evolution, and thus represents one way in which a philosophical position is used to synthesize religious and scientific thought. The distinction between evolution and Darwinism becomes important in this model because the Darwinian understanding of science and evolution is reduced to one factor among many in the cosmic development. The idealist resolution of the conflict between orthodox religion and Darwinism is represented by James McCosh, a Scottish scientist and minister who became president of Princeton University.

An interesting synthesis of Spencerian philosophy, idealism, and Christocentric faith appears in the writings of Henry Drummond. Drummond's views provide a point of transition to the twentieth century as his perspective is quite similar to that of Teilhard de Chardin. After a brief discussion of Teilhard, we will examine twentieth-century parallels to Fiske and McCosh.

John Cobb and Charles Birch represent the "in concert" model based upon an organic philosophy from the twentieth century (Whitehead and Hartshorne), while F.R. Tennant and Peter Bertocci represent an idealist reconciliation of Darwinism and religion. The appropriateness of the "in concert" label for this model is apparent in the work of A.R. Peacocke, who bases his perspective on Polanyi's study of science and religion, and suggests the metaphor of composer for God.

Finally, we will examine a constructive critique of this model by feminist theologians who generally work with the "in concert" approach. Rosemary Ruether and Elizabeth Gray are committed to a revision of the relationship of nature, God, and humanity, and to a critique of the hierarchical perspective usually at work in this model.

Evolution as God's Way of Doing Things

In chapter 3 we examined the opposition of religious thinkers to Darwinism in terms of their epistemological conflict with the demise of an external divine teleology in the biological world. Charles Hodge discerned the distinction between Darwinism and evolution in general, and suggested that Christians could be evolutionists without being consistent Darwinians. That option is represented in this chapter. As James Moore has noted, Christian Darwinists struggled with Darwin's ateleological vision of nature in which humanity itself evolved from other species.[1] The issue was, and is, how to reconcile God's beneficent purposes which should be evident in nature and Darwin's description of a world functioning quite well without God. This conflict was resolved primarily by broadening the definition of evolution in order to reduce the influence of Darwin's theory and relegate natural selection to a minor role in natural, especially human, processes.

John Fiske

John Fiske (1842–1901) achieved his reconciliation through the philosophy of Herbert Spencer. Fiske grew up in Connecticut, graduated from Harvard in 1863, took a law degree, and set up practice in Boston. Fiske had little commitment to law, and, when few clients appeared, he wrote freelance articles for national magazines. His readings included Humboldt's *Cosmos*, the positive philosophy of Comte, and Spencer's *Synthetic Philosophy*. In 1869, Fiske received a temporary appointment to lecture at Harvard on Comte, and he remained at Harvard until 1879 as lecturer and assistant librarian. When he did not receive a professorship, Fiske devoted himself to writing and lecture tours. Fiske's goal was to discover a cosmology which would incorporate physical, biological, psychological, and social phenomena into one system of laws.

This cosmology, presented in *Outlines of Cosmic Philosophy* (1874), reconciles science and religion through an epistemology which Fiske called "relativity of knowledge." Fiske echoes Kant by claiming that we can know things only in their relation to us, not absolutely. The Absolute cannot be known since our knowledge is dependent upon elements of likeness, difference, and relations. The deity and the world are known only as they affect our states of consciousness, and we cannot assume that these agents resemble our states of consciousness. Science thus deals only with particular orders of phenomena, and not with truths in all classes of phenomena. The task of philosophy is to study the whole by synthezising the deepest truths of the particular sciences into a universal doctrine. Truth can be established scientifically by balancing intuitions with empirical tests, by bringing together Hume's test of "uniformity of experience" with Kant's "inconceivability test," to reach a definition of "relative truth":

> When any given order among our conceptions is so coherent that it cannot be sundered except by the temporary annihilation of some one of its terms, there must be a corresponding order among phenomena ... because the order of our conceptions is the expression of our experience of the order of phenomena.[2]

Our conceptions are thus to be trusted as valid guides to the world as it affects us.

Idealism and positivism are consistently attacked for their failure to understand the implications of the relativity of knowledge. Neither position took a positive attitude toward objective existence. Idealism assumed that the possibilities of thinking were the measure for the possibilities of existence, and claimed that the unknown was a figment of our imagination. Positivism simply dismissed the question. Fiske follows Spencer and asserts that the relativity of knowledge depends upon an Unknown Reality independent of us:

> Our ineradicable belief in the absolute existence of Something which underlies and determines the series of changes which constitute our consciousness rests upon the strongest of foundations,—upon the unthinkableness of its negation.... Without postulating Absolute Being—existence independent of the conditions of the process of knowing—we can frame no theory whatever, either of internal or of external phenomena.[3]

Neither mind nor matter can fully account for the changes in our states of consciousness, and, since they are both phenomenal manifestations, Absolute Reality is not to be identified with either. Every phenomenon is the knowable manifestation, the objective existence, of the Unknowable Reality. The proper attitude toward this absolute, unknowable reality is religious.

Fiske's "Cosmic Philosophy" attempts "a Synthesis of scientific truths into a Universal Science dealing with the order of the phenomenal manifestations of the Absolute Power," and this synthesis begins with the fundamental laws of matter, motion, and force. The idea that matter is indestructible and motion is continuous is derived from the idea that matter is built up from our experience of force. The persistence of force is thus the deeper theorem. Three corollaries of this theorem eventually lead to evolution.

First, like forces cause like effects, and they are followed by an invariable order of succession. Second, the direction of motion is the result of resistances being balanced. The key corollary is the third which analyzes the rhythm of motion when two bodies attract each other:

> The mere coexistence of a vast number of bodies in the universe necessitates perpetual rhythm, resulting in a continuous redistribution of matter and motion.... The scientific demonstration further shows us that the change is always from an old state to a new state.[4]

This rhythm of motion gives us evolution in Spencerian terms as "the integration of matter and the concomitant dissipation of motion." Spencer's "law of evolution" is established as the overarching law of the universe, and at least an equal to Newton's law of gravity. Evolution applies not only to biological systems, but also to the whole inorganic universe such that wherever change is possible, it will be from a lower level of uniformity to a higher level of diversity. Fiske then supports this assertion with a long series of examples of growth from simple cells to mature species to the evolution of the planetary system. Along the way, special creation and the fixity of species are attacked since they have survived only because of theological dogmas which were assumed infallible, rather than by scientific verification. Science has verified "derivation by slow modification" which offers better explanations than creationism for why frogs do not exist on islands suited for them, and why old forms are used in human embryos.

Darwin's work is first addressed in the chapter on natural selection. Darwin is praised for his patience and restraint in publishing his theory, and for demolishing arguments for special creation:

> He was the first to marshal the arguments from classification, embryology, morphology, and distribution, and thus fairly to establish the fact that there has been a derivation of higher forms from lower; and he was also the first to point out the *modus operandi* of the change.[5]

Fiske talks of natural selection in terms of a "prodigious slaughter" in nature due to the geometric rate of increase and the struggle for life in which only the best adapted survive. Darwin's theory is successful because it explains facts otherwise unexplained, and the standard objections are easily answered.

Fiske moves quickly from Darwin and biology to sociology by adapting Spencer's concept of life as adjustment such that evolution becomes a process of adjustment. Life is to be understood as a perpetual balancing of external forces by internal forces. Drawing upon Lamarckian theories of evolution, Fiske describes four types of forces at work: external direct (adaptation to environment) and indirect (natural selection), and internal direct (heredity) and indirect (use and disuse of organs and capacities). Organisms survive and evolve by adjusting to these environmental forces, but for humans this adjustment is more mental than physical. Fiske suggests that the greatest obstacle to the acceptance of evolution is the kinship that is established between humanity and lower forms of intelligence. This obstacle can be overcome by focusing on social evolution in which the contrast is made between primitive and civilized humans. Civilized humanity has survived and is superior due to our capacity for rational and imaginative thought. Fiske thus dodges the essence of Darwin's *Descent*, and reclaims Spencer's doctrine of evolutionary progress. In a later writing, Darwin is praised for providing this higher view of humanity: "So far from degrading humanity, or putting it on a level with the animal world in general, the Darwinian theory shows us distinctly for the first time how the creation and the perfecting of Man is the goal toward which Nature's work has all the while been tending."[6]

Fiske's celebrated theory of infancy becomes the cornerstone of his evolutionary social history, which has the goal of bringing forth the human soul. The whole purpose of "the deadly struggle for existence" has been teleological: to bring forth from the brute a humanity with a soul to adjust us to the laws of nature, which are the same as the laws of God.

The third part of *Cosmic Philosophy* and much of Fiske's later writings focus on "cosmic theism," an effort to purify the Christian faith. The question is not whether there is a God, but whether there is an anthropomorphic, limited, personal God with quasihuman consciousness, volition, and contrivances. Fiske draws upon Comte's positivism and critiques it by arguing that religion has not been on the decline; rather there has been a process of "deanthropomorphization" in which human attributes are being stripped from the absolute and unknown Power which is manifested in phenomena. Anthropomorphic theism arose in nature worship in which the mind projects its attributes upon nature. These attributes were slowly stripped away as religion moved toward ancestor worship and to monotheism. Two forms of monotheism struggled with the issue of a personal God in terms of theodicy. The immanent God of the Stoics, Origen, and Athanasius was set in opposition to the remote deity of Plato, Lucretius, and Augustine. The

Augustinian God led to the rejection of Newton and Darwin because physical forces seemed to be substituted for the direct action of the deity. The distinction between divine action and natural law comes not from science but from the theology of the Latin church.[7] The remote anthropomorphic deity is either infinite in goodness or infinite in intelligence and power because the reality of evil limits one or the other of these personal attributes. Personality and inifinity are incompatible, and deanthropomorphization must continue as evolution reveals the sources and limitations of a quasihuman deity.

The immanent God resolves this problem by seeing every event flowing directly from the First Cause. For a cosmic theologian, the laws of nature express a mode of divine action: "All the dynamic phenomena of Nature constitute but the multiform revelation of an Omnipresent Power that is not identifiable with Nature."[8] The proper metaphor for understanding the workings of this power is an organism with an indwelling principle of life, rather than Paley's watchmaker. Even without a watchmaker, Fiske recognizes that we crave a final cause and must rely on a series of fragmentary conceptions and symbols. Science can provide us with such symbols as it discovers the unity of nature's forces: "The universe as a whole is thrilling in every fiber with Life. . . . Life as manifested in the organism is seen to be only a specialized form of the Universal Life."[9] The movement of this Universal Life is toward the perfection and salvation of humanity. Natural selection is to be understood metaphorically as sparing the unfit the miseries of life and perfecting humanity, thus restoring teleology to the evolutionary process: "Toward the spiritual perfection of Humanity the stupendous momentum of the cosmic process has all along been tending."[10]

Fiske has absorbed Spencer's optimistic vision of evolutionary progress, and has given it an altruistic and religious interpretation. Cosmic theism maintains a transcendent deity as an inscrutible Power, yet knows an immanent God through the manifest evolutionary process. Science thus comes to the aid of true religion, and is a threat only to anthropomorphic, personal concepts of God. Darwin's vision of science explaining natural processes without recourse to God is accepted on one level, yet science is limited in its area of explanation. Reality is an open secret, and the deity is more than the manifestations we know as the universe. Fiske thus rejects the label of pantheism, and establishes a position that is important for the "in concert" model: there is a transcendent aspect to this God who is immanent in evolution.

James McCosh

While Fiske followed Spencer and the biologist Joseph LeConte followed Hegel to locate an immanent deity in the evolutionary process, Henry Ward Beecher, Lyman Abbott, and James McCosh claimed a form of idealism to synthesize their religious faith with evolution. The key issue for these latter men was the design which we see in nature. The idealist position is evident in Beecher's aphorism that "design by wholesale is grander than design by retail" and McCosh's suggestion that we should "look on evolution simply as the method by which God works."[11] James McCosh (1811–94) provides an interesting study for this model because he shared with Charles Hodge many of the Scottish realist convictions but came to some different conclusions on evolution.

Born in Scotland and educated at Glasgow and Edinburgh, McCosh integrated the study of geology and biology into his training for the Presbyterian ministry. *The Method of Divine Government* was published in 1850 while McCosh was in the pastorate, and that book provided the credentials for his invitation to the chair of metaphysics and logic at the new Queen's College in Belfast. In 1868, McCosh was elected president of the College at Princeton in the midst of the American debate over Darwinism.[12]

McCosh took on the task of rescuing both science and religion from the naturalistic errors of some interpretations of Darwinism. He opposed the power which Fiske gave science over religion, and argued from the beginning of his work that science was valid only within its boundaries. The tenets of Scottish realism, however, could not be overlooked, and McCosh shared with Hodge the conviction that we can trust what our senses tell us about like producing like, about design in nature, and we can trust the knowledge we derive through inductive inferences.

While Hodge attacked Darwin for undermining divine design, McCosh was able to be more open to Darwinism because his concept of design was not limited to the special adaptations of which Paley had written. Already in his first work, McCosh set alongside the evidence of special adaptations another view of providential design: the principle of order. This idealist form of design was presented in the following manner: "Wisdom displayed in the prevalence of general laws and observable order in the world [such that] wherever we we find law, there we see the certain traces of a lawgiver."[13] McCosh had thus established a method of reconciling religion and Darwinism, even though his next book carried forth this idealist argument based on a transcendental morphology, which was quickly undermined by the publication of the *Origin*.[14]

McCosh turned to the relationship between religious thought and science in a Darwinian world with a series of lectures at Union Theological Seminary in New York, which were published in 1871 as *Christianity and Positivism*. The understanding of humanity and the gaps in the natural order set McCosh apart from the Darwinian position. While he recognized that Darwin's theory contained many truths, McCosh's position can be called at best "progressive creation."[15] Reflecting the influence of his Scottish realism, McCosh argued that there were qualitative differences between the inorganic and organic, the unconscious and the conscious, plant life and animal life. McCosh called upon Huxley and Wallace in support of his position that there was an unbridgeable gulf between human and animal intellectual capacity that cannot be explained by natural selection. McCosh held this position consistently throughout his life. In the realm of nonhuman nature, he was quite willing to allow evolution to be the causal process, but even there nature cannot run on its own and God is quite involved in the forces at work. The fixity of species was no longer a great concern, but McCosh could not see how human feelings, intelligence, and morality could have developed from natural causation: "Causation cannot create anything new; it cannot give what it has not within itself."[16] God had to be involved in the creation of humanity because God is the only cause which is equal to or greater than humanity:

> If anyone asks me if I believe man's body to have come from a brute, I answer that I do not know. I believe in revelation, I believe in science, but neither has revealed this to me; and I restrain the weak curiosity which would tempt me to inquire what cannot be known. Meanwhile I am sure, and I assert, that man's soul is of a higher origin and of a nobler type.[17]

The problem with both Darwin's method and natural selection was that Darwin established an either/or position: either natural law or supernatural power. McCosh suggests that this position was misleading:

> The supernatural power is to be recognized in the natural law. The Creator's power is executed by creature action. The design is seen in the mechanism. Chance is obliged to vanish because we see contrivance. There is purpose when we see a beneficent end accomplished. Supernatural design produces natural selection.[18]

The real question is whether God works with means or without means, and there is nothing inherently atheistic in saying that evolution is one of God's means. The laws of evolution are themselves expressions of a Final Cause:

> There is proof of Plan in the Organic Unity and Growth of the World. As there is evidence of purpose, not only in every organ of the plant, but in the whole plant . . . so there are proofs of design, not merely in the individual plant and individual animal, but in the whole structure of the Cosmos and in the manner in which it makes progress from age to age.[19]

In this sense, evolution does not undermine the concept of a Final Cause, but rather strengthens it with examples of the beneficence of God. Natural selection means not that nature makes a choice, but rather that God has chosen this process to integrate the diversity of nature in order to produce higher organisms and strengthen the race. With the appearance of Christ, humanity's struggle to survive was transformed into a spiritual struggle between good and evil. McCosh then incorporates Lamarckian elements in the development process, and suggests that humanity is moving toward perfection through education, agriculture, and commerce. As surely as the age of the struggle for existence was transformed into the struggle of good against evil, the divine plan is leading to the age of the Spirit in which God will be all in all.

Henry Drummond

The immanent God of Fiske and McCosh's idealist design leading to the age of the Spirit are synthesized in the writings of Henry Drummond (1851–97). Brought up in the Free Church of Scotland, Drummond was educated at New College, Edinburgh, and at Tübingen. When Dwight L. Moody brought his evangelistic missions to Great Britain, Drummond worked with him in 1874 and again in 1882. Drummond himself conducted missions to several universities in Great Britain and popularized evolution on the lecture circuits of America. His mixture of geology, biology, and revivalism made him a well-known speaker and writer in America, Britain, and Europe. While Fiske and McCosh directed their synthesis of religion and evolution primarily to university and seminary audiences, Drummond took his message to the masses. His *Natural Law in the Spiritual World* (1883) was both praised by church papers and condemned as a "fascinating but misleading and dangerous book."[20]

Drummond acknowledged the inspiration he received from Spencer, and claimed to do for natural science and religion what Spencer had done for natural law and and sociology. The distinction between the natural world and the spiritual world, which we shall examine in the next chapter, is a false distinction for Drummond since he discovered himself discussing spiritual laws in the terms of physics and biology. The focus should be not on individual phenomena but rather on law which integrates diverse phenomena and transforms knowledge into eternal truths. Drummond had tired of efforts to "reconcile" religion and science, and instead invoked the spirit of Bacon who discovered that deeper knowledge of science led one to religion. Drummond thus argued that

> what is required, therefore, to draw Science and Religion together again—for they began the centuries hand in hand—is the disclosure of the naturalness of the supernatural.... Thus, as the Supernatural becomes slowly Natural, will also the Natural become slowly Supernatural, until in the impersonal authority of Law men everywhere recognise the Authority of God.[21]

The proper relationship between the natural and the spiritual is one of identity, not the analogical distinction which Bushnell had attempted to establish: "Nature is not a mere image or emblem of the Spiritual. It is a working model of the Spiritual."[22]

The key to the identity of the spiritual and the natural is the Law of Continuity. Drummond recognizes that the threat of science to religion is not the facts of science but the method of science: law, harmony, and continuity. This experience of being threatened by the method of science is misplaced, however, since the Law of Continuity simply claims that God will not confuse us permanently. Given this assurance, the role of science is to purify religion and give it a solid foundation: "As the Natural Laws are continuous through the universe of matter and of space, so they will be continuous through the universe of spirit."[23] As we discover the various laws of the natural world and integrate them into the Law of Continuity, we are given a sure guide to the spiritual life. There may well be new laws for the spiritual world, but the natural laws are never abandoned. The power of law is its ability to point to the harmony of the unseen world:

> Law in the visible is the Invisible in the visible. . . . Law is great not because the phenomenal world is great, but because these vanishing lines are the avenues into the eternal Order. . . . [God] would simply project the higher Laws downward, so that the Natural World would become an incarnation, a visible representation, a working model of the spiritual. The whole function of the material world lies here.[24]

Evolution is the name science has given to this law, but religion calls it redemption, when properly understood. In *The Ascent of Man* (1894), Drummond sets out to correct the myopic understanding of evolution as simply a struggle to survive. There is indeed a process of natural selection which punishes individuals who are parasites on a community and thus survive for a while even though they are weak. The continual focus on natural selection, however, has distorted the true understanding of the law at work in the natural and spiritual world. Evolutionary theorists have focused too much on the "Villain" in the drama of life:

> Creation is a drama, and no drama was ever put upon the stage with one actor. The Struggle for Life is the "Villain" of the piece, no more; and, like the "Villain" in the play, its chief function is to re-act upon the other players for higher ends. There is, in point of fact, a second factor which one might venture to call the *Struggle for the Life of Others*, which plays an equally prominent part.[25]

The impact of Darwin was so great that the second struggle was overlooked by all except Spencer who balanced survival of the fittest with the care of offspring. Drummond rejects T.H. Huxley's claim that the the natural processes must be resisted since the continuity of nature must be maintained. When we focus on humanity, we discover a continuity as the reign of natural selection is being replaced with the reign of the law of love. The growth of altruism provides wisdom for the use of our knowledge of evolution, as both science and the Bible declare the mystery of the ascent of man.

This ascent was stimulated by the struggle to survive, and a price has been paid for this progress. The Hegelian biologist Joseph LeConte had rationalized the pain of the struggle by claiming that such "evil" is a real good, but Drummond rejects this solution. The pain of the struggle cannot be rationalized away, but its value can be discovered within the larger context: "To make a fit world, the unfit at every stage must be made to disappear; and if any self-acting law can bring this about, though its bearing upon this or that individual case may seem unjust, its necessity for the world as a whole is vindicated."[26] Natural selection thus leads to health, wholeness, adaptation, and the ascent of all. Sentimental moralists unnecessarily divert our attention by focusing on the negative aspect of evolution, and there is no support for their claim that the unfit are innocent.

This amoral struggle is, however, only half the story since there is also the "Struggle for the Life of Others." Drummond asserts that the center of life is affection, not the body or the intellect. The key to life is love and the most important point in evolution was the transition from "Self-ism to Other-ism." Where nutrition was the focus in the struggle for life, reproduction is the focus in the species' struggle for the life of others. Self-sacrifice and cooperation are essential factors in the evolutionary process that are not to be dismissed. Any individual must give up the self in order to reproduce and care for the infant. All nature cooperates in this sacrificial process: "The Seed is the tithe of love, the tithe which Nature renders to Man. When Man lives upon Seeds he lives upon love."[27]

Drummond offers a vision of the goal of this evolutionary process as it extends beyond the organic world into the spiritual Kingdom of God. With Fiske and McCosh, Drummond rejects pantheism because any growth process finds its explanation outside itself. An organism can be understood only in relationship to its environment, and that environment includes the Infinite Intelligence. The energies which direct and shape evolution are spiritual thoughts and ideals which use matter to manifest themselves. God is thus not to be found in the gaps of our knowledge, since that leaves God to the disorder in the world. God is both immanent in the evolutionary process as spiritual energy and transcendent to it as providing the law, the design, for the whole process. As evolution has moved from the inorganic to the organic kingdoms, it will continue to evolve into the spiritual kingdom in which the millions of people are treated as simple cells for the evolution of humanity from complexity to simplicity and unity. Drummond quotes from Tennyson's "In Memoriam" regarding "the one far-off divine event, To which the whole creation moves," and concludes:

> This is the final triumph of Continuity, the heart secret of Creation, the unspoken prophecy
> of Christianity. To Science, defining it as a working principle, this mighty process of
> amelioration is simply *Evolution*. To Christianity, discerning the end through the means, it
> is *Redemption*. These silent and patient processes, elaborating, eliminating, developing all
> from the first of time, conducting the evolution from millennium to millennium with
> unaltering purpose and unfaltering power, are the early stages in the redemptive work—the
> unseen approach of that Kingdom whose strange mark is that it "cometh without
> observation."[28]

The center and the goal of this process is Christ, the realization of the ideal of love. Evolution is the history of Christian salvation as humanity realizes within itself the "Perfect Ideal" which empowers and directs creation in the ascent of love.[29]

The Interconnectedness of Life

Drummond's optimistic vision of life as an ascent of love empowered by the inward spiritual presence of Christ did not capture the mind or spirit of the nineteenth century, partly because that world view lacked the support of scientists on both sides of the Atlantic Ocean. In the early twentieth century, there were several efforts to discuss evolution less in terms of natural selection and survival of the fittest and more in terms of novelty and ascent toward complexity. Henri Bergson's *Creative Evolution* (1911) rejected a mechanistic view of evolution in which variations are due to chance and suggested an *élan vital* which creatively urges living forms higher. Samuel Alexander's *Space, Time and Deity* (1920), C. Lloyd Morgan's *Emergent Evolution* (1923), and Jan Smuts's *Holism and Evolution* (1926) rejected Bergson's concept of a vital impulse being added to natural processes and argued for matter organizing itself into new forms of complexity from which emerge new properties unique to each level of organization. Alfred North Whitehead's *Process and Reality* (1929) struggled with the idea that something new "emerges" at each level of organization and argued instead that those properties were present already at the lower levels, but not in sufficient amounts to be obvious. For example, regarding human consciousness, the emergent evolutionists claim that consciousness is something unique to the organization of matter in humanity while Whitehead suggests that mental activity has been present always, but is a very small pattern in atoms and molecules. F.R. Tennant's *Philosophical Theology* (1930) presented a more empirical argument in which the teleological question was reshaped in terms of the order present in nature.

These six men represent a bridge between the nineteenth and twentieth centuries in the relationship between Darwinism and religious thought. In many ways, their efforts at philosophical reinterpretations of evolution and nature are quite similar to the efforts of those discussed in the first section of this chapter. The fundamental difference between these two groups is that evolution in general is widely accepted by the twentieth-century figures. The status of Darwinian evolution, however, is as questionable in their thought as it was in the biological science of their day. The active followers of Whitehead, Tennant, and "emergent evolution" have dealt with Darwinian evolution more directly, and so we shall focus on their perceptions of the relationship between religion and Darwinism. Before we do that, however, another figure must be discussed.

Teilhard's Vision

Pierre Teilhard de Chardin (1881–1955) has been an enigma to both friends and critics.[30] While this study has focused primarily on the Anglo-American scene, the French paleontologist's vision captured the imagination of many on both sides of the Atlantic, and his synthesis is often referred to as the pioneering effort to create a new relationship between religion and science. The impact of his ideas in both Europe and America has been due not simply to his synthesis of evolutionary science and religion but to the stamp of "scientific" which carries great weight in the minds of many. We are thus compelled to examine his work and to place it a broader perspective. While not meaning to diminish the importance of his vision, one can assert that Teilhard has remained more of a cult figure than a leader of a movement whose ideas are being developed and explored. Ian Barbour has suggested that Teilhard is best understood as offering a process philosophical theology similar in many ways to Whitehead's position, and process thought has become the primary framework in which Teilhard is mentioned but with little use or development of Teilhard's language system.

Teilhard was trained in France as a geologist and paleontologist and accepted ordination as a Jesuit priest. This background provides some clues as to the formative influences on his thought. The French intellectual climate and its struggle with the Roman Catholic Church tended to be isolated from the debates over Darwinism taking place in Britain and America.[31] Teilhard's effort to construct his world view through a synthesis of evolutionary cosmology and theology was shaped primarily by contemporary French philosophers and theologians rather than by Darwin's writings on evolution. The influence of Rousselot, Blondel, and Bergson is evident in many of his writings through the vision of a cosmic Christ at work as the "within" of matter.[32] Following his service as a stretcher bearer in World War I, Teilhard taught geology in Paris at the Catholic Institute, and explored the China deserts in 1923. Teilhard's conflict with his superiors arose over an evolutionary interpretation of original sin, and his license to teach was withdrawn. In 1926, he returned to China where he remained until the end of

World War II, when he went back to France, only to be denied once again a teaching position. Teilhard thus knew little of the "new synthesis" which reestablished the authority of Darwinian evolution. The last four years of his life were spent in New York, where he remained faithful to his vows and to the restrictions placed upon publishing his writings. This resulted in Teilhard becoming something of a cult figure when his *Phenomenon of Man* was published after his death, and some 14 other volumes have now been made available.

Teilhard was primarily a visionary, a seer, trying to help others see: "This work may be summed up as an attempt *to see* and *to make others see* what happens to man, and what conclusions are forced upon us, when he is placed fairly and squarely within the framework of phenomenon and appearance."[33] His efforts to create a new cosmology led Teilhard to explore the scientific discoveries of natural history and project them toward the present and the future. These explorations into the past led to the conclusion that this is a universe in the making, not simply a cosmos but a "cosmogenesis." Beginning with the fundamental elements of matter, Teilhard presents the "phenomenon of man" as a process of transformation of matter through life to the flowering of mind and society. The dynamic principle underlying this cosmology is the "law of complexification," a movement toward increasing complexity of structure which is accompanied by the development of greater internal unity and concentration. This trend toward increasingly centered complexity is empirically verifiable in atoms, molecules, organisms, and societies.

This trend is understandable in terms of the energy present in natural processes. Teilhard acknowledges the first two laws of thermodynamics (conservation of energy and increasing entropy), but moves to correct the physicist's picture of the cosmos by arguing that scientists have examined only the "without" of things, the external appearances of matter and energy. Taking humanity and the appearance of consciousness as the key to the world process, Teilhard suggests that there is another aspect of matter:

> It is impossible to deny that, deep within ourselves, an "interior" appears at the heart of beings, as it were seen through a rent. This is enough to ensure that, in one degree or another, this "interior" should obtrude itself as existing everywhere in nature from all time. Since the stuff of the universe has an inner aspect at one point of itself, there is necessarily a *double aspect to its structure*, that is to say in every region of time and space—in the same way, for instance, as it is granular: *co-extensive with their Without, there is a Within to things.*[34]

In order to overcome the traditional dualism between mind and matter, Teilhard asserts that "all energy is psychical in nature," and that there are two components to this energy. The "without" of matter is named "tangential energy" which "links the element with all others of the same order (that is to say, of the same complexity and the same centricity) as itself in the universe." The tangential energy gives shape to the outward form of the evolutionary process, and this is what science observes when it examines the organizations of matter in the process. The "radial energy" corresponds to the "within" of matter, and "draws it toward even greater complexity and centricity—in other words forward."[35] This second component of the total energy of the cosmos is responsible for both the movement to new and higher levels of complex organization and the increasing interiority and unity at these higher levels. Teilhard has invited science to widen its perception of natural processes by understanding them from the perspective of human consciousness. The nineteenth-century problem of how humanity could be the result of the evolutionary process has been resolved by asserting a second angle from which to view the process. As we shall see, this is essentially the position of process philosophy.

Teilhard's radial energy is responsible for the evolutionary advances described by the law of complexification. In the evolutionary process, there are "critical points" or "thresholds" which are crossed and at which new phenomena appear. The evolutionary "jumps" are accounted for by a theory of "involution" or "coiling up": "Regarded along its axis of complexity, the universe is, both on the whole and at each of its points, in a continual tension of organic doubling-back upon itself, and thus of interiorisation."[36] At various points, the quantitative changes accumulate to such an extent that a qualitative change occurs. The appearance of life and of humanity are significant examples. As carbon-based molecules organized themselves into cells, life burst forth into a profusion of forms which "grope" their way toward greater complexity and interiority. Teilhard acknowledges the "struggle for life" and "survival of the fittest by natural selection" as valid *but partial* explanations for the evolutionary process. They are not the final explanation for they overlook the "within" of life's process. Evolutionary development is a "groping," a process of "directed chance" in which large numbers of individuals try everything in their search for a specific target.

Teilhard thus follows in the tradition of the nineteenth-century reconcilers of religion and Darwinism by recognizing the role of natural selection but placing a greater emphasis on neo-Lamarckian aspects of evolution. Teilhard acknowledges in a footnote that he may be charged with being too Lamarckian in his emphasis on the "within," but he argues for a "symbiosis" between the two:

> It is only really through strokes of chance that life proceeds, but strokes of chance which are recognised and grasped—that is to say, psychically selected. Properly understood the "anti-chance" of the Neo-Lamarckian is not the mere negation of Darwinian chance. On the contrary it appears as its utilisation. There is a functional complementariness between the two factors; we could call it "symbiosis."[37]

As he moves to reflect on humanity as evolution becoming conscious of itself, Teilhard laments that many have not moved beyond the "old Darwinian hypothesis":

> For many, evolution is still only transformism, and transformism is only an old Darwinian hypothesis as local and as dated as Laplace's conception of the solar system or Wegener's Theory of Continental Drift. Blind indeed are those who do not see the sweep of a movement whose orbit infinitely transcends the natural sciences and has successively invaded and conquered the surrounding territory—chemistry, physics, sociology and even mathematics and the history of religions. . . . Is evolution a theory, a system or a hypothesis? It is much more: it is a general condition to which all theories, all hypotheses, all systems must bow and which they must satisfy henceforward if they are to be thinkable and true.[38]

In one of his last writings, Teilhard is so confident in the perspective provided by the "within" of things that he can call Darwinism a word with "only historic interest."[39]

While Darwinism as an issue is resolved by postulating radial energy which searches out all possibilities, the conflict between science and religion is also resolved by the "within" of things. It has long been recognized that Teilhard's vision of evolution is Christocentric, and there is no need to repeat those analyses. In the *Phenomenon of Man*, Teilhard's focus on Christ is minimized as he claims to be presenting a scientific treatise, yet he leaves little doubt as to his intentions.[40] After tracing the evolution of humanity and society, Teilhard argues that, since the process of complexification and interiorization has led to the personal as its highest form, the true extension of the process must be in the direction of "hyper-personalisation." The process of involution must converge upon some ultimate center of maximum consciousness, and Teilhard calls this the "Omega" since it will be found at the end of the evolutionary process. The further evolution of humanity cannot erase the distinctiveness of what the process has thus far produced, personality, so the ultimate goal will be the intensification of personality. Teilhard asks what name we can give to this radial energy which intensifies personality in a movement toward union, and his answer is love, the natural attraction of being to being. Love working through the Omega is thus both the power immanent in the evolutionary process and the transcendent goal toward which the process is moving.

In the Epilogue to the *Phenomenon*, Teilhard identifies this power and goal as "Christic," and this adjective reflects Teilhard's lifelong understanding of the movement of evolution through "Christ-the-Evolver":

> Regarded *materially* in their nature as 'universal centres', the Omega Point of Science and the revealed Christ coincide. But considered *formally*, in their mode of action, can they truly be identified with one another? On the one hand, the specific function of Omega is to cause the conscious particles of the universe to converge upon itself, in order to ultra-synthesize them. On the other hand, the Christic function (in its traditional form) consists

essentially in reinstating man, in restoring him, in rescuing him from an abyss. In the latter, we have a salvation through the winning of pardon; in the former, a fulfilment, through the success of an accomplished work. *In one case, a redemption; in the other, a genesis.* Are the two points of view transposable, for thought and for action? In other words, can one, *without distorting the Christian attitude,* pass from the notion of *"humanization by redemption"* to that of *"humanization by evolution"*?[41]

The similarities with Drummond's vision are quite striking. For both, the hope for the future is a synthesis through which the Christian faith is revitalized as Christ is seen sacramentally incarnated in, empowering and leading upward the world evolutionary processes until all attain a unity in Christ.

The Process Perspective: Cobb and Birch

Teilhard's vision captured the imagination of many religious thinkers, but his claim of being "scientific" and his language system failed to win him many disciples. The similarities between his vision and that of Whitehead have allowed many of Whitehead's followers to point to Teilhard as a pioneer, while basing their own vision on Whitehead's metaphysics. Two such people are Charles Birch, biologist at the University of Sidney, and John B. Cobb, Jr., professor of theology at the Claremont School of Theology. Birch and Cobb struggled in their early training to find a vision of nature that made sense to them, and they both discovered the basis of that vision at the University of Chicago in the late 1940s. While they have both set their views in conversation with Teilhard, they have both claimed that a more secure philosophical foundation is necessary to establish a vision of nature, science, and religion. That philosophical basis was discovered in Whitehead's process philosophy as mediated through Charles Hartshorne. Birch and Cobb have recently come together to coauthor *The Liberation of Life* (1981), which offers a comprehensive process vision of nature.

Like Teilhard, Cobb struggled with the loss of a coherent "vision of reality" early in his career. In an article first written in 1959, Cobb claims that "the distinctiveness of the Judeo-Christian vision of reality lies in its vision of the world as creation," but that vision has lost its power in the world of modern science.[42] The concept of the world and the self as created by and dependent on a creator was undermined, not by the rise of modern science itself, but by Hume's discovery that the religious assumptions of science were not justified by the data of experience:

Experience, for the first time in our era, undertook to interpret itself as self-explanatory, as requiring no cause, ground, or support outside itself. Immediately, the ideas of "cause" and of anything "outside experience" became radically problematical. The phenomenal flux is experienced *as* the world, the only world whose existence is known, and the application thereto of the category of creation is at best dubious, at worst, utterly meaningless.[43]

Cobb rightly notes that, in the Anglo-American scene, Hume was not taken seriously and Kant's idealism was not that influential. The shock was felt primarily through Darwinian science:

> The wider implication of Darwin's evolutionism was that blind forces immanent in nature account for the complex order we now observe. In the context of the Newtonian world view, this meant that God, if posited at all as the cause of the world, was only the initiator of a much simpler and less impressive world than ours. It also meant that man was a part of the mechanical world of matter in motion, with only the remotest relation to God. No wonder that Darwinism appeared as synonymous with atheism to many sensitive Christians![44]

Pragmatism, existentialism, and the theologies of Bultmann, Barth, and Tillich were varying responses to this modern vision, but they each failed to establish a valid method of exploring God's relationship with the world of modern and Darwinian science. While Cobb has higher regard for Boston Personalism and Wieman's naturalism, they too fail to provide the systematic foundation needed.

The modern world vision of Hume and Darwin raises the fundamental issue of how God is a cause in this world. The biblical language about God and Newtonian science led to discussing God's relation to the world in terms of efficient causation, with God as an agent both in creating and sustaining the world through the laws that govern it. The result of this was an understanding of God intervening in the world's processes to effect certain purposes. Hume denied that law is imposed, since we experience only a regular succession of phenomena rather than a direct connection between a cause and an effect. Since a cause is an antecedent member of an observable regular succession, the cause must be observable, and it must be a phenomenon that occurs occasionally. Since God is neither sensually observable nor an occasional phenomenon, there is no place for God in the modern scientific understanding of events. Cobb suggests that this Humean view of causation is correct, but it is incomplete. After discussing a non-Humean view of causation which understands persons as patients who are acted upon and who are influenced by past events, a third notion of causation is asserted which accepts Hume's rejection of necessary causal links and affirms the influence of past events in human experience. The image is of a person who carries out some action: the scientist can observe the action in Humean terms, but there is another, unseen aspect influencing what is seen. There is the real inner influence of past events upon the person who is seen acting outwardly. Cobb believes that this view of causation, which takes seriously the concept of influence, provides a way of conceiving God's relationship with the world:

> Similarly, if God acts or functions as an efficient cause, it is not through overt, sensible, observable actions. He acts by constituting himself in such a way that other events, such as human experiences take account of him. By constituting himself in a particular way God

affects the way in which he is taken account of by others. In some instances this leads indirectly to overt, sensible, observable actions.[45]

Behind the emphasis on the experience of influences lies Whitehead's metaphysics which describes a subjective side to all aspects of reality, including atoms and molecules. Where Teilhard asserted the "within of things," Whitehead argued for an experience of "feeling" at all levels of reality.[46] Every occasion "prehends" or "feels" the previous occasions, and reality is a process of interrelatedness in which the present is a process of unifying past experiences. Efficient causation occurs through "incarnation" as we enter into one another's experiences. In many ways, process thought is an aesthetic interpretation of reality, a focus on the quality of our experiences. Every occasion is an occasion for "enjoyment," with the greater enjoyment being found in the greater diversity of experiences that are "prehended" in an occasion and brought into a unity. This enjoyment can never be forced, but the choice is not made in a vacuum. There is a lure present in every occasion: "God is the divine Eros urging the world to new heights of enjoyment."[47] The primordial nature of God maintains and confronts the world with unrealized possibilities. Creative transformation is thus the essence of the world process as God calls us forward to actualize novel possibilities. God does not control the realization of those possibilities, but God experiences the world and provides both the unrest and the order as we are lured forward.

Evolution becomes an essential part of process thought at this point:

> When we have seen that the call forward in conscious experience is continuous with the total process of growth in human personality, we are prepared to recognize that this process in its turn is continuous with that of growth throughout nature, indeed with life itself as it has been embodied in the whole evolutionary process.[48]

Rather than provide an *apologia* for evolution within the framework of traditional theism, the process perspective recognizes evolution to be an essential aspect of the world process. Birch and Cobb argue that evolution must affect the way we understand ourselves:

> One response to the implications of evolutionary theory is a bifurcation of reality that tries to create a protected sphere for the human wholly separate from the rest of nature. It has profound effects on human self-understanding which we find incredibly damaging. We take evolutionary history seriously in the effort to understand humanity, its future, its relations to other living things and to the life that is inwardly experienced.[49]

While acknowledging the inspiration from Teilhard, they set themselves apart from his vision by criticizing Teilhard's insensitivity to the relationship between ecology and evolution, and his Omega as a single goal for the evolutionary process. The process view demands a greater appreciation for all that interacts and influences events, and for the openness of the future direction which events might take. These two points form the basis of a process response to Darwinian evolution.

Following in the tradition of Fiske and Teilhard, Birch and Cobb offer a perspective on the organization of the world from the origin of molecules to human society. A hierarchy of levels of organization which have their own ecology is recognized as the product of a process of aggregation, multiplication, and diversification. Each level (atoms, molecules, organisms) provides the necessary conditions for the emergence of the next level. Darwin is properly recognized as providing the inspiration for focusing on the relationship between the organism and the environment: "Ecology is the study of all those complex interrelations referred to by Darwin as the conditions of the 'struggle for existence'."[50] The struggle to survive is portrayed as a dynamic process of adaptation and "spreading the risk" through genetic and environmental heterogeneity. Drawing again upon the *Origin*, Birch and Cobb take up the metaphor of "the web of life" to describe the interdependence of all nature, especially as seen in the self-sustaining system of nutrition. Any sense of an order's being imposed from above is rejected in favor of order as a result of the dynamic struggle which Darwin described. The life of an organism represents the appearance, maintenance, and disappearance of order. The appearance of humanity has resulted in an organism which has the power to disrupt the normal cycles of order, and thus humanity has the power of sustaining life on earth.

With this concept of the interconnectedness of life established, the concept of evolution itself is addressed. The modern synthesis of Darwinian natural selection and genetic recombination is recognized as being not tautological because it focuses on the relationship of populations of organisms, chance mutations of DNA, and the environment. Natural selection is not a chance process, but "an ordering process which brings design out of randomness."[51] Purpose is seen to be at work in evolution as the intelligent adaptation of behavior to an environment which encourages the passing on of the genetic information of the successful organisms. Humanity is recognized as continuous with this web of life, but the appearance of culture introduces new elements into the process of adaptation.

At this point the process model breaks with Darwin and many of his followers. The vision of evolution which Darwin presented was deeply immersed in a mechanical model of life which is evident in Darwin's effort to demonstrate that evolution was completely determined by natural law. The vitalist solution of Bergson and the emergent model of Morgan are both dismissed as not really explaining anything. The mechanical, vitalist, and emergent models are based on "substance thinking" which defines the world in terms of independent, discrete individuals and attempts to account for the appearance of qualitative change in the world without the essence of the entities changing. The process model redefines the problem:

> What is to be explained, then, is why things happen as they do. And the explanation will consist in analysis of the causal relations among events and of the component occurrences which make up the larger ones.... Our argument is that it is now time to seek the explanation of behaviour at one level in terms of behaviour at other levels and to recognize that behaviour at any level is to be accounted for in terms of complex interacting. This complex interacting is an event, not a substance.[52]

Darwin's mechanistic model of evolution examined only the external relations of substances, but a true ecological model sees relations as internal to events from the atomic level to human societies. An event, whether sodium chloride or a human being, is what it is because it takes account of, and interacts with, its environment at a given moment.

This process of "feeling" the environment gives value to every event, regardless of its level of organization. The evolutionary process is a movement toward more complex events which are more capable of experiencing enjoyment because they are able to feel more aspects of the environment. The essence of the evolutionary process is not a ruthless struggle, but the urge to live and experience more: "Life is bound up with an urge to live. It is not a mere fact; it is a value. That is, being alive is valuable in itself."[53] As every event experiences its environment, there is a creative response to the given conditions which strives to meet the unrealized possibilities. At every level of organization, there is the discovery of novelty, new possibilities, and this experience of novelty forms the basis of an ecological ethic.[54] Every event has intrinsic value as it experiences novelty and enjoyment, but ethical decisions can be made on the basis of relative levels of richness of experience. At the subatomic, atomic, molecular, and aggregate levels, the subjective experience of events can be safely ignored and these can be treated in terms of their instrumental value. As we move to cells and plants, we discover complex societies and a new level of internal relations, but primarily instrumental worth. In animal life, however, a new level is reached as conscious feeling begins to appear, and that source of richness of feeling moves us toward greater intrinsic worth. The criterion of richness of experience also allows for distinguishing levels of intrinsic value at the human level, and it is the responsibility of the community to make the difficult decisions which maximize the quality of human life experiences.

This hierarchical, evolutionary view of life experiences the divine presence as both immanent and transcendent. Process thought rejects traditional theistic claims for God as "Cosmic Moralist," or "Unchanging and Passionless Absolute," or "Controlling Power," or "Sanctioner of the Status Quo," or as "Male."[55] There is no justification for those descriptions of God from what we know of the world process. Rather, God is present maintaining and confronting each event with the possibilities for greater enjoyment, and feels the result of which possibility is chosen in each event:

> Each stage of the evolutionary process represents an increase in the divinely given possibilities for value that are actualized. The present builds upon the past but advances beyond the past to the degree to which it responds to the divine impulses. . . . God's success as the goad toward novelty increases the present enjoyment in the world by stimulating the emergence of life.[56]

Wieman's distinction between created goods and the creative good which brings them into being is drawn upon to distinguish between living things and Life. Birch and Cobb argue that Life, rather than living things, is to be trusted:

> To trust life is to allow the challenging and threatening elements in our world to share in constituting our experience. It is to believe that they can enter into a creative interchange with what our past experience brings into the situation. It is to trust that the outcome of allowing the tension of the old and the new to be felt can be a creative synthesis which cannot be predetermined or planned.[57]

Life is "the cosmic principle" which "actualizes creative novelty" and "works for higher order in the midst of entropy." There is no distant goal toward which Life moves, for its "teleology is simply the creation of values moment by moment." Life works through the evolutionary process to bring order at successive levels of creation, and works for new organization of human life. Life overcomes old restrictions which have become repressive, and creates new possibilities for order and meaning.

The religious symbol for Life is God. To speak of hopes for an end other than extinction is to speak of evil and redemption, and that is to speak of God. Whitehead's language is used to expand the religious meaning of Life as God:

> In his primordial nature, God proffers values. In his consequent nature, he conserves values. . . . All that is of value, that has become real in the world, is saved in God's consequent nature. This is the way God "saves the creation."[58]

> True perfection consists not in excluding everything but in including everything. The Primordial Nature of God is the inclusion within God of the entire sphere of possibility, realised and unrealised in the universe. God so orders possibilities that they may be realised in the world, each in its due season. It is this ordering that establishes the effective relevance of novel possibilities and thus makes life possible in the world. But like all living things, God not only acts on others, but also takes account of others in the divine self-constitution. The Consequent Nature is God's perfect responsiveness to the joys and suffering of the world.[59]

This "panentheistic" view understands the relationship between God and the world as a dynamic interaction in which God lures events to greater possibilities.

For those who would attempt to reconcile religion with Darwinian evolution, the meaning of evil is a significant problem. Process thought offers its own answer, which is ultimately little different from those of the nineteenth century. Evil and suffering in the evolutionary process are the result of God luring the world toward richer experience, which also makes possible the experience of discord and pain. In this sense God is responsible for suffering, even as God is responsible for the enjoyment we experience. Cobb remains close to Whitehead in his explanation:

> The struggle for survival and the law of the jungle also need not appear as peculiar problems for theodicy.... The struggle for existence is a part of the means whereby greater values have been realized, and it itself reflects and expresses the fundamental drive for more abundant life which is part of the divine contribution to the evolutionary process.[60]

Biblical images are incorporated into Birch's discussion of the "travail of nature" in which he reduces the aspect of "struggle" in the adaptive process of evolution but recognizes the cost of harmful genes. The Christian, however, has a perspective from which to understand these two "costs of creation":

> Then, too, the Christian has a special perspective; for he knows that redemptive love was and is costly. It cost the sacrifice of the Son of Man on a cross. Christianity reveals the Cross as central to the meaning of human life. Evolutionary studies are revealing this same cross pattern woven deeply into the very fabric of creation.[61]

God's persuasive love accepts the cost, the pain, of existence in order that nature may grow in the experience of enjoyment toward an open future.

The evolutionary vision of life presented by process thought represents a parallel with the Spencerian "cosmic theology" of Fiske in that both have borrowed liberally from a comprehensive philosophical perspective in order to construct a world view which synthesizes religious and scientific thought. Fiske, Cobb, and Birch have accepted to some degree the Darwinian version of evolution but modify it according to their philosophical foundation. They also reject some elements of the traditional views of divine power in order to accommodate the workings of God to what is known of the evolutionary process. This revised understanding of divine power allows the "in concert" model to explain evil as the price we pay for also having the possibility of happiness and enjoyment.

A Wider Teleological Argument: Tennant and Bertocci

A twentieth-century parallel to McCosh's idealist argument for design and order in evolution has been provided by Peter Bertocci, student and interpreter of F.R. Tennant's "wider teleological argument." As we saw above, McCosh learned from Darwinism that Paley's design argument was no longer tenable, yet McCosh claimed that an order is evident in the natural laws which govern the evolutionary process, and such order points to an Orderer. McCosh's position was rooted in Scottish commonsense realism, yet an empirical approach can lead to a similar claim. F.R. Tennant (1866–1957) studied the sciences at Cambridge and taught science before being ordained in the Church of England and appointed university lecturer in philosophy of religion at Cambridge in 1907. Tennant's philosophical roots are in the British empirical tradition of McTaggart and Ward, but his greatest impact has been in North America, especially at Boston University, through the work of Bertocci and Edgar S. Brightman. No doubt his influence here is due in part to the Scottish realism tradition and the popular acceptance of some form of the wider teleological argument for God.

In *Philosophical Theology* (1930), Tennant argues that nature, when allowed to speak for itself, with no preconceived ideas of God, suggests design. No one line of argument is conclusive, yet epistemological, teleological, aesthetic, and moral arguments collectively produce a forceful argument for a Designer. This claim is based upon an epistemological argument in which Tennant accepts some of the epistemology of Locke and Kant. Knowledge comes through "rapport" between true subjects and objects. We receive data through the senses, and come to understanding through the mind's activities of recognition, memory, assimilation, and differentiation. Our perception is thus rooted in both the objective and subjective worlds. The mind does have an active role, as Kant suggested, but our perceptions are not independent of the objects themselves.[62] Tennant retains Kant's distinction between the noumenal and the phenomenal since there must be something which is aware of the act of knowing. This leads to an uncertainty with regard to our perceptions of the world since there is always the possibility that the mind does not mirror reality:

> Our knowledge of the external world is, from its very foundations, a matter of more or less precarious and alogical analogy rather than of self-evidence; of hope and venture that have been rewarded. Its certainty or necessity is practical not logical; its exact intellectual status is that of "probable" belief.[63]

Thinking is thus a teleological experiment in which we search for clues that are known when found. Both science and religion follow this method of interpreting our experiences; the difference between them is found in the concepts which are read into the experiences. All knowledge is thus subjective as it involves creatively reading into the data the concepts which are of interest to us. In the scientific realm, Darwin is held up as a great example of the creative use of imagination and teleological experimentation in order to discover a new association of ideas. Only when the goal is reached do logical connections take over the thinking process, and "truth" is the most reasonable hypothesis for understanding the data.

Although critical of Tennant's distinction between the phenomenal and noumenal in the knowing self, Bertocci accepts and develops Tennant's basic epistemological position. Bertocci begins with a religious, rather than philosophical, position which he then seeks to understand in the world of Darwinian evolution. The need to understand evolutionary thought in the philosophy of religion is apparent from Bertocci's definition of religion: "The essence or core of religion is the personal belief that one's most important values are sponsored by, or in harmony with, the enduring structure of the universe, whether they are sponsored by society or not."[64] "Creative uncertainty" is the religious stance toward the world as faith and reason work together to establish a reasonable course of action to guide us into an uncertain future. Reason is not the antagonist to faith since faith needs to be guided, and faith is essential to reason in order to make a commitment to some path in life. Since there is always more than we can possibly know, uncertainty is inherent in the human condition. "Growing, empirical coherence" is the criterion of truth upon which we can risk our lives and make our commitments.[65] Bertocci thus follows in one tradition of nineteenth-century philosophy of science which claimed that "consilience" was a criterion for truth.

Both science and religion search for coherence in meaning and are concerned with issues of order, chaos, and causality. The problem arises when science makes the philosophical claim that its concern for mechanical predictability and regularity provides the whole answer. Religion responds by calling upon other philosophical positions which claim that we have the best explanation when we understand the goals and purposes toward which events are moving. Rather than separate science's concern for accuracy and religion's concern for purpose, Bertocci asserts that they both must be held accountable for the whole of human experience. In an act of faith, science and religion are accepted as providing partial interpretations of the human experience. We reach a greater understanding of the human experience when we synthesize both of these perspectives and the interpretations they provide.

In order to discern the data which both science and religion interpret, Bertocci presents a detailed study of the theory of evolution. The presentation is consistent with the concept of truth as empirical coherence, as Bertocci recognizes the power of evolution to be its ability to correlate vast amounts of data; it also leaves fewer facts to be explained than does the theory of special creation. Along with the process thinkers, Bertocci follows the interpretation of "survival of the fittest" as a creative process of peaceful adaptation and integration into an ecological niche, and rejects the perspective that sees "nothing but goodness" in genetic mutations. The data of evolution can be interpreted in a variety of ways, but Bertocci argues for an "empirical coherence" which recognizes a variety of data, and enables "one to speculate *without leaving known facts out (and without distorting them)* about the interconnection of man and the universe and the nature of the universe as a whole."[66] This method allows us to take into consideration the distinctive aspect of the human being: imaginative construction of future possibilities which can be acted upon in the present.

From the perspective of "empirical coherence," which recognizes the validity and necessity of teleological explanations, Bertocci develops Tennant's "wider teleological argument" from human experience to God. The classical arguments for the existence of God are recognized as having some value, but the empirical approach searches for an explanation which harmonizes the facts of the world and human experience. The force of the argument is "cumulative" in that it rests not on the individual and specific adaptations from which Butler and Paley argued for a Designer, but rather "on the interconnectedness of physical nature, life, and human experience." Tennant notes that particular adaptations may be explained scientifically, and are inadequate support for a teleological interpretation of the world. There is, however, "a general order of Nature" which is maintained by natural causes.[67] Bertocci describes this "general order of Nature" as "the ultimate conditions which make harmonies possible. It stresses not the mere fact of survival of the fit, but it points to the *arrival* of the fit (or fit-able) in the first place."[68]

Tennant discusses five traditional arguments for the existence of God in terms of how they point to a "a general order of Nature," though he rejects the claim that they are each sufficient for proving the existence of a Designer God.[69] The epistemological argument for the adaptation of thought to things does not in itself prove a teleological order, but it does become one piece of evidence when we recognize that the world is intelligible rather than chaotic. The teleological argument of Paley was undermined by Darwinian evolution, but it provided a broader basis for teleology in the direction and plan of the process of evolution. Third, the fact that the inorganic world contained whatever was necessary for the appearance of organic life points to an intelligent principle at work. Fourth, the aesthetic argument that beauty is a human value which is present but not inherent in a mechanical explanation of nature forms another link in the argument for a Designer of nature who enjoys beauty. Finally, Tennant offers a lengthy discussion of the moral argument which suggests that, because nature has produced beings with moral sensitivities from nonmoral nature, the natural processes are contributing to some larger purpose. Tennant concludes:

Theism no longer plants its God in the gaps between the explanatory achievements of natural science, which are apt to get scientifically closed up. Causal explanation and teleological explanation are not mutually exclusive alternatives; and neither can perform the function of the other. It is rather when these several fields of fact are no longer considered one by one, but as parts of a whole or terms of a continuous series, and when for their dovetailing and interconnectedness a sufficient ground is sought, such as mechanical and proximate causation no longer seems to supply, that divine design is forcibly suggested.[70]

Bertocci expands Tennant's argument to include seven "links" in the wider teleological argument, and, consistent with the structure of his argument, begins with evolution. Link one, "The Purposive Interrelation of Matter and Life," argues against the reduction of life to its material substances. Life does indicate processes at work which cannot be described purely in terms of physical and chemical processes. While there is a qualitative difference between living and nonliving things, the force of Bertocci's argument lies in the harmony between those two orders. Mechanical explanations fail to explain the coordination needed to produce complex organs such as the eye, but "emergent" and "creative" evolution do not explain the fact that life does appear from nonlife. The coordination and interrelationship between the physical and living orders which is necessary for the appearance and maintenance of life leads Bertocci to conclude that "a Mind" is responsible for the appearance of life and its variations. There is no other way to understand the physical and biological evolution of the world except through an orderly mind using ordered means to accomplish its ends. This creative Intelligence is not completely successful, however, since natural processes of decay and selection do continue.

The second link in Bertocci's argument, parallel to Tennant's first, is forged through reflection on the relationship between human thought and the world. There is a process of human adjustment to the world which cannot be explained in terms of chance or mechanical causality. If we reflect on the fact that our minds are attuned to and supported by the world, we are forced to recognize the work of a purposeful Intelligence who provides the conditions for human thinking. As we reflect further, we discover that moral effort as well as thought is supported by the order present in nature. If nature placed strict limits on human freedom, there would be little room for moral growth. At the same time, if there were no order upon which we could depend, then we could not learn from our experiences. We discover that there is a balance between freedom and order which provides some hope for our quest for increase in values which, in the fourth link in the argument, are supported by nature. We must, however, recognize the limits nature sets for the things we can do, and these limits act as guides for the formation of our values.

The fifth link in this argument is a lengthy and significant turning point for now we can inquire into the nature and goal of this Mind at work in nature. The first four links pointed to a Mind who has designed a world good for human life since the world supports our efforts to achieve values. The creation of values is the essence of the world process, and humanity is encouraged to be cocreators:

> The deepest values in human experience are never those which, as it were, another implants in us. They are those we have a share in developing. Whatever other interests the cosmic Mind may have in the creation of value, at the human level the values he has in mind *must* include the *co*-creating of values by human beings. Again, that human beings should be co-creating values in his universe is *the* value attending all other values.[71]

This process of cocreating values is the growing center for humanity since the values are transmitted through social institutions as we struggle and face new opportunities and thus form our character. Character formation is the value of values, and is dependent upon having value possibilities maintained over time. The cosmic Mind not only creates value possibilities but also maintains them by establishing principles for what ought to be done to realize these values. Bertocci concludes that the creative Mind pointed to by the first four links seeks our happiness by preparing a realm in which men and women may enable each other to realize the best possible lives through the power of God's creative love.

The uniquely human experience of moral order thus complements the evolutionary argument for a wider teleological order in nature. Bertocci concludes his argument with brief discussions of the aesthetic and religious experiences of humanity. The religious experience acts as confirmation of, rather than being sufficient for, the whole argument for a Personal Source of Value in the world. The previous links provide a context for understanding the religious experience, rather than forcing the "revelation" to stand isolated from the rest of human experience. Religious experience affirms something "More" (William James) than the natural world, and that experience confirms where the six previous links have led us.

The reality of evil does not undermine the validity of this argument for a cosmic, personal Designer who wills good for humanity. Bertocci argues that much of the evil in the world is the result of our misuse of the freedom God has given us. Other evil can be understood as a stimulant for humanity's growth in character. The natural order required for the support of such growth also produces some evil. There is, however, an amount of evil left in the world that cannot be explained as human error or as a stimulant for growth. Bertocci is thus led empirically in a direction similar to process thought: God is not omnipotent. The whole movement of the evolutionary process has been toward a world that sustains human values, and so we cannot doubt God's goodness. The slow and sometimes unsuccessful process of evolution is to be understood as God's struggle against something within God's own self, a Given, that resists the immediate realization of all that God wills.[72]

From this empirical argument, we discover that we live in an adventurous universe, a cosmic experiment, with contingency at the core of reality. God, as a friendly cosmic Mind, is constantly struggling to maintain the stability that does exist, and also to improve the possibilities for creating values. The theological concept of creation refers precisely to this sense of dependency of all the world upon God. While some claim that we do not know how God creates, Bertocci argues that the facts of cosmic evolution and human experience are adequate expressions of the meaning of creation. At the level of physical nature, God's activity of maintaining and creating values is evident in the laws of physics and chemistry. The grand order of nature provided the possibilities for the appearance of living species, and God enjoyed the realization of those values. While God's efforts at maintaining aspects of this creation are not always successful, the process of evolution points to a cosmic Mind which introduces new value into the universe wherever there is an opening for the kind of value living things represent. The cosmic Lover suffers with humanity and provides the order in which the painful but joyful creative process of evolution searches for goodness.

Emergent Levels of Reality: A.R. Peacocke

A number of the epistemological and methodological issues raised by the empirical approach have been developed in the work of Michael Polanyi. As was noted in chapter 1, Polanyi pioneered the sociological study of science and its personal dimensions. These concerns were systematized in a general study of epistemology, *Personal Knowledge* (1958), in which Polanyi developed the distinction between science and religion as being one of motives and interests. Polanyi also attempted to resurrect Morgan's concept of "emergent evolution" in terms of structural hierarchies, each of which has its own unique properties.[73] Polanyi's concern for scientific methodology and for the significance of structural hierarchies has been incorporated into the work of Arthur Peacocke, Dean of Clare College, Cambridge, who has blended his training in molecular biochemistry with religious studies. Since the sociological and linguistic study of science and religion represents a growing edge in the field (especially Barbour's work), we shall briefly examine Peacocke's line of argument.

In his 1978 Bampton Lectures, Peacocke recognizes that religion and Darwinian science had reached a "truce" through the use of the "two books" concept in which science and religion had little to do with each other. Due to changes in both scientific and religious thought, that "truce" is no longer tenable. Religious thinkers have come to see that, however one conceives of God, God is experienced through our lives as biological organisms. The sociology of science has recognized that scientists are committed to "believing" in such things as atoms, while religious persons also believe that they make meaningful assertions about a reality which we encounter.[74] Drawing on Polanyi, Peacocke argues that both enterprises abstract from human experience, and thus they should complement each other as we move toward a fuller understanding of human life. Science and religion are both personal activities in that they involve imagination and intuition within the context of a community of people. Both science and religion search for and provide models of intelligibility, but differ in their "interests." Peacocke argues that science and religion are both asking "why are things the way they are?" and thus they are "interacting approaches to the same reality."[75] Religious thought can no longer remain unaffected by scientific knowledge since science provides the most reliable answers to our what, how, and why questions of the world. Since they are both exploring the nature of reality, the insights from science and religion should "be in harmony or at least mutually enriching."[76]

With the methodological perspective established, Peacocke moves to locate humanity within the immensity of the universe as now understood by science. Humanity can be seen as a rather amazing product of the evolutionary process. Given the emergence of consciousness in humanity, there is a need to reclaim a teleological direction to the evolutionary process since this is the kind of universe that produces personal consciousness which transcends the universe. The emergence of consciousness is thus both a problem in explaining the universe and a clue to the answer. In a discussion of "Chance and the Life-Game," Peacocke rejects Jacques Monod's attempt to raise chance to a metaphysical principle since chance in biological processes is precisely what would be expected if all the possibilities in the universe were to be explored. The work of Prigogine and Eigen has demonstrated from thermodynamic principles that ordered molecular structures are highly probable, and thus Peacocke argues that the "interplay" of chance and law is creative as it allows new forms to emerge and evolve.

How is this interplay of chance and law to affect our understanding of divine creativity? The fascinating image of God as a "composer" is suggested. God can be understood metaphorically as a composer of a Bach-like fugue which reaches "its consummation when all the threads have been drawn into the return to the home key of the last few bars—the key of the initial melody whose potential elaboration was conceived from the moment it was first expounded."[77] Peacocke supports this image of divine creativity by drawing upon the Eastern religious image of Shiva as Lord of the Dance of creation, the "play" of the creator from Hinduism, and Wisdom as a woman playing at God's side in Proverbs.

The hierarchies which have resulted from this play are examined, and emergence is argued as an essential concept. Rejecting methodological, ontological, and epistemological reductionism, Peacocke claims that nature itself demands that we talk of boundaries and interfaces at which new configurations result in emergent qualities not present in "lower" levels. The view of Teilhard and process philosophy that elementary matter is already "mental" is thus rejected because it accepts, to some extent, a reductionist position which is not necessary.[78] Borrowing an illustration from Polanyi, Peacocke argues that we cannot derive the mechanical principles for the working of a steam engine from its parts, nor can we derive the specific sequence of a DNA chain from the laws of chemistry. The cosmic process is truly "creative" in that we cannot deduce or predict the laws governing matter in higher levels of organization before that level of integration is reached.[79] The metaphor of God as agent in the creative process is suggested within a panentheistic biological model where God is like a woman who creates new forms and meanings within herself.

The complementary relationship between science and religious thought moves to a more complex level when Peacocke addresses the emergence of humanity from the evolutionary process. With the appearance of humanity, there is a "unique transition" as "evolution becomes history." The claims of sociobiology are recognized as valid if they are seen as describing certain restraints or natural limits within which humanity must live. We have always had to come to terms with our basic biological needs, our own finitude and death, the reality of suffering and the unrealized possibilities in human life. Peacocke concludes that neo-Darwinism and sociobiology present no new challenge to religious thought for there has always been the threat of reductionism and the naturalistic fallacy. Religious thinkers are, however, challenged to recognize the complexity of human nature and its biological and genetic foundation. This recognition has religious consequences. It

> is this kind of genetically based creature that God has actually created as a human being
> through the evolutionary process. God has made human beings thus with their genetically
> constrained behavior—but, through the freedom God has allowed to evolve in such
> creatures, he has also opened up new possibilities of self-fulfillment, creativity, and
> openness to the future that require a language other than that of genetics to elaborate and
> express.[80]

Peacocke does not claim to be doing "natural theology" in the British tradition of Paley and others by deriving religious convictions from nature, but he argues that the metaphors and beliefs of religion must be set alongside the changing perspectives of nature and humanity. Science has presented an image of the world in which there are hierarchies of levels of organization, and Christian religious thought must take cognizance of these, without being captive to them. At each level of organization, metaphors for the divine presence must be discovered. The God who "explores" and "composes" at the lower levels of the open-ended process of emergence appears as suffering love at the level of personal consciousness in the Christ who mediates the meaning of creation.

A Concluding, Feminist Critique

In this lengthy chapter we have examined a type of response to Darwinian evolution which accepts certain aspects of Darwinism but claims that Darwinism must be "corrected" in order to provide an accurate world view. The basic belief in this model is that the religious understanding of the world must be in harmony with the scientific world view, even if that requires modifications of the scientific perspective and a revision of traditional understandings of God. The continuity of these variations on the "in concert" model is important to recognize if we are to claim any sense of historical perspective on the relationship between science and religious thought. With Fiske, Birch, and Cobb we have examined an approach to reconciling Darwinian science and religion which is rooted in a philosophical tradition amenable to an evolutionary world. With McCosh, Tennant, and Bertocci we have seen an effort to establish an idealist concept of natural order which requires a Designer for complete explanation. Drummond and Teilhard present similar visions of Christ leading cosmic evolution onward and upward. Peacocke is more aware than the other twentieth-century figures of the historical perspective, and he has called upon the tradition to justify the need for a new approach to synthesize science and religion, free from the metaphysical constraints of Teilhard and process philosophy and based on the role of metaphors in science and religion.

Even as these men have called upon us to move beyond the nineteenth-century mechanistic roots of Darwin's theory, many women are now calling us to examine the masculine bias in the epistemology, methodology, and ontology of modern science, and of Darwinism in particular. Ruth Hubbard, Evelyn Fox Keller, Sandra Harding, and Donna Haraway, among others, have raised questions as to the values that may be discovered in the foundations and implications of Darwinian evolution. While Birch and Cobb attempted to co-opt some of these issues, they were unable to integrate the essential insights into their own work.[81] The questions concern not simply the attitudes toward women and the place women are assigned in an evolutionary history, but also the masculine goal of scientific objectivity and a view of nature which reflects and supports repressive social structures which are defined in terms of competition and hierarchy. The feminist perspective has moved into the discussion of the relationship between science and religion very slowly.

That dialogue has been carried on by two women, Rosemary Ruether and Elizabeth Gray, who have written of the impact of hierarchical thinking on our understanding of and relationship to the web of life. Ruether has argued that scientific reason took on the patriarchal, dualistic characteristics of the God of traditional Christianity which knows and dominates nature from the outside. The basic paradigms of science and religion need reworking such that God is not an "alienated male ego outside the visible world, but as Divine Matrix (Logos-Sophia) of existing beings," and reason serves to bind humanity and nature together. Gray has recognized that Darwin's work initially established an ecological perspective which firmly rooted humanity in nature, but Darwin's insight was lost as men interpreted it to show that men are the most highly evolved species, and the goal for the whole evolutionary process.[82] We thus end up with the evolutionary process as a hierarchy ("holy order") which can be understood only from the perspective of men who are on top. The Spencerian language of "survival of the fittest" then comes to shape our whole perception of reality. While the men in this chapter have attempted to revise the Spencerian language, they are still caught within a hierarchical structure which legitimates "up" and "down" thinking.

The feminist perspective calls us to take seriously the ecological model of interdependence of all forms of life.[83] Gray claims that the male perspective has not been sufficiently empirical to become the basis for a new vision of nature:

> Not only are we interconnected in ways we have not understood; life is also coordinated and symbiotic. We have been blinded to this by our patterns of male competitiveness and by our notions of "survival of the fittest."
> Diversity and interdependence are motifs in creation which weave together like a Bach fugue. You cannot understand the one without the other. Yes, there is conflict. Yes, there is competition. But we need to readjust our mental models or paradigms so we are able also to perceive coordination in all these systems as more fundamental than conflict. We must put aside our mental filters which let us see nothing but conflict and competition. We must see the world as it is—powerfully diverse and full of conflict as well as powerfully interdependent.[84]

The "in concert" model strives to be empirical in the way science and religious thought are related, but there is the question of how we understand "the world as it is." Some claim that such concerns are insignificant, and we shall now examine that model.

6

Religion *above* Darwinism

The fourth model for the religious responses to Darwinism completes the description of the fundamental options for discussing the relationship between scientific and religious thought. In many ways, this is the most traditional model since its roots are in Galileo and Bacon's concept of the "two books" of God. The advocates of "religion *above* Darwinism" argue that religion is to be understood as a sphere of inquiry separate from science. The representatives of this model usually understand the issues of scientific methodology and Darwinian evolution, but claim that scientific discoveries have little impact on true religious faith when those discoveries are stripped of metaphysical claims. Evolution is accepted in a more-or-less Darwinian form as an accurate description of natural processes, but the religious claim is that there is more to understanding life than science and its methodology. The representatives of this model often have been advocates of Darwinian science in the name of religion, and have opposed the other three models of religious responses in the name of both religion and science since the other models tie religious thought much too closely to the conclusions of the scientific method. The "religion *above* Darwinism" model welcomes Darwin's liberation of science from religious presuppositions since religion must be based upon faith, not scientific world views.

The nineteenth-century representatives of this model continue to be sources of debate as to their true position. The primary figures are the Presbyterian botanist who taught at Harvard, Asa Gray; his student, Chauncey Wright; and the Congregationalist minister G. Frederick Wright. Gray's acceptance of Darwinian science in relation to the questions of design and teleology is still debated, but he was one of the few American scientists who argued for the methodological neutrality of science. Chauncey Wright will be discussed briefly because he articulated the philosophical neutrality of science, and may well have learned this from Gray. G. Frederick Wright became a friend of Gray late in Gray's life, and articulated Gray's position with more theological skill. Separate from the "Gray school" and with a deeper understanding of the religious and philosophical issues, Borden Parker

Bowne of Boston University argued for a Darwinian understanding of the relationship between science and religious thought from the perspective of personal idealism. Bowne and the "Gray school" made some of the earliest attempts at bringing an end to the warfare of science and religion over Darwinism while maintaining the intellectual integrity of both.

In the early twentieth century, the methodological separation of science from religion was forcefully argued by Karl Barth and Emil Brunner. Their European "neo-orthodox" position will be discussed briefly as a background to the thought of the American Reinhold Niebuhr, whose analysis of the human condition challenged those who attempted to build a metaphysic out of Darwinism. The contemporary Roman Catholic position also falls into this model, although it represents a struggle to overcome any radical separation of science from religion. The major twentieth-century figure on the American scene is Langdon Gilkey, whose roots are in the neo-orthodox tradition, and who has argued for this model in the contemporary scientific creationism debates. In a more detailed study, advocates of existentialist positions and of linguistic analysis could also be discussed, but they argue essentially the same position as these others.

Early Attempts at Ending the Warfare

Asa Gray

Asa Gray (1810-88) has long been recognized as one of the first American proponents of Darwinian evolution, even though he and Darwin differed over the understanding of design. Gray's primary credentials were in the area of botany where he established his authority in 1847 with a manual on botany. Early in his career, Gray was exposed to the materialist philosophy of William Lawrence, the transcendentalism of New England, and German idealism. Following his graduation from medical school in 1831, Gray lived in New York where he reclaimed his religious faith by joining the "New School" Bleeker Street Presbyterian Church in 1835. Gray's rationalism and empiricism led him to reject the idealist concept of the "great chain of being" which provided an ideal pattern for the plant world. At the same time, Gray argued that the Bible was not intended as a book for science.[1]

When Gray accepted a teaching position at Harvard in 1842, those influencing his thought in the period leading up to the publication of the *Origin* included the British empiricist Jeremy Bentham, the Swiss vitalist A.P. DeCandolle, and, of course, Paley. Paley's design argument was accepted by Gray, and it was the basis for Gray's rejection of Chamber's *Vestiges*. Gray argued that like produces like, and this demonstrates not only a Creator but also a Governor, even if his work is done through natural laws. Gray's rejection of German idealism led to continual conflict with Louis Agassiz when Agassiz came to Harvard in 1848, for Gray argued that the connection between species was genetic, not idealist. Gray had been prepared for the publication of the *Origin* through correspondence with Darwin, and Gray became the leader of Darwinian evolutionary thought in America.[2]

The interpreters of Gray's response to Darwinian evolution have divided themselves into two camps: those who focus on Gray's project of reclaiming divine design in the variations among offspring and those who focus on Gray's methodology, which makes a distinction between science and religious thought.[3] The first group has a valid point, but they fail to take seriously Gray's effort to separate the conviction of divine design from empirical science. Gray wrote to Darwin in the midst of their debate over design that "design must after all rest mostly on faith."[4] Darwin and Gray agreed that the products of nature look designed, that such design is related to an organism's ability to survive, and that the results do come through natural laws. Gray claimed out of his religious faith, not scientific method, that purpose must be read into nature. Contrary to Hodge, Darwinism is not essentially atheistic, because science in and of itself does not make philosophical or religious claims one way or the other. Gray's position is obviously based on a different understanding of the epistemology and methodology of science, and he established this position in a series of mainly anonymous articles and reviews which were published as *Darwiniana* in 1876, and in his 1880 Yale lectures, *Natural Science and Religion*.

Gray's argument moves through three phases. First, he establishes the methodological distinction between science and religion in which science studies the "how" of nature, the secondary causes, and religion focuses on the "why" question, the primary causality and design. Second, he argues for the validity of Darwinism as a science parallel to Newtonian physics in its ability to provide "true causes" and consilience of inductions. Third, Gray reconciles his understanding of evolution with divine providence.

In his March 1860 review of the *Origin*, Gray contrasts the assumptions and method of Agassiz and Darwin. Agassiz is criticized for referring both the origin and the distribution of species directly to divine will, since that effectively removes both from the realm of science. Darwin avoids Agassiz's excessive theism:

> Studying the facts and phenomena in reference to proximate causes, and endeavoring to trace back the series of cause and effect as far as possible, Darwin's aim and processes are strictly scientific, and his endeavor, whether successful or futile, must be regarded as a legitimate attempt to extend the domain of natural or physical science.[5]

Where Agassiz's idealism forces him to offer something other than a scientific answer to the question of "how," Darwin's focus on the physical connections between species allows him to consider the "how" without denying or affirming an ultimate "why." Science may well eventually tell us how changes in form take place, but the question of "why" stands exactly as it did before the theory of derivation through natural selection:

> Since natural science deals only with secondary or natural causes, the scientific terms of a theory of derivation of species—no less than of a theory of dynamics—must needs be the same to the theist as to the atheist. The difference appears only when the inquiry is carried up to the question of primary cause—a question which belongs to philosophy.[6]

Darwinism raises no new problems since religious thinkers had already conceded to geologists and physicists precisely what they have to concede to Darwinian evolution: that there is a nature with fixed laws. Scientific and religious questions should be explored independently, each according to its own method, rather than intermixing the different kinds of arguments. The question of design and the role of divine providence belong to the philosophers and theologians, and science can neither establish nor overthrow them.[7]

Once he has distinguished between scientific and religious questions, Gray argues against both scientists and theologians in favor of Darwinism as excellent science in the tradition of Newtonian physics. Hodge and other creationists thought that they had the advantage because their inductive approach provided "proof" where Darwinism gave only probabilities. Gray rejects this claim because creationism is also a hypothesis which, like evolution, is assumed in order to account for what is observed and can be tested only indirectly. The strength of Newton's theory of gravitation was its ability to explain the facts that are known, and to answer most tests put to it.[8] Darwinian evolution is excellent science because it provides "real causes" to explain adaptations and unity of types. Natural selection harmonizes these facts quite well without speculating as to the actual origin of organs and variations. The true test of all scientific theories is this ability to harmonize what is known. The creationist hypothesis is not immune to this test, even though it wants to "mix up revelation with scientific discussion": "Agreeing that plants and animals were produced by Omnipotent fiat does not exclude the idea of natural order and what we call secondary causes."[9] A successful scientific hypothesis must give real and known causes, and describe their actual operation in nature. Darwin's natural selection succeeds where all others give quite empty and unclear explanations.

Gray reconciles his religious convictions with Darwinism by assuming that Darwin does not deny an intelligent first cause for the system he has described. Darwinian evolution is not inherently atheistic since its explanation rests on proximate causes, which can be quite compatible with theistic views. Gray is not surprised that the *Origin* is attacked as atheistic, but he is concerned that it is denounced by scientists who assume that a genetic relationship between organisms is incompatible with an intellectual relationship established through God. Darwinism is no more theistic or atheistic than Newtonian physics:

> It would be more correct to say that the theory in itself is perfectly compatible with an atheistic view of the universe. That is true; but it is equally true of physical theories generally. Indeed, it is more true of the theory of gravitation, and of the nebular hypothesis, than of the hypothesis in question. The latter merely takes up *a particular, proximate cause,* or set of such causes, from which it is argued, the present diversity of species has or may have *contingently* resulted; that the actual results in mode and measure, and none other, must have taken place. [10]

Even though Newtonian science does assume a universal and ultimate physical cause which works necessarily, Gray notes that few claim any longer that it leads to atheism or pantheism. The concept of "mediate creation" in which God's design works through what we call secondary causes has long been accepted by religious thinkers. [11] Darwinism is a similar theory, and similarly does not necessarily lead to atheism.

Gray's acceptance of Darwinism was eased by the conviction that the *Origin* is a scientific work in which Darwin does not reveal his philosophy and religion. Gray's struggle to maintain belief in design and divine providence in a Darwinian world took a variety of forms. Initially, Gray was convinced that Darwin could give Paley's teleology "a further *a fortiori* extension" in which the watch sometimes makes better watches, and thus Darwin would assume an idealist design of natural laws "ordaining when and how each particular of the stupendous plan should be realized." [12] In contrast to those who claimed that design could be proven, Gray argued that design cannot be demonstrated in nature, but rather that we have to infer design from the results which seem to be adapted. We import our religious faith into the interpretation of nature. Nature echoes our faith at various points, but faith is never founded upon nature itself. On this philosophical and theological level, Gray offers his famous advice and metaphor to Darwin:

> Wherefore, so long as gradatory, orderly, and adapted forms in Nature argue design, and at least while the physical cause of variation is utterly unknown and mysterious, we should advise Mr. Darwin to assume, in the philosophy of his hypothesis, that variation has been led along certain beneficial lines. Streams flowing over a sloping plain by gravitation (here the counterpart of natural selection) may have worn their actual channels as they flowed; yet their particular courses may have been assigned; and where we see them forming definite and useful lines for irrigation, after a manner unaccountable on the laws of gravitation and dynamics, we should believe that the distribution was designed. [13]

That Darwin aided in the British publication of the articles in which this argument appears no doubt gave Gray a sense of assurance that Darwin accepted this imagery. Gray soon learned that Darwin could not accept the notion that each particular was designed, and the two parted company on this matter as Gray could not accept as proven the philosophical position that design is not the ultimate explanation for the specific path of natural selection. The choice for Gray was either pure chance or design. Gray reveals at this point his lack of understanding of Darwin's use of "chance," since Darwin meant simply that the law explaining a "chance" event was unknown, not that there was no scientific law involved.

Gray was not able to appreciate this type of argument, and divine providence was introduced to explain Darwin's "chance" variations. The concept of natural selection was quite acceptable as it explained the effects of natural forces on the variations that do appear in nature. Gray continually argued, both scientifically and religiously, that the source of those variations has never been explained. Natural selection is an external force which works on the variations, but does not produce them. After Darwin had refuted Gray's metaphor for design, Gray offered a different metaphor to explain the relationship between natural selection and design of variations:

> Natural selection is not the wind which propels the vessel, but the rudder which, by friction, now on this side and now on that, shapes the course. The rudder acts while the vessel is in motion, effects nothing when at rest. Variation answers to the wind: "Thou hearest the sound thereof, but canst not tell when it cometh and whither it goeth."[14]

Variations are not the result of the work of the environment, but rather arise from within. Gray would be proven correct on this point scientifically, but his faith in design rested on the assumption that only God could direct such changes. The theist can never relinquish divine providence, and Gray's religious demand for an immanent as well as transcendent providence led him into a "God of the gaps" position which was vulnerable to the discovery of how variations do arise.

Gray maintained that he was a Darwinian scientist and an orthodox religious man. He did follow Darwin in separating the work of science from religious presuppositions, and recognizing the work of natural laws to shape the world as we see it now. Gray's concern over design at times reflected a "common sense" philosophy, but ultimately design is a matter of faith. Gray established this position and criticized both the creationists who failed to understand the scientific revolution, and the philosophers who attempted to erect a religious or social system on Darwin's theory of natural selection.

Chauncey Wright

Gray's argument for the "metaphysical neutrality" of science was developed by one of his students, Chauncey Wright (1830–75). Wright is recognized today as one of the leaders of American pragmatic philosophy, and his place in this study relates to his view of the relationship between religion and science, which he may have learned from Asa Gray. As a student at Harvard from 1848 to 1852, Wright studied under Gray, and, while living in Cambridge following graduation, Wright heard the scientific debates over Darwinism and participated in the philosophical debates of the Metaphysical Club.[15] Wright echoed Kant's distinction between scientific and ethical questions, but his pragmatic pluralism did not recognize Kant's transcendent realm of absolute ideas. Wright's pluralistic world view distinguished between the various activities of the human mind, and demanded that those activities be methodologically separate. In one of his last conversations, Wright made a clear distinction between scientific, metaphysical, and moral thought. Nature can indeed refer to the harmony of things, but we must keep separate the laws of nature and the moral order:

> The laws of this harmony are of a wholly different order, *different in meaning*, out of the other's sphere, neither contradictory to nor in conformity with those of the scientific cosmos: though involving them as the laws of living structures involve those of matter generally, or as the laws of mechanical structure involve those of its materials and surrounding conditions. Mechanical structures, living structures, artistic and moral structures, are all fittings to ends; and these though not absolute accidents (since nothing in the cosmos is absolutely accidental), yet relatively to any discoverable principles of the cosmos, are accidents.[16]

The moral, aesthetic, and scientific interests of humanity are distinct realms of discourse, and science is not to be burdened with ethical or religious presuppositions.

Wright defended Darwinism as a science from the attacks of the creationists such as Mivart, from those such as F.E. Abbot who would attempt to create a religion of Darwinism, and from those who shaped a metaphysical world view based on evolutionary theories, such as Spencer and Fiske. In February 1860 Wright confessed to a close friend that he had read the *Origin* while teaching in Agassiz's school for women, and found it a better account of nature than Agassiz's theory: "I believe that this development is a true account of nature, and no more atheistical than that approved theory of creation, which covers ignorance with a word pretending knowledge and feigning reverence."[17]

Wright felt himself following in the line of the British empiricists, and this tradition culminated in Darwin's work. The method of the empirical scientist is careful and patient observation, and Wright distinguished this from the "elaboration of vague definitions" in the writings of Spencer and Fiske. Wright corresponded with Abbot, at Abbot's invitation, and criticized Abbot's attempt to build religion on science, since such efforts are pure speculation. More importantly, religion is a practical and aesthetic concern which has little to do with pure science:

> True science deals with nothing but questions of facts,—and in terms, if possible, which shall not determine beforehand how we ought to feel about the facts; for this is one of the most certain and fatal means of corrupting evidence. If the facts are determined, and, as far as may be, free from moral biases, then practical science comes in to determine what, in view of the facts, our feelings and rules of conduct ought to be; but practical science has no inherent postulates any more than speculative science.[18]

In a critical review of St. George Mivart's *The Genesis of Species* (1871), Wright demonstrated a better understanding than Gray of Darwin's use of "accident" in reference to variations. Mivart established his criticism of Darwin on the distinction between essential and accidental forms of life, but Wright clarified what Darwin had left confused. Darwin

> has not said often enough, it would appear, that in referring any effect to "accident," he only means that its causes are like particular phases of the weather, or like innumerable phenomena in the concrete course of nature generally, which are quite beyond the power of finite minds to anticipate or to account for in detail, though none the less really determinate or due to regular causes.[19]

Wright's pluralistic world view in which science and religion are separate realms of human endeavor led him to criticize all attempts to either fetter science with religious presuppositions or to create a religious faith on the facts of science. In this effort he carried forth the epistemological and methodological Darwinian revolution as he learned it from Gray.

G. Frederick Wright

Another Wright, G. Frederick, of no relation to Chauncey, carried Gray's argument into the realm of religious discourse. G. Frederick Wright (1838–1921) has not received as much critical recognition as the other two men, but his adaptation of Gray's thought suggests one way of discussing religious thought under this model.[20] Wright maintained a dual career of Congregationalist minister and glacial geologist. Educated at Oberlin College into the revivalism of Charles Grandison Finney and "New School" Calvinism, Wright became the pastor of the Congregational church in Bakersfield, Vermont, in 1862, and relaxed from his ministerial duties by studying Kant and Hamilton, and exploring the effects of glaciers on New England topography. In 1872, Wright moved to Andover, Massachusetts, and then back to Oberlin in 1881, to take up a teaching position in New Testament. Throughout this period, Wright contributed articles and books on theological issues and glacier studies, and a series of articles on the relationship between science and religious thought. Wright's relationship with Gray began in 1874 when Wright sought out the reviewer of Hodge's *What is Darwinism?*, and their friendship led to Wright encouraging Gray to publish *Darwiniana*.

Wright's articles on science and religion were initially written for *Bibliotheca Sacra*, and were collected in book form as *The Logic of Christian Evidences* (1880) and *Studies in Science and Religion* (1882).

Following Gray and Chauncey Wright, Wright's primary concern was to establish a methodology by which both religious thought and science can be pursued. Wright rejects Bushnell's distinction between nature and the supernatural and argues that nature refers to both the causally connected sequences which appear in time and to the forces which produce the phenomena. "Supernatural" refers to phenomena such as providence, grace, and miracles which originate outside the chain of natural forces. Where science studies the natural sequences and their forces, the doctrines of Christian faith refer to the supernatural facts. Both science and religion use the inductive method of inference and analogy, but religion affirms that there are phenomena which must be taken into consideration even though science's law of parsimony sets them apart from their sphere of study: "Supernaturalism affirms naturalism to be inadequate, in view of all the facts, and establishes itself upon such residual phenomena as remain after natural causes have been made to do their utmost in solving the problem."[21] Wright does not base this position on a Kantian distinction between noumena and phenomena or a strict concept of secondary causality. He does talk of "secondary causes," but in terms of Mill's "permanent possibility of phenomena" as being all there is between God and humanity.[22]

Science and religion both use the inductive method of inference and analogy, and so they work under similar restrictions. The process of moving from facts to conclusions which apply outside the range of those facts leads to "a belief" which is at best probable, never absolutely certain. The process of observation and explanation produces hypotheses that coordinate isolated phenomena into a system that reveals a larger meaning. Science and religion use this method, but the methods of verification are to be determined by the subject matter. For science, the network of hypotheses is at various stages of verification, and so science assumes a faith in its theories in order to test them and see which hypotheses solve the greatest problems. The principle of verification in religion is based on the assumption, from Jonathan Edwards, "that the Creator works in accordance with the highest wisdom for the *highest good of being*." There are no complete proofs of this religious assumption either, since we have a limited perception of the total world. Our faith, thus, cannot be proven from external evidences and we have to depend on a prior belief based in revelation. We assume that God has designed the world for the good of being and shape our religious life accordingly. Although Wright claims that science and religion work with similar methodologies, there is a natural limit provided by the subject matter of both spheres of inquiry, which provide two volumes of divine wisdom.[23]

With this structure of epistemology and methodology, Wright argues that Darwin and his theory of evolution are excellent examples of the scientific method. Natural selection and the struggle for existence provide the best explanation for the adaptations and structures we see in nature, and are based upon "a real analogy or true cause."[24] Wright criticizes the creationists for committing scientific suicide when they assert "so God has made it." Such a claim is

> suicidal to all scientific thought, and would endanger the rational foundation upon which our proof of revelation rests. We are to press known secondary causes as far as they will go in explanation of facts. We are not to resort to an unknown cause for explanation of phenomena until the power of known causes has been exhausted. If we cease to observe this rule there is an end to all science and of all sound sense.[25]

Darwin followed in the footsteps of Newton in using the law of parsimony, in arguing for the power of secondary causes as far as they go, and in not speculating on "the ultimate facts of observation." The true scientist "does well to remain an agnostic," and to "divest [himself] of theological presuppositions of any kind in reference to the material machinery by which the diversity of animal and vegetable life has been produced."[26] To those who object that Darwinism is a "mere theory," Wright responds that all science and religion work with analogies. Wright similarly rejects other objections to Darwinism on the basis that those scientists and theologians do not understand scientific methodology.

Wright argues on two levels, methodology and design, that Darwinism and orthodox religion are compatible. In one of his more famous articles, "Some Analogies between Calvinism and Darwinism," Wright suggests some methodological similarities between the two.[27] The theologian works with revelation as the scientist works with data, and both look for patterns of order and meaning. As the Calvinist faith denies optimistic progress to humanity, so too does Darwinism deny a theory of universal progression. Any advantages gained, whether physically or morally, are local adjustments to the conditions of existence. Where Darwinism affirms the organic connection of humanity, Calvinism's doctrine of original sin has "illustrative analogies" to Darwinian heredity. There is also an analogy between the religious concepts of foreordination and free will and the Darwinian paradox of "chance" and evident design. Next, Darwinism and Calvinism limit speculative reason since they work with probable hypotheses and moral evidence in which absolute knowledge and proof are not available. Lastly, they accept the reign of law appropriate to their disciplines. Wright continually refers to these as "analogies" because he accepts the use of analogies as appropriate to the inductive method, and, in another article, rejects all efforts to draw closer parallels between science and religion. He criticizes those who would reconcile their faith and science by drawing parallels between the Bible and science since the Bible, following the Westminster Confession, is only for what is necessary for salvation. The creation stories assert divine agency in opposition to polytheism, but the mode of that creation is left for scientific research. The biblical stories and language should be allowed to do their work in the moral sphere, not in the scientific sphere which has its own language. With regard to evolution and the Bible, Wright suggests that "evolution has just about as much to do with the question of the general validity of Christian evidences as the nebular hypothesis has with the question of whether Mary Queen of Scots was guilty of murder."[28]

Darwinian evolution is also compatible with an orthodox religious understanding of divine design in nature. Wright again insists that design cannot be proven from the adaptations we see in nature since design is a question of first and final causes, and those causes are not within the sphere of science. The theist claims that there is a design in nature, and the real question is whether we can interpret that design given the phenomena in nature as describe by Darwin. Wright rejects the attempts of some who see an optimistic, "pietistic" design, because it is based on a very narrow range of facts.

The heart of Wright's argument is that the reality of secondary causes does not undermine design since what is used to accomplish a goal has nothing to do with the reality of a design. Darwinism simply forces theists to reevaluate when design enters the process, and to modify to some degree the interpretation of that design. We assume that the system is designed for "the good of being," but that is known only in the mind of God since only God can see to what good all the uses are put. In this context, Wright offers his "analogy of a saw mill" as a rejoinder to Darwin's "stone house" argument against divine design.[29] A saw mill exists for the production of timber, but the existence of a specific mill depends upon a variety of factors (labor costs, nearness to market, ease of getting raw materials, use of refuse). The profits from the mill may come from the sale of timber, or the sale of sawdust as fuel, of scraps for play houses or for kindling. Each of these could be used as explanations for the existence of the mill, and, from their respective angles of perception, each could be quite correct. Wright suggests this as an analogy for our perspective on nature as a whole. We may argue that incidental advantages are the sole reason for the universe, but we are limited in our perception of the whole. Darwinism has not discarded final causes, but asks one particular question of the universe. The question of final causes is left for religion to ponder.

In later writings, Wright makes more explicit this dualistic view of the universe. Matter and mind are "separate orders of being," and, since design is inferred through analogy with the the human mind, design is a distinct question. Matter has independent existence, but is under partial control of the divine mind which is expressed through the laws of nature.

Wright provides a good summary of the "Gray school" perspective in his Lowell Lectures:

> This view of the relation of God to the universe both leaves room for science and revelation and sets limits to their scope. It is the duty of science to take into consideration all the facts, and to suffer the inferences to be guided by the survey. It is the duty of those who believe in revelation to recognise the divine ideas incorporated in the laws of the material universe.[30]

Darwin is to be thanked for freeing the scientific world from bondage to mere bookkeeping empiricism, and for revealing the true nature of scientific methodology. Otherwise, he has raised no new problems for religious faith.

Borden Parker Bowne

The methodological dualism of Gray and G.F. Wright was based in the Calvinist religious tradition in which the dualism was overcome partially in the faith of the believer, completely only in the mind of God. A different philosophical and religious tradition which works with the "religion above Darwinism" model is represented by Borden Parker Bowne (1847–1910). Bowne grew up in a Methodist home in New Jersey, graduated from New York University, and was ordained in 1872 to the Methodist church in Whitestone, Long Island. Bowne's thought was shaped through a year of study in Europe with Ulrici and Lotze where he discovered personalism and sharpened his skills in attacking scholars who ventured outside their fields to do philosophy. In 1876 Bowne accepted a position in the philosophy department at Boston University where he remained for 30 years and established "personal idealism" in American thought.[31]

Bowne's career was bracketed with books on the philosophy of Kant and Herbert Spencer, and this fact gives a clue as to Bowne's primary interests: what are our assumptions about reality, and how is knowledge possible? The skills in criticism Bowne acquired in Germany shaped his response to Spencer. If Spencer and evolution were to be valued for their reasoning, then they are to be attacked on the basis of reason. Spencer's *First Principles* was used by Bowne as "a 'cadaver' on which his students might acquire dissection practice." Bowne was highly critical of the wide acceptance of Spencer in American thought, and claimed that because Spencer "had painted a big picture with a big brush many persons have considered him a great painter."[32] Spencer's epistemology was based on a scheme of recognition, and Bowne asserted that this scheme ruled out all knowledge since we must first have knowledge of something to which we can relate new knowledge. Spencer was equally imprecise with regard to evolution, and fell into what Bowne called the "logical fallacy." Spencer saw the past as simple and the present as complex, so he called the simpler age homogeneous. Bowne wondered how Spencer could draw that conclusion.

Bowne's understanding of the relationship between science and religion reflects his debt to Kant and Lotze. In the preface to *Metaphysics* (1882), Bowne claims to save idealism *and* to make a place for inductive science. This would be done through

> the distinction between phenomenal and ontological reality. The latter belongs to metaphysics and must finally be viewed as active intelligence. The former is the field of experience and is perfectly real in that field; that is, it is common to all and is no individual illusion. And everything we can do in the way of discovering uniformities of coexistence and sequence in that field is so much clear gain. The discovery of these uniformities is the great work of inductive science; and this study it can pursue without being molested or made afraid of metaphysics. Of course, when the scientist sets up these uniformities as self-sufficient and self-executing laws, he then becomes a metaphysician; and criticism is in its full rights when it reminds him that such doctrine is not science but bad metaphysics.[33]

This long quotation reveals several aspects of Bowne's position that shape his response to Darwinism. Bowne is an idealist, and reality can be known only through the conceptions we form. This does not deny the trustworthiness of our sense experiences, but thought and sense experience are different kinds of reality. Thought, the noumenal reality, is real since it has "causality and substantiality." Sense experiences, the phenomenal realm, "are real in the sense that they are no illusions of the individual, but are abiding elements in our common sense experience."[34] Bowne is critical of the naive beliefs of common sense realists, such as Hodge, who discover the nature of things in sense experience. Sense experiences reveal only their effect upon us, never what something is. Common sense realists overlook the variety of sense qualities and complex nature of objects as science reveals them to us. If realists were more critical, they would recognize that epistemological certainty is found "not [in] the ontological existence of material and mechanical things, but rather [in] the coexistence of persons, the community of intelligence, and the system of common experience."[35]

Bowne's "personalism" is the key to overcoming the subject-object dualism of Kantian idealism. Personal idealism is the framework in which common sense, science, and philosophy are held together:

> They are not mutually contradictory or indifferent realms, but rather mutually supplementary aspects of the mind's effort in the attempt to understand itself and its experience. All conflicts between them, then, are entirely the outcome of misunderstanding and ignorance.[36]

Our experiences can be understood only when they are integrated into one inclusive system of meaning which is formed around volitional and intelligent purpose and causality. The duality of subject and object, noumenal and phenomenal reality, is overcome through one "basal power," "one world ground" upon which all is dependent. As our mind organizes the "flitting and discontinuous impressions" into rational principles, we discover that the objects harmonize with our laws. Since this harmonization does happen, Bowne claims that an objective rational order must exist which parallels our subjective thinking. The mental activity of a person overcomes the Kantian duality by discovering one reality that encompasses both subject and object in a thought world.

The key to this thought world is causality, which can be understood in three ways: (1) as the determination of the consequent by its antecedent; (2) as the mutual determination of different things; (3) as the self-determination of a free agent. Inductive science focuses on the first meaning of causality. Science has its "cause" when it can refer to antecedents which form a group of events that "explain" the consequent. The "cause" in this sense is the order in which events occur. Bowne claims that this scientific explanation gives us practical knowledge, but it does not provide a complete understanding of "the cause."[37] A true understanding of causality is reached when we understand the "dynamic determination" of antecedents and consequents. Scientific causality explains an event as being pushed out of the past, but dynamic causality looks toward the future as intelligence choosing things to be. The human mind is not satisfied with only the scientific explanation since the mind must eventually refer events to a personal purpose and volition for a complete explanation. Our experience tells us that laws do exist, since events are not totally random, and that there is mutual interaction under laws as things make adjustments to each other. While science can explain the laws by which interactions occur, the personal mind requires "a unitary being which posits and maintains them in their mutual relations."[38] Everything has its being and true cause through this one reality.

From this understanding of the varieties of causality and their resolution in personalism, Bowne is able to distinguish clearly between the activities of science and religion. Two distinct questions may be asked about any event. We may ask the scientific question of how it came about in an order of law, or we may ask the philosophical and religious question of what it means in a scheme of purpose. The two questions are distinct and should not be confused. In contrast to the creationists, Bowne asserts that order in nature can and should be studied without reference to teleology. Teleology is never causal in itself, and it would not arise as a part of the scientific process. The theist's claim that order and adaptations point to a design somewhere assumes nothing as to how the effects are produced. The scientist is free to discover the answer in natural laws, and poses no threat to the theist's intellectual perception, which is not tied to sense experiences. In many ways, science has done theists great service by freeing us from ignorance and superstition. The error which is often made is to elevate science into a philosophical system, and thus to fall back into a naive common sense realism. Science is to limit itself to descriptions and allow philosophy to explore the world-ground which operates through the laws of nature. Theists, on the other hand, are guilty of bad logic when they "make the order of law a reason for denying purpose. The way in which events occur in an order of law is one thing; the meaning of such events in a scheme of purpose is forever another."[39] Neither the scientist nor the theologian is to fall into a crude, simplistic common sense realism.

Bowne is consistent with his personalism and his critical stance toward inappropriate philosophy when he deals specifically with evolution and Darwinism. Evolution must be examined because it seemed to be a denial of purpose and required a new conception of the way purpose is realized. Bowne's position does not require a close reading and analysis of Darwin since Bowne is not arguing for or against Darwin on scientific grounds. The focus of Bowne's analysis is the philosophical precision and appropriateness of Darwinism and other theories of evolution. "Evolution" may be either a biological theory or a cosmic formula:

> It may be a description of the genesis and history of the facts to which it is applied, and it may be such a description, plus a theory of their causes. In other words, it may be a description of the order of phenomenal origin and development, and it may be a theory of the metaphysical causes that underlie that development. The former is evolution in a scientific sense; the latter is metaphysical doctrine.[40]

As a scientific theory, evolution describes the phenomenal order and the relationships among things, but is silent about causation in the philosophical sense. The theory is open to scientific proof and debate, and anyone can agree with it.

Given this understanding of evolution as science, Bowne correctly perceives that the "conflict over evolution" is actually "a battle of philosophies" in their metaphysical interpretation of the theory. There are two common fallacies in this battle of philosophies. Materialist metaphysics construes nature as "a self-contained and self-sufficient system; and natural laws have been viewed as self-executing necessities."[41] The fallacy here is that there is no logical connection between natural causation and a uniform, progressive law of evolution. Natural causation can be a "purely kaleidoscopic effect," but "if the system does not thus proceed, it is not because it is natural, but because it is confined by its laws and the relation of its parts to orderly and progressive movement."[42] Those laws and the relations of the parts can be understood only by reference to the world-ground beyond the phenomenal appearances. Bowne is obviously attacking Spencer's philosophical evolution here.

The second fallacy in this battle of philosophies is the fallacy of the universal. Here we see the nominalist aspect of Bowne's idealism for he, like Darwin, rejected talk of higher and lower species and denied that a "species" exists as anything apart from the individuals. At the scientific level, the question of the transformation of species is whether the present forms can be traced genetically to earlier forms, and whether they converge at some common origin. At the philosophical level, the issue is what the individual things are themselves and what power produces them. The scientific issue has had such great interest outside science because of the assumption that a "genetic connection would mean identity of nature in successive members of the series."[43] That is the great fallacy of bad evolutionary metaphysics. Evolution may tell us of the progression from the simple to the complex, but it cannot identify humanity with monkeys. They are each individuals to be understood in relation to metaphysical causes or a teleological scheme or purpose. The scientific and metaphysical, teleological issues must not be confused.

Natural selection and the creationist argument are both subject to Bowne's criticism of the fallacy of the universal. Bowne charged that natural selection can be tautological since, when stripped of its anthropomorphisms, it is reduced to survival of the fittest, which is tautological in its short form. The tautological character of natural selection and the survival of the fittest is overcome when they are referred to specific environments, which Darwin meant, but Bowne criticizes those who attempt to universalize Darwin's metaphors into metaphysical principles.[44] The conflict of "special creation" with Darwin's theory also would been have diminished through a better understanding of the debate between nominalism and realism. The creationists attempt to build their science on unrelated and lawless acts of divine intervention, but they should simply see each individual as special because each is the result of purposeful activity of the world-ground. This personalism protects Bowne from the absolute, impersonal idealism of Agassiz, who had to deny evolution since it contradicted the creation of ideal and fixed species.[45]

Bowne resolves the conflict of religion with Darwinism by separating knowledge of causality into spheres having their own integrity. Science deals with phenomenal reality and it should not make metaphysical or teleological claims since its methodology will not answer those questions. The questions of metaphysics and teleology are valid since they are required to satisfy the mind, but they must not demand that science deal with them. Darwinism does give practical information on the way nature works, but this knowledge is limited and must not be universalized. From a faith position and in response to the needs of the mind, Bowne claims that we can talk of natural laws because the divine will is consistent in its methods. The divine transcends the natural order in the sense that the many depend on it, and is immanent in the sense that the many exist in and through its power. Science studies the surface appearances of the many, and religion studies the one ground of all existence. Each sphere of inquiry has its own integrity, and the warfare between science and religion is brought to an end.

Pluralistic Epistemology Established

The "religion above science" model established by Gray and Bowne quickly became the working model for most scientists in the twentieth century since it fit quite well with Darwin's own method and allowed them to pursue their research programs with little worry for religious implications of their work. This position came to be so taken for granted that few efforts to argue for it are made until proponents of the other three models force the issue. In the area of religious thought, however, the arguments of the nineteenth-century proponents of this model have tended to be forgotten and few references to Gray, the Wrights, and Bowne are found in twentieth-century religious thought.

Rise of Neo-Orthodoxy in Europe: Barth and Brunner

The epistemological and methodological distinction between science and religious thought was raised anew in this century in Europe and in North America by the "dialectical" theologians, now usually referred to as "neo-orthodox" as an indication of their efforts to reclaim some traditional Reformation arguments. Karl Barth (1886–1968) is recognized as the leader of the European neo-orthodox movement and its call for a renewed focus on the revelation of God in Christ. Barth's Christocentric thought excluded many of the issues of the relationship between religion and science since God is to be known only as revealed in Christ, and not through natural theology. This is evident in his discussion of the doctrine of creation in which little discussion is found of Darwin and evolution and the creation stories are a "saga" which tell of God's absolute sovereignty over creation. Nothing in the human study of creation can reveal God's intentions, so religion need not concern itself with scientific issues.[46] Barth's radical distinction is reflected in many contemporary religious thinkers who have little interest in contemporary scientific thought.

A more creative engagement with scientific issues is found in Barth's contemporary Emil Brunner (1889–1966). Brunner also rejected much of the liberalism of nineteenth-century thought, but, unlike Barth, he was also concerned with addressing religious questions to those outside the faith. Where Barth began with the objective revelation of God in Christ, Brunner began with a doctrine of humanity. Brunner criticized Barth for an objectified faith in which knowledge of God is an objective revelation. Truth lies not in an objective revelation nor, as in the nineteenth century, in the content of human, subjective faith, but in the encounter between revelation and faith. Brunner draws upon Martin Buber's *I and Thou* (1922) to maintain the dialectical approach to our knowledge of God. Brunner's concept of "truth as encounter" is a more personal understanding of the divine-human relationship, and it led him to break with Barth on epistemological grounds. Barth's emphasis on Christ as the only way God is known eliminated any other relationship humanity might have with God. Brunner argued that God does encounter humanity in nature, and that such encounters are necessary in order for humanity to know Christ as the primary encounter between God and humanity. In traditional theological terms, Brunner argued for a general revelation in which there is "a point of contact" between God and humanity that prepares us for the special revelation in Christ.

This difference between the two broke into the open with the publication in 1934 of Brunner's *Nature and Grace*, which was made available in English with Barth's reply of *Nein!*.[47] Where Barth argued that human reason had been so distorted by sin that the sole source of knowledge of God was the biblical witness to Christ, Brunner argued that human reason does function quite well in scientific and cultural pursuits and that we must acknowledge the biblical witness to the praise of God in creation. Though human reason has been distorted and the knowledge of God in creation cannot bring salvation, we can discern something of God in nature:

> The world is the creation of God. In every creation the spirit of the creator is in some way recognisable.... Wherever God does anything, he leaves the imprint of his nature upon what he does. Therefore the creation of the world is at the same time a revelation, a self-communication of God.[48]

Humanity turns this knowledge into an idol, but that distortion does not eradicate the partial knowledge of God that can be gained through an understanding of the "orders" in nature and society that God has created. The laws of nature do reveal the power of God to preserve the creation, but natural laws cannot reveal the redeeming power of God which we find only in Christ. Brunner thus argued that he was following in the tradition of Calvin by using analogies from nature to understand the supporting presence of God, which is available to all humanity. The knowledge of Christ, however, is necessary for a true and complete understanding of nature's relationship to God. If there is no way to talk of God's relationship with nature, Brunner wondered how we could ever talk of God's revelation in Christ when the first biblical witness is to creation.

Brunner's more systematic efforts to outline an epistemology and doctrine of creation argued for a "dualistic" approach to knowledge in which scientific and religious knowledge are distinguished. Scientific study is valuable, but it is unable to give complete knowledge of God. Our human reason can give us reliable knowledge of the world, but God is not of the world, so human reason fails at that point: "The sum total of all that in principle is accessible to man is called the "world"... The unconditioned mystery does not belong to the world; it is Supramundane. To say that it is Supramundane and that it can only be known through revelation, really mean the same thing."[49]

The Christian doctrine of creation is an affirmation of God's transcendence, lordship, and mystery, and thus is an article of faith based on revelation. Scientific inquiry must be seen as distinct from the knowledge of God since "it makes practically no difference whether a [scientist] is a Christian or not."[50] Brunner claims that the "dualism of scientific knowledge and religious knowledge" must be maintained to properly understand the relationship of science and religion. God has created humanity with the power of reason to accurately understand the natural world, but this knowledge is always growing and transforming itself, and so is never a complete and final truth. Brunner's dualism affirms the place of science and allows us to appreciate the valuable, but limited, role of analogy. Science can never reveal the God of creation, but we can discover some analogies:

> In the material world there is a mathematical order which bears witness to the thought of the Creator. Here there is life which is a reflection of Him who is Himself the true Life; in the material world there is the mystery of the whole of organic life, with its wonders of nature— seeing eyes, hearing ears, a purposeful organization which indicates a creative planning spirit behind it all; there is the marvel of spontaneity and freedom, which is a picture of Him who is Himself unconditioned, absolute freedom.[51]

Brunner is sensitive to the fears of the "analogy of being" which makes a too direct connection between knowledge of the created world and the Creator, but he argues that analogy is the basis of communication and understanding. On the basis of analogical knowledge, the laws of nature are seen as God's orders of creation which indicate that the Creator is a God of order. To know this part of God's creation is to know something of God's will. The traditional distinction between God as the primary cause and the secondary causes of nature, however, is not accepted. Brunner argues that the distinction is not helpful because it attributes a causal relationship between Creator and creation where there is none, and it is dangerous because it establishes an independent creation, separate from divine preservation. The value of analogy is that God is continually present supporting and upholding creation through the natural orders.

This continual presence of God shapes Brunner's response to Darwinism.

Brunner is critical of those such as Barth who rely upon the first two chapters of Genesis for their understanding of creation since that narrative could imply the absence of God from the creation once it was set in motion, and can lead to unnecessary conflicts with science: "The Christian statement on creation is not a theory of the way in which the world came into being—whether once for all, or in continuous evolution—but it is an 'existential' statement." There is thus "no difficulty in bringing creation and evolution into agreement with one another," especially when we accept a form of "creative evolution." Brunner is quite specific on the use of "agreement" here, rather than "identity":

> Yet this agreement must not be confused with identity. Evolution, even creative evolution, is a phenomenon which we are able to observe, something which is in the foreground of empirical fact, something which the botanist and the zoologist can establish over and over again. . . . But he can never thus prove Creation. Creation remains God's secret, a mystery, and an article of faith, towards which the fact of creative evolution points, but which is never contained within it.[52]

The basis for this possibility of agreement is found in an appendix where Brunner notes that the Bible gives a world view which cannot be reconciled with that of modern science, but that world view has nothing to do with revelation. Again drawing upon an analogy, Brunner suggests the relationship between evolution and creation is like that of the relationship between a chemical analysis of a painting and the aesthetic judgment of it as a work of art. The two perspectives are not mutually exclusive, but "on different planes." The person of faith assumes that God created the world in such a way that it appears as a causal sequence to the scientist, but the person of faith sees more:

> The Creation is the invisible background of Evolution; Evolution is the visible foreground of Creation. Faith alone grasps that invisible aspect; science grasps this visible aspect. Evolution is the mechanism of creation; creation is the spiritual source and Final Cause of Evolution.[53]

Like many in the previous model, Brunner denies that evolution is to be identified with Darwinism since the evolutionary process includes aspects which can not be explained according to Darwin's mechanism, especially the appearance of life, and such mysteries point beyond the process itself. This is particularly true with regard to humanity: the causal explanations of Darwinian evolution are inadequate to explain the spiritual uniqueness of humanity. Brunner claims that he is making a choice here as to which scientists he follows, but he makes little use of creative evolution except as an analogy to the mystery behind the appearance of humanity from the apes. The essence of his argument is the dualistic epistemology, and the more complete understanding which faith provides.

Reinhold Niebuhr

Brunner's method of recognizing the place of nature in partially indicating the character of God and of saying both a yes and a no to the results of modern science won him a receptive audience in North America in the 1930s. One prominent American theologian who reflected Brunner's dialectical method was Reinhold Niebuhr (1892–1971). Born in Missouri to an Evangelical minister and his wife and graduated from Eden Theological Seminary and Yale Divinity School in 1915, Niebuhr was ordained in the Bethel Evangelical Church in Detroit where he remained for 13 years before being called to Union Theological Seminary in New York as professor of Christian ethics. Niebuhr had little interest in the epistemological and methodological issues which were central at Yale and chose not to work on the doctorate. His writings reflect his primary interest in the social and ethical issues which were raised by his experience in the industrialized Detroit of Henry Ford. *Moral Man and Immoral Society* (1932) was a critique of liberalism's optimism regarding human nature and the hopes that love would transform social institutions. Niebuhr's political and social realism shaped his analysis of the human condition and theological interpretation of history. Since science and evolutionary thought reflect and shape humanity's efforts to understand our place in the world, they too came under Niebuhr's scrutiny.

Niebuhr's thought is profoundly dialectical, and he resists efforts to move beyond the dialectic. The 1939 Gifford lectures, *The Nature and Destiny of Man*, provide a systematic background for Niebuhr's method which he revised and extended in later works. Humanity is to be understood dialectically, and the first dialectic is that of nature and spirit. We live on the borderline of the natural and spiritual worlds, and this places us in an ambiguous situation. As a creature of nature, we are subject to the laws and limitations of the natural world, and we must learn to accept them as God-given. On the other hand, we can transcend these limitations through our self-consciousness. As spirit, we can know and order the structures of the universe that physically constrain us, and see them as instruments for our creativity. This ability to transcend ourselves through self-consciousness launches us on a search for meaning beyond ourselves since the search for meaning transcends the rational problem of understanding the relationships among things. Our efforts to secure meaning in life become evil as they lead to idolatry of "some vitality of existence, or even some subordinate principle of coherence" being taken as the principle of meaning. Humanity is constantly tempted to overcome the dialectic of freedom and necessity by denying "the limited character of our knowledge, and the finiteness of our perspective."[54]

In one of his few "philosophical" essays, Niebuhr expands on the epistemological implications of this understanding of human nature. The basic characteristic of reality is its coherence, and reality is known through conceptual frameworks which organize things and events. Though there is one cosmos, there are many ways of organizing our knowledge of it:

> In the one world there are many worlds, realms of meaning and coherence; and these are not easily brought into a single system. The worlds of mind and matter have been a perennial problem in ontology, as have subject and object in epistemology. There must be a final congruity between these realms, but most of the rational theories of their congruity tend to obscure some truth about each realm in the impulse to establish total coherence.[55]

The dialectical relationship of the various realms of knowledge must be maintained in order to neither destroy the uniqueness of things and events, nor remove contradictions, nor subjugate them to the demands of a rational system, nor eliminate freedom which cannot be conceived in natural and rational schemes of thought. Science and religious thought are thus to be held in a dialectical relationship as two realms of coherence.

Niebuhr argues that science in the twentieth century has tended to expand into the realms of metaphysics and history. The extension of human confidence in science into the other realms is an effort to secure ourselves against the fundamental ambiguity of human existence. The strength of science is its empirical method and its "humility before the fact," but these have given it an "aura" that makes science synonymous with truth. In the search for a coherent structure of meaning, the scientific description of temporal processes is often taken as the metaphysical principle for explaining all things, as in Bergson's creative evolution. Darwinian evolution comes to be seen as invalidating the myths of religion and thus removing any need for the religious perspective. Religious thinkers should not insist on the scientific accuracy of our religious myths. We should avoid any possible conflict with science by seeking to reclaim the "permanent" myths in our religious stories which deal "with aspects of reality which are supra-scientific rather than pre-scientific."[56] Scientific analysis may observe life processes and describe their causal sequences, but there will always be a depth dimension, human freedom, which reason can never fully explain:

> Man is rooted in the world of natural necessity, out of which he arises to various levels of freedom. He also has a biological structure which is subject to scientific scrutiny, but the self in the heights of its freedom over structure and necessity is not a spatial object. It knows itself introspectively and in its dramatic dialogue with others. But every effort to make it an object among other objects reduces its stature. . . . It is because this transcendent responsible self is so inaccessible to science that a scientific culture is so prone to deny it, in order to reduce the human world to a dimension which can be grasped by the "scientific method."[57]

Science tells many little truths in the interest of its one great lie "that spatio-temporal realities are self-contained and self-explanatory and that a scientific description of sequences is an adequate analysis of causes."[58]

The religious response to the elevation of evolution to a metaphysical principle should be neither the creationists' "theological obscurantism" nor liberalism's resolution of the mystery by "some call it evolution and others call it God." Both of these responses to Darwinism are inappropriate within Niebuhr's method for they refuse to accept the limitations placed upon humanity and attempt to overcome the paradoxical ambiguity of the human condition.[59] Niebuhr is particularly harsh on the creationist position at this point for it corrupts the doctrine of creation into a theory of secondary causation which inevitably comes into conflict with the scientific account of natural causation: "This corruption of religion into a bad science has aroused the justified protest of a scientific age. It has also helped to tempt science to become a bad religion by offering natural causation as an adequate principle of ultimate coherence."[60] The proper religious response is to assert the biblical understanding of creation which maintains the mystery in a realm beyond natural and rational causalities: "We are deceivers yet true, when we say that God created the world. Creation is a mythical idea which cannot be fully rationalised."[61] Nature cannot be fully rationalized, by Darwin or anyone else, because the mystery of human freedom transcending the natural determinations cannot be explained through natural causation. Niebuhr draws on Whitehead's argument for novelty and Lovejoy's discussion of the failure of the "great chain of being" to rationally organize the world and asserts that "the idea of creation is not in conflict with any scientific account of natural causation."[62] The paradox of natural necessity and human freedom injects an aspect of mystery and novelty in creation for which a Darwinian evolution of humanity from the brutes does not account.[63]

Niebuhr's most extensive critique is directed toward those who would expand evolutionary theories into the realm of human history which, though rooted in the processes of natural causation, transcends natural determinism through the freedom we have as human beings. Niebuhr rephrases his "little truths/big lie" concept to focus on history: The "falsehood was that historical processes and natural processes were sufficiently identical to make the scientific method applicable to both fields."[64] The primary culprit in this "big lie" was Darwinism and its extension into ethics and the direction of history. On the one hand, Spencer and the social Darwinists attempted to transfer "survival of the fittest" into a moral ought as a law of nature with which one must not interfere, especially when it was extended to laissez-faire economics. On the other hand, Fiske and others transformed Darwinism into an optimistic view of historical and religious progress:

> Darwinism seemed to crown the whole structure of modern interpretations of a progressive history by proving natural forms to be as subject to development as historical structures. It also proved an historical relation between the human "animal" and its "mammalian" forebears. These were all "scientific" discoveries, consequent upon an empirical

observation of historical and natural sequences. Modern culture drew some illicit, though seemingly plausible, conclusions about these discoveries. It concluded that history was but an extension of the natural process so that evolution in biological forms was supposed to give the final proof of modern man's confidence in historical progress.[65]

For Niebuhr and the "neo-orthodox" in general, human history is taken as the primary arena of divine activity, and so history must be understood properly. The Bible is not a record of the evolutionary ascent of humanity, and Christ is not the symbol of progressive history. The illusion of progress supposedly justified by Darwinian evolution is a distortion of both science and history. Darwin is not to be held responsible for this distortion, but those who eliminate the common human experiences and "facts of a different order" are to be corrected. The way to confront the distortions, while not disregarding the evidence of science (as do "modern Barthians"), is through two propositions:

> 1) A radical distinction between the natural world and the world of human history must be made, however much history may have a natural base. The justification for this distinction lies in the unique character of human freedom [which cannot be reduced] to the coherence of nature. 2) Human history must be understood as containing within it the encounters between man and God in which God intervenes to reconstruct the rational concepts of meaning which men and cultures construct under the false assumption that they have a mind which completely transcends the flux of history, when actually it can only construct a realm of meaning from a particular standpoint within the flux.[66]

The illusion of a progressive history represents a simple coherence and meaning which attempts to overcome the ambiguity in the dialectic of natural necessity and human freedom. The simple facts, before which science is to be humble, of humanity being encountered with creative possibilities, of being judged and renewed, have no place when science is improperly extended into the realm of history.

There are some obvious echoes of Brunner's position here, both in the methodological distinction and the focus on the personal encounter as the essence of religious faith. Niebuhr also follows Brunner in rejecting Barth's blindness to "general revelation," and argues that, while the God we encounter as creator, judge, and redeemer cannot be proven through analyses of the rational coherences in nature, such analyses can point to a freedom, mystery, and meaning which transcend the natural processes. Only in a realm of knowledge above the conceptual schemes of Darwinian science can these ambiguities be appreciated, if not resolved.

Development of the Roman Catholic Position

During the time when Niebuhr was attempting to combat the two distortions of Darwinian evolution, the Roman Catholic Church was moving toward an "official" opinion which accepted Darwinian evolution as not contradictory to the tenets of faith. The history of the Roman Catholic response to Darwinism has been well documented, but deserves mention for it has become a representative of the "above" model.[67]

The discussion of "the Roman Catholic position" presents some difficulties for it involves both statements by individuals and the "official" declarations of the popes. As we saw in chapter 3, the initial popular as well as semiofficial response was in opposition to Darwinism. The ongoing debate between individual scientists and theologians prepared the way for an official, though limited, acceptance of modern views of natural science and evolution. We shall examine briefly the course of this debate.

The personal and official Roman Catholic responses to science in general and Darwinism in particular are based upon the epistemological and methodological distinction between spirit and matter which can be seen holistically from a religious perspective. Where Niebuhr maintained the paradoxical situation of humanity, Roman Catholic thought seeks a resolution of the dualism, even if such a coherence is not possible in human knowledge.[68] This approach to knowledge and especially to the human being as both spirit and matter led to an immediate rejection of Darwin's theory of human evolution even before the *Descent* was published. In an 1860 Council in Cologne and the 1869 Vatican Council, the implications of Darwin's theory for humanity were rejected. The fact that the theory itself was not addressed left the door open for scientists and theologians "to distinguish materialistic transformism from a theistic transformism which takes into account the essential difference between man and the other creatures of the material world."[69] A leader in this movement was John A. Zahm, physics professor at Notre Dame, who initially opposed Darwinism but moved to clarify the scientific issues and distinguish them from extensions of evolution into metaphysics and ethics. In two books published in 1896, Zahm argued that Augustine and Aquinas were theistic evolutionists and derivative creationists, even though they did not have the biological basis for their views. As a scientific theory, evolution was as well founded as Newton's theory and "is in perfect accordance with science and Scripture, with Patristic and Scholastic theology," and would come to be accepted for apologetic purposes by the church.[70] Zahm did not urge "acceptance" of Darwin's theory, but he demonstrated that the theory did not necessarily conflict with doctrine. This line of argument was overwhelmed by the opposition, and by 1899 Rome opposed further distribution of *Evolution and Dogma*, even though there was no "official" banning of the book. Opposition to the evolutionary theory received further official but noninfallible support from the 1909 Biblical Commission which opposed any evolutionary origin of humanity.

A breakthrough in the Roman Catholic position occurred with the publication in 1931 of John A. O'Brien's *Evolution and Religion* for it received an *imprimatur* from an American bishop. The *imprimatur* gave an official clearance for the contents of the book, which reasserted Zahm's position that Darwinian evolution did not conflict with doctrine. This movement toward the acceptance of evolution as scientific theory received official support from Pope Pius XII, who gradually removed theological opposition in a series of addresses and the encyclical *Humani generis* (1950). In a 1941 address to the Pontifical Academy of Science, Pius XII reasserted the distinction between the animal world and humanity, but he recognized the scientific uncertainties and opened up the possibility that humanity could physically descend from a lower creature while God intervened to make this new being unique. The 1950 encyclical took this position one step further and asserted that the physical origin of humanity from other living matter is theologically permissible, though all humanity must have come from one historical pair:

> Thus, the teaching of the church leaves the doctrine of evolution an open question, as long as it confines its speculation to the development, from other living matter already in existence, of the human body. (That souls are immediately created by God is a view which the Catholic faith imposes on us.) In the present state of scientific and theological opinion, this question may be legitimately canvassed by research, and by discussion between experts on both sides.[71]

It must be remembered, however, that in the midst of this "official" change of opinion, the writings of Teilhard were being barred from publication.

Pius XII's position shifted the tone of the Roman Catholic debate over Darwinian evolution. In the manner of all representatives of this model, the discussion quickly left behind the scientific theory to articulate an epistemological and methodological position which prevented evolution from becoming a metaphysical doctrine. The Roman Catholic position understands that truth is one since all truth comes from God, but there are legitimate methodological distinctions in the search for that one truth which may be known only by God. The distinction between reason and revelation is rooted in Aquinas's thought, and is reclaimed in the dialogue between modern science and religion. Karl Rahner argued in the 1950s that there is "a genuine plurality of realities in man which are not reducible to one another," and the recognition of these pluralities gives science a domain of inquiry which is relatively independent of religious thought:

> Revelation itself enters a sphere of reality which is also determined by other forces, which indeed derive from God, the author of Revelation, but which on that account cannot, in the actual form they take and in their special character, simply be derived from Revelation, which itself cannot simply be identified with God as he is in himself.... A genuine dialogue ensues between two ultimate authorities which have a common origin only in God himself, but which in their created reality stand irreducibly separate from one another.[72]

The plurality of realities not only gives the scientist a working autonomy, but also prevents evolution from becoming a metaphysical or religious position regarding the ontological status of humanity. In a scientific context, Philip Fothergill's *Evolution and Christians* (1961), which received the *nihil obstat* and *imprimatur,* claimed that evolution and religion are "true and valid spheres of knowledge" but revelation is necessary for a complete understanding of humanity:

> The Christian religion is authoritative and is based on Revelation, Reason and Tradition which spring ultimately from its Founder. The Christian religion gives a sufficient explanation of man's nature in terms of his ultimate end which is to see God. On the other hand, science has no means of determining man's end, and without Revelation it cannot obtain a complete picture of the nature of man.[73]

Evolution is quite competent to describe the secondary causality at work in nature, but that knowledge must be completed by revelation for a full understanding of the meaning of life.

This dualism of scientific and religious knowledge was made official in the documents of Vatican II in the early 1960s as a way both of reducing tension between the church and the world and of encouraging scientific research for the benefit of humanity. "The Pastoral Constitution on the Church in the Modern World" (*Gaudium et Spes*) asserts "the autonomy of earthly affairs" to discover the order and laws within each sphere of knowledge and activity:

> Therefore, if methodical investigation within every branch of learning is carried out in a genuinely scientific manner and in accord with moral norms, it never truly conflicts with faith. For earthly matters and the concerns of faith derive from the same God. Indeed, whoever labors to penetrate the secrets of reality with a humble and steady mind, is, even unawares, being led by the hand of God, who holds all things in existence, and gives them their identity.
>
> Consequently, we cannot but deplore certain habits of mind, sometimes found too among Christians, which do not sufficiently attend to the rightful independence of science. The arguments and controversies which they spark lead many minds to conclude that faith and science are mutually opposed.[74]

The plurality of spheres of knowledge which attain coherence in God has become "the Roman Catholic position" on the relationship between religion, science, and Darwinism. Most recently the position of Vatican II has been demonstrated through the testimony of a Roman Catholic biblical scholar, Bruce Vawter, who appeared in the Arkansas case against creation science. Science does provide valuable knowledge for human conduct and its technologies can improve the human condition, but only so long as they do not assert their supremacy as forms of knowledge to the exclusion of the religious answer to the "whence" and "whither" of human existence.[75]

Langdon Gilkey

The last representative of the "above" model is Langdon Gilkey, professor of theology at the University of Chicago Divinity School, who provides a fitting conclusion to this section for his intellectual roots are in the thought of Brunner, Niebuhr, and Paul Tillich, but he has moved beyond them to search for a philosophical position which can interrelate the scientific and religious spheres of thought. In his first major work, *Maker of Heaven and Earth* (1959), Gilkey claims that the Christian doctrine of creation answers the human experiences of dependence and temporality. The doctrine faced serious problems when it was closely linked with the scientific world view of the biblical period, and those problems were not eased with a philosophical identification of the divine with the natural processes. Gilkey argues that the basic problem is that Christians have been confused as to what the doctrine of creation is all about, and so he sets out to interpret the doctrine correctly. Much of his life's work has focused on that issue.

Gilkey's basic move was to make the epistemological distinction which permeates this chapter:

> The best way to understand what is the subject matter of the doctrine of creation is to distinguish between certain basic kinds of questions that men ask. People ask many kinds of questions about the origin of things, and these are often radically different from each other in meaning and intention. Consequently the answers to these questions can be in quite distinct realms of discourse.[76]

The scientific realm of discourse is concerned with relations between finite things in space and time, and thus can never deal with questions of an ultimate origin. The metaphysical level of truth deals with questions of the nature of reality itself, and this is distinct from the religious dimension, which deals with the existential issue of the ultimate meaning of a person's life. The religious idea of creation is thus an answer to the mystery of the meaning of our life as finite creatures. The conflicts between science and religion have occurred because these epistemological distinctions have not been fully appreciated, and this resulted in the biblical world view being confused with the religious meaning to which it witnessed.

This epistemological pluralism is supported by Gilkey's analysis of the traditional doctrine of *creatio ex nihilo*. This doctrine affirms, among other things, that God is the source of all that there is, and that the divine act of creation is "a totally unique act." Since it is a unique event, creation cannot be described in the same way as natural processes. Science can provide valid information about the world God has created, but not about the beginnings of the natural world. Scientific explanations and the doctrine of creation refer to events on different levels of being, and thus can never conflict. Gilkey supports this position through a discussion of the way the Christian doctrine of creation was responsible for the rise of modern science: the doctrine removed the gods from the things of nature and asserted that nature must be known empirically. This has resulted in a scientific causality which provides different answers than are required when we ask about ultimate causality. Since science examines the relations among finite things, its concepts and terms cannot be used in religious discourse as that would reduce God to a finite force in the world. God is the creative source and ground of all that is, but this religious dimension is not observable by science: "God's creative activity is not part of a finite sequence among finite entities, a sequence that is available to sense experience and testing because it can be manipulated by the scientist."[77] The religious question of ultimate meaning does not contradict our knowledge of nature, but complements it with a "deeper dimension."

Gilkey claims that religious discourse must make a limited use of analogies, but *creatio ex nihilo* denies even the use of analogies to describe the divine "how" of creation. The Thomistic distinction between primary and secondary causality was the most effective effort to establish analogical thinking about the creation, but Gilkey warns that it too can be misunderstood as reducing God's relationship to the world to finite terms or even as denying the immanence of God. (We shall see that Gilkey reclaims this distinction in the contemporary debate over creationism.) A more effective analogy for the creation is found in human and historical events where we talk of "why" an event occurred. With echoes of Niebuhr, this focus on history and human intentions is argued as the best way to overcome our concerns with the scientific "how's." While religious persons must accept the scientific method as the best available means for understanding the observable world around us, we cannot accept it as a complete understanding of reality since science provides us with only an understanding of causal necessity. Our own experiences, however, demonstrate that freedom, intention, and purpose are also aspects of everything that happens. The deterministic explanations of science must be balanced and complemented with an understanding of human and historical events in order that we gain a fuller perspective on reality. The proper way to think of creation is not in scientific terms, but as an analogy of the freedom and purpose of human historical action. The use of paradoxical analogies drawn from historical experience and expressed in the language of creation myths protects the religious answer from claiming that it is to be tested by scientific evidence. The validation of meaning in this realm of discourse is the "ability to provide a meaningful context for those basic intuitions which are taken to be the ultimate certainties of our experience."[78]

Gilkey concluded *Maker of Heaven and Earth* with a call for philosophical reflection on how we are to reconcile the various realms of discourse, and followed it with attacks on the weakness inherent in neo-orthodoxy's acceptance of these realms: while it accepted the modern scientific world view, neo-orthodoxy continued to use biblical language to describe the "mighty acts of God" without discussing how those acts relate to its modern world view.[79] The language of the Bible and of orthodoxy was univocal in that it understood God "acting" as did any secondary cause, but neo-orthodoxy has failed to recognize the shift to analogical thinking demanded by its scientific world view, and fails to give any concrete meaning to God "acting" in this world. Liberalism in the nineteenth century had overcome this problem by identifying God's activity with evolution, but the neo-orthodox rejected this and attempted to graft their biblical language onto the scientific language of causality as seen through the eyes of faith. Gilkey rejects this move for it leaves religious discourse essentially separate from the lives of modern people and their view of the world, and he calls for the discovery of dimensions of ultimacy in modern life.[80]

Darwinism and other theories of evolution are discovered to function in two different ways in the search for ultimacy in the modern world view. On the one hand, the philosophical and religious assumptions of Darwinian evolution were experienced as an attack on a religious world view. On the other hand, some ontological implications of Darwin's theory were elevated into myths which were substituted for the religious meanings of life. In both cases, Darwinism was seen as confirming and symbolizing the triumph of modern science. Those who felt this scientific theory as an attack saw Darwinism replacing divine activity by deterministic causal sequences and random variations. In a 1960 article, Gilkey claimed that "it was because Darwinism seemed to make man a child of blind Fate, rather than of God, that it became the center of heated if short-lived controversy."[81] (Gilkey learned that the controversy was alive and well in 1981 when he was called as a witness against the Arkansas creation science bill.)

In a widely anthologized article, Gilkey reclaims his earlier position of the distinction between scientific and religious realms of knowledge.[82] The basic confusion of both Darwinians and their opponents is to regard the religious and scientific explanations as equivalent, mutually exclusive theories. As we saw in chapter 3, creationists are confused about the role of theories in modern science and the method of causal explanation. They have also confused, according to Gilkey, questions of ultimate and proximate origins:

> They ignored the distinction (interestingly, ignoring this is a typical *modern* fallacy) between the *primary* causality of a First Cause, with which philosophy or theology might deal (where did it *all* come from?), from *secondary* causality, causality confined to finite factors—how, for example, did present forms of life arise out of *other* forms of life?[83]

This confusion leads to the conclusion that science deals with all the truth, and, when God and ultimate origins are left out, then science must be asserting that there is no God. Gilkey rightly points out that this is not simply a warfare between science and religion, but a complex issue of how these two forms of knowledge interrelate. Scientists have also accepted this model of mutually exclusive theories, and the scientific culture which has resulted demands some forms of religious meaning.

Darwinian evolution has not only been experienced as a deterministic threat to religion but has also been turned into a myth that champions human freedom to control our destiny. Gilkey again echoes Niebuhr's paradox of freedom and necessity in his analysis of the relationship of Darwinism and religion.[84] One of the ironies of Darwin's theory, having disposed of Paley's God, was "to find the liberal's immanent God of inevitable progress resurrected" through evolutionary theory.[85] Cosmic evolution, whether the nineteenth-century version of Fiske or the twentieth-century naturalistic versions, has become a myth to replace religious meaning in life. In the writings of Julian Huxley and Teilhard de Chardin, for example, evolution leaves the the realm of science and offers "a framework of ultimacy within which both public history and private destiny make sense."[86] Gilkey argues that the move to provide a framework for meaning based on Darwinian evolution overlooks the determinism inherent in Darwinism, and thus the essential paradox of human life is improperly dismissed. In this scientific culture, then, religion is needed as much as ever to provide symbolic forms by which humanity "comprehends the nature of historical passage into the future, and so the forces that shape the future for good or for ill."[87]

Gilkey has worked to move beyond the simple neo-orthodox separation of spheres or realms of knowledge to find a philosophical perspective from which scientific knowledge and religious symbols can be interrelated ontologically. The impact of modern science and Darwinism has been so significant that religious truth has been forced to be reinterpreted in terms of symbolic truth which vaguely asserts something about reality. This symbolic truth is caught in the dilemma of having little place within a scientific culture but having no meaning when separated from or placed above this culture. The way out of this dilemma is not to transform science into a religious myth, but to analyze the scientific process itself for the questions it raises about an ultimate meaning. Gilkey discovers in science a great passion and commitment to know, to control and manipulate, to rise above human limits and know the truth "objectively," and to remake the world with this knowledge. These "whiffs of ultimacy" in science create a paradox in which scientific knowledge points us toward determinism, while the creativity of science points toward a free and autonomous self *which the scientific method can never know.* Where modern science has defined the human problem in terms of the inability to know and control the forces outside of ourselves, Gilkey argues that the true question is the mystery and ambiguity of the self which is excluded by the scientific method.[88] This paradox between freedom and control has shaped the basic characteristics of Western culture: that all life is relative to and explained by a complex network of finite causes, and yet humanity is autonomous in its direction and future.[89]

In order to address this paradox, Gilkey incorporates some of the process philosophy of Whitehead to construct a viable doctrine of God and an understanding of nature and history in his *Reaping the Whirlwind* (1976) and *Message and Existence* (1980). He rejects, as did Wieman, Whitehead's separation of creativity from God on the basis that creativity in natural and historical processes is part of God's presence in the world. Gilkey does not follow Wieman and others in identifying God and process, but argues that the flux of nature and history is intelligible only as it is understood analogically as the manifestation of a divine ground which is in but not of the flux, the source and power of all life that transcends time. Gilkey maintains his belief that this God is not to be found objectively and known scientifically in the natural processes; instead God appears through the order, power, and creativity of nature and history. Given the limitations of ordinary human discourse, the concepts of process thought taken symbolically are as close as we get to providing the link between religious language and the modern scientific world view.

In this chapter we have examined a response to Darwinism which argues for an epistemological and methodological plurality in which science and religion have their own spheres of inquiry, and the results of one need not bow to the other. The advocates of this model in both the nineteenth and twentieth centuries have been critical both of attempts to combat Darwinian science in the name of religion and to replace the religious perspective with an evolutionary myth. Though he differed with Darwin on the meaning of design, Gray correctly believed that he was faithfully representing Darwin's epistemology and methodology, and he symbolizes the efforts of the representatives of this model to support the modern scientific method against opponents on both sides. The ability to distinguish between realms of knowledge, and to maintain the conviction of a "general revelation" in nature provided a firm religious and philosophical perspective from which to face any new scientific theory. As Gilkey put it, the other models tend toward a univocal understanding of religious and scientific language which is difficult to maintain with integrity. The use of analogical and metaphoric language has been a consistent approach in this model to ease the difficulties of religious talk in a scientific culture since metaphor and analogy do not tie religion to any one scientific theory.

The strength of the "above" model is that it allows the spheres of knowledge their own integrity. The weakness of this model is that it tends to cut off dialogue between science and religion since religion need no longer be concerned with science except as scientific theories are extended into myths, or as religion attempts to interfere with the free inquiry of science. As we have discovered in the recent debates over creationism and sociobiology, this isolation of religion from scientific discourse tends to leave religious persons with a poor understanding of the history and philosophy of science, and thus little understanding of the issues involved. The effective use of this model requires an understanding of science by religious thinkers and an understanding of religious thought by scientists so that each appreciates the issues the other faces.

7

Expanding Our Perspective:
A Fifth Model?

This study has sought to establish a method for analyzing the relationship between science and religious thought by focusing on the specific scientific and philosophical issues raised by Darwinian evolution and devoloping models for organizing religious responses to them. Darwinism was an epistemological and methodological revolution in that it claimed the freedom of science to do its work unfettered by religious presuppositions and demands for certain types of conclusions. Though this revolution began with Galileo and Newton, its significance was not strongly felt in Anglo-American thought until Darwin extended it to biology, which had long been the last domain of "doxological" science. The primary issue in the relationship between science and religious thought is epistemological: what are the accepted canons for explaining our experiences of nature? The epistemological presuppositions one has shapes whatever religious stance is taken towards science and the knowledge it provides us about the world.

The suggestion was made that the establishment of models is the most effective approach for recognizing both the plurality of positions which can be taken regarding the relationship between science and religious thought and their historical continuity. The hermeneutic chosen for establishing these models is rooted in the epistemological revolution of modern science. That hermeneutic can be used in any discussion of the relationship between science and religious thought, not only to analyze the religious responses but also to understand how philosophical and religious assumptions affect science. The process of analysis involves a close study of the scientific theory under question in which the significance of that theory is determined in light of previous theories and the epistemological and methodological claims it makes. Models of the relationship can then be articulated along epistemological lines: (1) opposition in favor of the old paradigm, (2) acceptance and transformation into a religious myth which then encourages research to support the myth, (3) synthesis of the new scientific world view with traditional religious concepts based on a flexible philosophical perspective, or (4) an epistemological pluralism which requires little rethinking of religious concepts and allows science the freedom to discover the natural laws which the Creator has established for managing the natural world, so long as no metaphysical claims are made which encroach upon religion's domain.

The religious responses to Darwinism were taken as a case study for this theoretical structure, and were examined in terms of their relationship to the epistemological and methodological revolution of Darwinian science. The "religion *against* Darwinism" model suggested that opposition to Darwinism in both the nineteenth and twentieth centuries is rooted epistemologically in a common sense realism which "knows" that God's design is present everywhere in nature. In this model, Darwinism is as much bad science as it is a threat to religious faith, and the epistemological paradigm revolution of which Darwin was the culmination has to be resisted in order for science and religion to work together in praise of God.

Even as the opponents of Darwinism looked to science for confirmation of their religious faith, the "religion *of* Darwinism" model embraces Darwin's revolution out of the conviction that science provides the only valid source of truth, and that becomes a religion. The "of" model rejects traditional religious concepts of God and replaces them with its own myth of human meaning rooted in an evolutionary world view in which nothing of significance transcends the natural processes.

The religion *in concert* with Darwinism model accepts some aspects of the Darwinian revolution but seeks to reclaim a close relationship between traditional religious thought and scientific concepts. Neither the epistemology nor the content of Darwin's theory is completely accepted in this model, as they must be "corrected" to attain harmony with previous philosophical commitments regarding the nature of reality or modes of divine presence.

The "religion *above* Darwinism" model is the truly Darwinian position for it works with a pluralistic epistemology that distinguishes between scientific and religious realms of knowledge. This model accepts a scientific description of natural processes without reference to divine guidance since science does not and can not provide a complete understanding of reality. The advocates of this model also follow in the Darwinian tradition of suggesting that analogies may be useful for developing meanings rooted in our common experience.

The usefulness of this theoretical approach to issues in science and religion is not limited to Darwinism. For example, the variety of responses to Heisenberg's Uncertainty Principle can be understood through a similar analysis. In the late 1920s, Werner Heisenberg developed a revolutionary theory regarding the limitations of scientific observation. He argued that nature, at the atomic level, introduces uncertainty into our scientific measurements. We can measure the position or velocity of an electron quite accurately, but the nature of the experiment precludes the possibility of precisely determining both in the same experiment, since measuring the position changes the velocity, and vice versa. Heisenberg developed a mathematical formula for determining the amount of uncertainty in our measurements, and this came to be known as the Heisenberg Uncertainty Principle.[1] Heisenberg went on to argue that there is indeterminacy in nature itself, not simply in our measurements, and this led to a variety of responses which can be analyzed according to the models suggested above.

The "religion against science" model is well illustrated by Albert Einstein, who could not accept this revolution in the determinacy of the world. Einstein's famous aphorism, "God does not play dice," was his response to the Uncertainty Principle. Einstein's faith was in the harmony and determinism of natural law, and he could accept no challenge to that world view.[2] Arthur Compton would represent the "of" model as he celebrated Heisenberg's theory as finally restoring free will to human action, since we are no longer absolutely determined by the machinelike supreme Intelligence many called God.[3] The synthesis approach has had many representatives. Charles Hartshorne reflected on the Uncertainty Principle in relationship with Whitehead's philosophy and declared that the only God he could accept was the one Einstein rejected since that God allows unpredictable novelty.[4] William Pollard went one step further and reinstated God's providential control in the indeterminacies Heisenberg discovered.[5] From the perspective of Eastern religions, Fritjof Capra's very popular *The Tao of Physics* (1975) would also fit nicely with this group. The representatives of the "above" model are legion, as many scientists and theologians have argued that Heisenberg's theory referred to epistemology at the atomic level, and, while analogies could be drawn to other levels of knowledge, there could be no direct line drawn to human experience.[6] William Temple presented this position in his Gifford Lectures when he claimed that physics should be of little interest to religious thinkers, while religious thought must be free from and able to challenge scientific theories, which are always changing.[7]

A Fifth Model?

Having suggested the value of these four models for analyzing the relationship between science and religious thought, the inevitable question is whether there might be a fifth model which more closely resembles H. Richard Niebuhr's fifth typology, "Christ the Transformer of Culture." It would appear that one might be possible, but little has been done systematically. In following Niebuhr, such a model could establish a more creative relationship between science and religious thought. This fifth, "transformist" model operates on the belief that divine creativity and power work through the cultural structures in which we live. At the same time, there is the recognition that our cultural forms are "corrupted" and contradictory, and only approximate the good for which they are intended. This model is thus less concerned with the conservation of the old forms than with renewal and integration through a reasoning faith which recognizes the partial and incomplete nature of our knowledge and its historical relativity. For the person in this fifth model, there is always a "leap of faith," making a commitment to the way the world can be, in the decisions which we must make regarding our social structures and the understanding of truth.[8]

How might a "transformist" model appear in the relationship between science and religion? This fifth model would take seriously the epistemological and sociological analyses of science and religion, since these are cultural forms through which the divine is present as a transforming power. Because this model recognizes that our knowledge is historical, relative, and fragmented in its understanding, it would acknowledge the epistemological pluralism of scientific and religious discourse but seek a way to move beyond a dualistic attitude. A dialogue between science and religion could be based in the faith that science itself is being transformed, and that part of that transformation is the overcoming of our fragmented knowledge of the world. The fifth model would distinguish itself from the "against" and "above" models by incorporating, metaphorically, the ecological perspective of modern science in its religious thought. This model would not, however, be dependent upon scientific thought for its basic world view, thus distinguishing itself from the "of" and "in concert" models, since it is aware that such a world view is "corrupted" and partial at best. The "transformist" model would always emphasize the presence of a faith commitment toward the understanding of reality which scientific and religious thought seek together.

A few recent efforts can be found which attempt to move toward such a model, but they are suggestive at best for moving from epistemology to an ontology. James Gustafson has approached the need for a new model from the "above" perspective. Following in the tradition of the "Gray school" and Gilkey, Gustafson suggests a model which establishes an analogical congruence between religious concepts and significant scientific theories, but he admits that he can provide only a minimal description of such a model.[9] Ian Barbour has attempted to provide a sounder philosophical basis for a new model from the "in concert" perspective. The basis for Barbour's approach is a "critical realism" which recognizes the partial nature of scientific and religious models of nature and God because they are formed around metaphors which always include an "is not" character in their reference. Barbour's analysis has led him to reject a blending of scientific and religious models since they refer to different entities and participate in different paradigms. The creative relationship between science and religion comes at the level of recognizing and discerning the partial truths about the world which each provides. Since the Christian paradigm does refer to God as Creator and does evoke attitudes toward nature, models of God must be found which are appropriate to the scientific understanding of the world which has been created by God, and Barbour argues that the process metaphysic of Whitehead and Hartshorne is most capable of providing this.[10]

The "critical realist" epistemology is also the foundation for A.R. Peacocke's recent effort to argue that "science and religion are interacting and mutually illuminating approaches to reality." In his earlier work, which was discussed above in chapter 5, Peacocke had argued for the value of metaphors in synthesizing scientific and religious thought. In his 1983 Mendenhall Lectures, Peacocke adds an epistemological introduction in order to suggest how his use of metaphors provides "intimations of reality."[11] Following Barbour's argument, Peacocke claims that scientific and religious models provide partial but valid representations of reality, and thus are "candidates for reality." Where Barbour then moves to place these models within paradigms of science and religion, and thus deny that they refer to the same entities, Peacocke is reluctant to follow for he fears that to recognize the social nature of the metaphors and models will undermine the claim that they provide a way to reality. Reality in the light of the sciences is then presented as an evolved hierarchy of systems in which each level is equally "real," but levels of complexity increase as we move up the hierarchy. The concern for religion appears at a high level in the hierarchy, and will have to take account of, but not be subservient to, the scientific understanding of the reality of the lower levels. The sciences are to be engaged in dialogue regarding the limited and partial knowledge they have of nature, and to restrict that knowledge to its appropriate levels.

Have we found the fifth, "transformist" model for the relationship between science and religion? The work of Barbour and Peacocke is suggestive of some lines along which such a model might be developed, but a few questions must be raised. First, the use of "critical realism" may be more helpful than other options, but it leaves the problem of how metaphors and their models can be "candidates for reality." As we have noted, metaphors always include an element of "is not" in their reference, and we are left with a negative statement about the nature of reality. It would seem that we have little true confidence when we can say that reality is only "something like" our analogy. On the other hand, the "transformist" model recognizes the fragmented and contradictory nature of our knowledge, and so "critical realism" may be an appropriate approach to science and religion.

Second, the fear of the sociological study of science and religion is legitimate since it does complicate matters. If we follow Niebuhr, however, the "transformist" model does affirm the value of the forms of culture, particularly as we become aware of the fragmented knowledge and historical relativity and move to examine the values at the heart of the scientific community and in the models which are proposed for understanding reality. [12] The fifth model would affirm that the understanding of reality through the scientific and religious communities can be renewed as we reconstruct the metaphors and models and move even closer to reality. Such a "transformist" position would allow us to recognize that, for example, a hierarchical world view may reflect certain values in the scientific community, and may not be a particularly true "intimation of reality." As we noted at the end of chapter 5, the hierarchical world view tends to sever the close relationship between humanity and the rest of nature and lead to relationships between men and women that are oppressive.

Each of the models we have examined, including "critical realism," is an attempt to gain some certainty about our understanding of reality in light of our scientific and religious knowledge. If we are to find a "transformist" model, the question must be raised as to the place of faith in each of these approaches to reality. The "critical realist" notes that physicists are committed to believing in the existence of electrons, even as their understanding of the electron has changed over the years. The "transformist" model affirms the presence of a faith commitment at the heart of our approach to reality. There is a danger, however, which religious thought must protect against: to abandon that faith commitment as religious thought looks to scientific metaphors and models for certainty in its knowledge. If we are to find a fifth model, that faith commitment needs to be recognized as an essential aspect of the scientific and religious communities. [13] We must ultimately make our decisions as to the nature of the knowledge which we have through science and religion, and commit ourselves to the belief that we do have an understanding of reality.

Notes

Chapter 1

1. James R. Moore's *The Post-Darwinian Controversies: A Study of the Protestant Struggle to Come to Terms with Darwin in Great Britain and America, 1870–1900* (Cambridge: Cambridge University Press, 1979), Part I, provides an excellent survey of the literature.

2. Alfred North Whitehead, *Science and the Modern World* (New York: Free Press, 1925); Michael B. Foster, "The Christian Doctrine of Creation and the Rise of Modern Natural Science," *Mind* ns 43 (1934): 446–68; Robert K. Merton, *Science, Technology and Society in Seventeenth-Century England* (New York: Harper and Row, 1970).

3. R.G. Collingwood, *The Idea of Nature* (New York: Oxford University Press, 1945, 1981); R. Hooykaas, *Religion and the Rise of Modern Science* (Grand Rapids, Mich.: William B. Eerdmans Publishing Co., 1972); Eugene M. Klaaren, *Religious Origins of Modern Science* (Grand Rapids, Mich.: William B. Eerdmans Publishing Co., 1977).

4. See, for example, John Dillenberger, *Protestant Thought and Natural Science* (Garden City, N.Y.: Doubleday and Co., 1960) and Harold Nebelsick, *Theology and Science in Mutual Modification* (New York: Oxford University Press, 1981).

5. The classic studies are Bert James Loewenberg's "The Controversy over Evolution in New England, 1859–1873," *New England Quarterly Review* 8 (1935): 232–57 and "Darwinism Comes to America, 1859–1900," *Mississippi Valley Historical Review* 28 (1941): 339–68.

6. Herbert Hovenkamp, *Science and Religion in America, 1800–1860* (Philadelphia: University of Pennsylvania Press, 1978) and Ferenc Morton Szasz, *The Divided Mind of Protestant America, 1880–1930* (University, Ala.: University of Alabama Press, 1982).

7. Michael Ruse, "The Relationship between Science and Religion in Britain, 1830–1870," *Church History* 44 (1975): 505–22 and *The Darwinian Revolution* (Chicago: University of Chicago Press, 1979), pp. 63–74, 239–50.

8. Lenn E. Goodman and Madeleine J. Goodman, "Creation and Evolution," *Zygon* 18 (1983): 3–43; Alice B. Kehoe, "The Word of God," in *Scientists Confront Creationism*, ed. Laurie R. Godfrey (New York: W.W. Norton and Co., 1983), pp. 1–12; George M. Marsden, "Understanding Fundamentalist Views of Science," in *Science and Creationism*, ed. Ashley Montagu (New York: Oxford University Press, 1984), pp. 95–116.

9. Ernst Benz, *Evolution and Christian Hope*, trans. Heinz G. Frank (Garden City, N.Y.: Doubleday and Co., 1966) and Hans Schwarz, "The Significance of Evolutionary Thought for American Protestant Theology," *Zygon* 16 (1981): 261–81.

10. The classic study is Ian Barbour's *Myths, Models, and Paradigms* (New York: Harper and Row, 1974) which incorporates the earlier works of Max Black, *Models and Metaphors* (Ithaca: Cornell University Press, 1962) and Mary B. Hesse, *Models and Analogies in Science* (Notre Dame: University of Notre Dame Press, 1966).

11. See also the work of Earl MacCormac in *Metaphor and Myth in Science and Religion* (Durham, N.C.: Duke University Press, 1976).

12. See the work of Frederick Ferré, "Mapping the Logic of Models in Science and Theology," *Christian Scholar* 46 (1963): 9–39 and "Metaphors, Models, and Religion," *Soundings* 51 (1968): 327–45.

13. This tendency has been analyzed in relation to the model of God as Father by Sallie McFague in *Metaphorical Theology: Models of God in Religious Language* (Philadelphia: Fortress Press, 1982).

14. See the study of John Angus Campbell, "A Rhetorical Analysis of *The Origin of Species* and of American Christianity's Response to Darwinism." Ph.D. diss., University of Pittsburgh, 1968.

15. An excellent analysis of Darwin's use of metaphors and the problems they created is provided in Robert M. Young, "Darwin's Metaphor: Does Nature Select?" *Monist* 55 (1971): 442–503. The influences of Scottish epistemology and aesthetics is discussed in Edward Manier, *The Young Darwin and His Cultural Circle* (Dordrecht: D. Reidel Publishing Co., 1978).

16. See the discussion in Young, "Darwin's Metaphor," pp. 483–86.

17. Michael Polanyi, *Science, Faith and Society* (Chicago: University of Chicago Press, 1946, 1964) and Harold K. Schilling, *Science and Religion: An Interpretation of Two Communities* (New York: Charles Scribner's Sons, 1962).

18. The classic study is Thomas S. Kuhn's *The Structure of Scientific Revolutions*, enlarged ed. (Chicago: University of Chicago Press, 1962, 1970); cf. Martin Rudwick, "Senses of the Natural World and Senses of God," in *The Sciences and Theology in the Twentieth Century*, ed. A.R. Peacocke (Notre Dame: University of Notre Dame Press, 1981), pp. 241–61.

19. See, for example, Thomas F. Torrance, *Theological Science* (Oxford: Oxford University Press, 1969) and *Divine and Contingent Order* (Oxford: Oxford University Press, 1981).

20. Rosemary Ruether, "A Feminist Perspective on Religion and Science," and Rubem A. Alves, "On the Eating Habits of Science," in *Faith and Science in an Unjust World*, Vol. 1, ed. Roger L. Shinn (Philadelphia: Fortress Press, 1980), pp. 41–46, 56–58.

21. Moore, *Post-Darwinian Controversies*, pp. 12–16, 110–22.

22. Charles Coulston Gillispie, *Genesis and Geology: A Study in the Relations of Scientific Thought, Natural Theology, and Social Opinion in Great Britain, 1790–1850* (Cambridge: Harvard University Press, 1951), pp. ix–xi and Neal C. Gillespie, *Charles Darwin and the Problem of Creation* (Chicago: University of Chicago Press, 1979).

23. George M. Marsden, *Fundamentalism and American Culture* (New York: Oxford University Press, 1980), p. 214.

24. H. Richard Niebuhr, *Christ and Culture* (New York: Harper and Row, 1951).

25. Ian G. Barbour, *Christianity and the Scientist* (New York: Association Press, 1960), pp. 86–89.

26. Ian G. Barbour, "Science and Religion Today," in *Science and Religion Today: New Perspectives on the Dialogue* (New York: Harper and Row, 1968), pp. 3–29.

27. The report is found in *Faith and Science in an Unjust World*, Vol. 2, ed. Paul Abrecht (Philadelphia: Fortress Press, 1980), pp. 7–27; for commentary, see J. Robert Nelson, *Science and Our Troubled Conscience* (Philadelphia: Fortress Press, 1980), pp. 31–58.

28. A.R. Peacocke extended the six models of the WCC to eight, but they too are variations on the two basic models, in *The Sciences and Theology in the Twentieth Century*, pp. ix–xviii. In the same volume, Eileen Barker developed eight models in "Science as Theology—The Theological Functioning of Western Science," pp. 265–79.

29. See, for example, Samuel Regester Neel, Jr., "The Reaction of Certain Exponents of American Religious Thought to Darwin's Theory of Evolution." Ph.D. diss., Duke University, 1942; Herbert W. Schneider, "The Influence of Darwin and Spencer on American Philosophical Theology," *Journal of the History of Ideas* 6 (1945): 3–18, *A History of American Philosophy*, 2nd ed. (New York: Columbia University Press, 1963), pp. 278–336; Stow Persons, "Evolution and Theology in America," in *Evolutionary Thought in America* (New Haven: Yale University Press, 1950), pp. 422–43; Eric C. Rust, *Evolutionary Philosophies and Contemporary Thought* (Philadelphia: Westminster Press, 1969).

30. See discussions in Alvar Ellegard, *Darwin and the General Reader* (Goteberg: Elanders, Boktryckeri Aktiebolag, 1958); David Lack, *Evolutionary Theory and Christian Belief* (London: Methuen and Co., 1957); John Dillenberger, *Protestant Thought and Natural Science*; Robert M. Young, "The Impact of Darwin on Conventional Thought," in *The Victorian Crisis of Faith*, ed. Anthony Symondson (London: SPCK, 1970), pp. 13–36; Jon Harlan Roberts, "The Impact of Darwinism on American Protestant Theology, 1859–1890." Ph.D. diss., Harvard University, 1980. John C. Greene has demonstrated some historical development and continuity regarding the three issues in the nineteenth and twentieth centuries in *Darwin and the Modern World View* (Baton Rouge: Louisiana State University Press, 1961).

31. Ian G. Barbour, *Issues in Science and Religion* (New York: Harper Torchbooks, 1971), pp. 80–114.

32. Ibid., pp. 365–419.

33. Richard H. Overman, *Evolution and the Christian Doctrine of Creation* (Philadelphia: Westminster Press, 1968), especially pp. 69–116.

34. Stephen Toulmin, "Contemporary Scientific Mythology" in *Metaphysical Beliefs*, ed. Alasdair MacIntyre (London: SCM Press, 1957), pp. 13–81.

35. Morse Peckham, "Darwinism and Darwinisticism," *Victorian Studies* 3 (1959): 19–40; reprinted in Morse Peckham, *The Triumph of Romanticism* (Columbia, S.C.: University of South Carolina Press, 1970).

36. For differently nuanced but similar analyses, see Langdon Gilkey, *Religion and the Scientific Future* (New York: Harper and Row, 1970) and Huston Smith, *Beyond the Post-Modern Mind* (New York: Crossroad Publishing Co., 1982).

37. Moore, *The Post-Darwinian Controversies*, p. 214.

38. Leo Sandon, "Darwinism and Religious Thought in America," lecture in *Darwinism Reconsidered* series, Florida State University, October 19, 1982.

Chapter 2

1. Charles Darwin, *The Origin of Species*, 6th ed., introd. Sir Julian Huxley (New York: New American Library, 1958), p. 450.

2. There are many introductions to Darwinism. The following are helpful: Peter J. Bowler's *Evolution: The History of an Idea* (Berkeley: University of California Press, 1984); Loren Eiseley's *Darwin's Century* (Garden City, N.Y.: Anchor Books, 1961); John C. Greene's *The Death of Adam* (Ames: Iowa State University Press, 1959); Michael Ruse's *The Darwinian Revolution* and *Darwinism Defended* (Reading, Mass.: Addison-Wesley Publishing Company, 1982); G. Ledyard Stebbins's *Darwin to DNA, Molecules to Humanity* (San Francisco: W.H. Freeman and Co., 1982).

3. Stephen Jay Gould, "Darwin's Dilemma," in *Ever Since Darwin* (New York: W.W. Norton and Co., 1977), pp. 34–38.

4. Charles Darwin, *The Descent of Man, and Selection in Relation to Sex*, 1st ed. (Princeton: Princeton University Press, 1981), p. 152.

5. See Arthur O. Lovejoy, *The Great Chain of Being* (Cambridge, Mass.: Harvard University Press, 1936).

6. See Arthur O. Lovejoy, "The Argument for Organic Evolution Before The *Origin of Species*, 1830–1858," in *The Forerunners of Darwin, 1745–1859*, by Bentley Glass et al. (Baltimore: The Johns Hopkins University Press, 1959), pp. 356–414 and Ernst Mayr, "The Nature of the Darwinian Revolution," *Science* 176 (1972): 981–89.

7. Gillispie, *Genesis and Geology*, pp. 149–83.

8. See, for example, Barry G. Gale, *Evolution without Evidence* (Albuquerque: University of New Mexico Press, 1982); Stephen Jay Gould, "Darwin's Delay," in *Ever Since Darwin*, pp. 21–27; H.E. Gruber and P.H. Barrett, *Darwin on Man* (New York: E.P. Dutton, 1974); Ruse, *Darwinian Revolution*, pp. 184–88.

9. Darwin, *Origin*, p. 74.

10. Ibid., p. 88.

11. Ibid., pp. 155–56.

12. Ibid., pp. 404–5.

13. Ibid., p. 449.

14. Peter J. Bowler, "Darwinism and the Argument from Design: Suggestions for a Reevaluation," *Journal of the History of Biology* 10 (1977): 29–43.

15. Julian Huxley, *Evolution: The Modern Synthesis*, 2nd ed. (New York: Harper and Row, 1942, 1963).

16. E.O. Wilson, *Sociobiology: The New Synthesis* (Cambridge, Mass.: The Belknap Press, 1975), pp. 3–4; cf. Richard Dawkins, *The Selfish Gene* (Oxford: Oxford University Press, 1976).

17. Robley Light, "Chemistry and Evolution: A New Modern Synthesis?" lecture in *Darwinism Reconsidered* series, Florida State University, September 14, 1982; John Gribbin and Jeremy Cherfas, *The Monkey Puzzle* (New York: McGraw-Hill, 1982) and "Updating Man's Ancestry," *The New York Times Magazine*, August 29, 1982, pp. 22–25, 55.

18. See the discussion in Bowler, *Evolution*, pp. 319–21.

19. An interesting discussion of Barbara McClintock's struggle for acceptance is found in Evelyn Fox Keller's *A Feeling for the Organism: The Life and Work of Barbara McClintock* (New York: W.H. Freeman and Company, 1983); for Frances James's work, see "On Nature Vs. Nurture: The Redwing Experiment," *Florida State University Bulletin, Research In Review* 77 (June, 1984): 3–5, 10.

20. Stephen Jay Gould, "Darwinism and the Expansion of Evolutionary Theory," *Science* 216 (1982): 382.

21. Niles Eldredge and Ian Tattersall, *The Myths of Human Evolution* (New York: Columbia University Press, 1982); Anthony Arnold, "Emergence of Hierarchical Structure in Evolutionary Theory," lecture in *Darwinism Reconsidered* series, Florida State University, September 21, 1982; Stephen Jay Gould, *The Panda's Thumb* (New York: W.W. Norton and Co., 1980).

22. Gould, "Darwinism," p. 386.

23. Bert James Loewenberg, "The Mosaic of Darwinian Thought," *Victorian Studies* 3 (1959): 3–18.

24. Stephen Jay Gould, "Worm For A Century," in *Hen's Teeth and Horse's Toes* (New York: W.W. Norton and Co., 1983), pp. 120–33.

25. Daniel S. Simberloff, "Is All Biology a Footnote to Darwin?" lecture in *Darwinism Reconsidered* series, Florida State University, September 28, 1982.

26. The following works have been most helpful: Gillespie, *Charles Darwin and the Problem of Creation*; David L. Hull, "Charles Darwin and Nineteenth-Century Philosophies of Science," in *Foundations of Scientific Method: The Nineteenth Century*, ed. R.N. Giere and R.S. Westfall (Bloomington: Indiana University Press, 1973), pp. 115–32; *Darwin and His Critics* (Cambridge, Mass.: Harvard University Press, 1973); "The Metaphysics of Evolution," *British Journal for the History of Science* 3 (1967): 309–37; *Philosophy of Biological Science* (Englewood Cliffs, N.J.: Prentice-Hall, Inc., 1974); Ruse, *The Darwinian Revolution*, "Philosophical Aspects of the Darwinian Revolution," in *Pragmatism and Purpose: Essays Presented to Thomas A. Goudge*, ed. L.W. Sumner et al. (Toronto: University of Toronto Press, 1981), pp. 220–35.

27. William Whewell, *The Philosophy of Inductive Science*, Vol. 2 (London: Parker Publ., 1840), p. 116; quoted in Ruse, *Darwinian Revolution*, p. 89.

28. In addition to Ruse and Gillespie, see Gruber and Barrett, *Darwin on Man* for a discussion of the notebooks.

29. See also Robert M. Young, "The Impact of Darwin on Conventional Thought," in *The Victorian Crisis of Faith*, ed. Anthony Symondson (London: SPCK, 1970), pp. 13–36.

30. Hull, *Darwin and His Critics*, p. 14.

31. Gillespie, *Charles Darwin and the Problem of Creation*, p. 53.

32. Michael T. Ghiselin's *The Triumph of the Darwinian Method* (Chicago: University of Chicago Press, 1984; reprint of 1969 edition with new preface) is an extensive but ahistorical exposition of Darwin's method.

33. Ruse, *Darwinian Revolution*, pp. 174–201.

34. The role of metaphors in Darwin's thought has been discussed in chapter 1, and the references there should be noted. See Ruse, *Darwinian Revolution*, p. 198, for a helpful schematic diagram of how the three elements of the new philosophy of science interact.

35. Hull, *Philosophy of Biology*, pp. 45–66; Ruse, *Darwinian Revolution*, pp. 238–39.

36. Hull, *Darwin and His Critics*, pp. 67–77; Ruse, *Darwinian Revolution*, pp. 237–38, 270–71.

37. See discussions in Bowler, *Evolution*, pp. 202–5, 327–34; Gould, "Darwin's Untimely Burial," in *Ever Since Darwin*, pp. 39–45; Hull, *Philosophy of Biology*, pp. 66–100; Ruse, *Darwinism Defended*, pp. 131–42.

38. Hull, *Darwin and His Critics*, p. 63.

39. See Dov Ospovat, "God and Natural Selection: The Darwinian Idea of Design,"*Journal of the History of Biology* 13 (1980): 169–94; William E. Phipps, "Darwin, the Scientific Creationist," *The Christian Century* 100 (1983): 809–11; also the discussions in Gillespie, *Charles Darwin and the Problem of Creation;* J.C. Livingstone, "Darwin, Darwinism, and Theology"; and Moore, *Post-Darwinian Controversies.*

40. Hull, *Philosophy of Biology*, pp. 101–24; also see articles in *Studies in the Philosophy of Biology*, ed. Francisco Jose Ayala and Theodosius Dobzhansky (Berkeley: University of California Press, 1974).

41. Ruse, *Darwinian Revolution*, p. 184.

42. See Michael E. Ruse, "Two Biological Revolutions," *Dialectica* 25 (1971): 17–38; also Ayala and Dobzhansky, and Hull, *Philosophy of Biology*, pp. 125–41.

43. See Hull, *Darwin and His Critics*, pp. 451–53; Ghiselin, *Triumph*, pp. 45, 59; John C. Greene, "The Kuhnian Paradigm and the Darwinian Revolution," in *Science, Ideology, and World View* (Berkeley: University of California Press, 1981), pp. 33–53; Ruse, "The Revolution in Biology," *Theoria* 36 (1970): 1–22, and "Two Biological Revolutions."

Chapter 3

1. Quoted in Arthur N. Foxe, *The Common Sense from Heraclitus to Peirce* (New York: The Turnbridge Press, 1962), p. 136. See also S.A. Grave, *The Scottish Philosophy of Common Sense* (Oxford: The Clarendon Press, 1960) and E. Brooks Holifield, *The Gentlemen Theologians* (Durham, N.C.: Duke University Press, 1978), pp. 110–18.

2. Sidney E. Ahlstrom, "The Scottish Philosophy and American Theology," *Church History* 24 (1955): 257–72.

3. Quoted in Foxe, *Common Sense*, p. 140.

4. Ibid., p. 148.

5. See Grave, *Scottish Philosophy*, pp. 136–42, 209–12; Bozeman, *Protestants in an Age of Science* (Chapel Hill: University of North Carolina Press, 1977), pp. 5–12; Hovenkamp, *Religion and Science in America*, pp. 3–13.

6. Bozeman, *Protestants*, p. 99–154; Marsden, *Fundamentalism and American Culture*, pp. 14–20, 110–14.

7. Charles Hodge, "The Unity of Mankind," *Princeton Review* 31 (1859): 105.

8. Charles Hodge, "The First and Second Adam," *Princeton Review* 32 (1860): 339.

9. See Joseph E. Illick, III, "The Reception of Darwinism at the Theological Seminary and the College at Princeton, New Jersey," *Journal of Presbyterian History* 38 (1960): 152–65; Daryl Johnson Freeman, "The Attitudes of the Princeton Theologians Toward Darwinism and Evolution from 1859–1929," Ph.D. diss., University of Iowa, 1968, pp. 17–119; Gary S. Smith, "Calvinists and Evolution, 1870–1920," *Journal of Presbyterian History* 61 (1983): 335–52.

10. Charles Hodge, *Systematic Theology*, Vol. 1 (New York: Scribner, Armstrong, and Co., 1877), p. 1.

11. Ibid., p. 9.

12. Ibid., pp. 22–23.

13. Ibid., p. 216.

14. Ibid., p. 224.

15. Ibid., p. 285.

16. Hodge, *Systematic Theology*, Vol. 2, p. 14; *What is Darwinism?* (New York: Scribner, Armstrong and Co., 1874), pp. 30–34.

17. Hodge, *What is Darwinism?*, p. 39.

18. Ibid., p. 53.

19. Hodge, *Systematic Theology*, Vol. 2, pp. 14–15.

20. Hodge, *What is Darwinism?*, p. 169.

21. Ibid., p. 134.

22. Hodge, *Systematic Theology*, Vol. 2, p. 27.

23. For surveys of Roman Catholic responses to Darwinism, see John Rickards Betts, "Darwinism, Evolution, and American Catholic Thought," *Catholic Historical Review* 45 (1959): 161–85; John L. Morrison, "A History of American Catholic Opinion on the Theory of Evolution, 1859–1950," Ph.D. diss., University of Missouri, 1951.

24. Orestes Brownson, "Darwin's Descent of Man," (1873) in *The Works of Orestes A. Brownson*, ed. Henry F. Brownson, Vol. 9 (Detroit: Thorndike Nourse Publisher, 1884), p. 496.

25. Brownson, "Science and the Sciences," (1863) in *Works*, Vol. 9, p. 263.

26. Ibid., p. 266.

27. Brownson, "The Cosmic Philosophy," (1872) in *Works*, Vol. 9, p. 454.

28. Brownson, "Darwin's Descent of Man," p. 485.

29. Ibid., p. 495.

30. See Brownson, "Primeval Man," (1869), "Hereditary Genius," (1870), and "The Primeval Man Not a Savage," (1873) in *Works*, Vol. 9, pp. 318–32, 401–17, 457–34.

31. See Conrad Cherry, *Nature and Religious Imagination* (Philadelphia: Fortress Press, 1980), pp. 158–230; David L. Smith, *Symbolism and Growth: The Religious Thought of Horace Bushnell*, AAR Dissertation Series 36 (Chico, Calif.: Scholars Press, 1981).

32. Horace Bushnell, "Science and Religion," *Putnam's Magazine* 1 (1868): 267.

33. Horace Bushnell, *Nature and the Supernatural as Together Constituting The One System of God* (New York: Charles Scribner, 1858), p. 36.

34. Ibid., p. 37.

35. Ibid., p. 253.

36. Bushnell, "Science and Religion," p. 271.

37. An interesting historiographical review has been provided by William E. Ellis, "Evolution, Fundamentalism, and the Historians," *The Historian* 44 (1981): 15–35. Historical studies of the American creationism debate over Darwinism are provided by John R. Cole, "Scopes and Beyond: Antievolutionism and American Culture," in *Scientists Confront Creationism*, ed. L. Godfrey, pp. 13–32; Dorothy Nelkin, *The Creation Controversy: Science or Scripture in the Schools* (New York: W.W. Norton, 1982); Ronald L. Numbers, "Creationism in 20th-Century America," *Science* 218 (1982): 538–44.

38. The literature analyzing contemporary creationism is growing rapidly. The following are are most helpful: Stephen G. Brush, "Creation/Evolution: The Case AGAINST 'Equal Time'," *The Science Teacher,* April 1981, pp. 29–33; *Creation/Evolution*, a journal devoted to the debate; "Creationism, Science, and the Law," a collection of articles in *Science, Technology, & Human Values* 7 (Summer 1982); Niles Eldredge, *The Monkey Business* (New York: Washington Square Press, 1982); Roland Mushat Frye, ed., *Is God a Creationist? The Religious Case Against Creation-Science* (New York: Charles Scribner's Sons, 1983); Douglas J. Futuyma, *Science on Trial: The Case for Evolution* (New York: Pantheon Books, 1983); Laurie Godfrey, ed., *Scientists Confront Creationism*; Philip Kitcher, *Abusing Science: The Case Against Creationism* (Cambridge, Mass.: The MIT Press, 1982); Roger Lewin, "Creationism Goes on Trial in Arkansas," *Science* 214 (1981): 1101–4, "Creationism on the Defensive in Arkansas," *Science* 215 (1982): 33–34, "Where Is the Science in Creation Science?" *Science* 215 (1982): 142–46, "Judge's Ruling Hits Hard at Creationism," *Science* 215 (1982):381–84; Ashley Montagu, ed., *Science and Creationism*; William R. Overton, "Creationism in Schools: The Decision in McLean versus the Arkansas Board of Education," *Science* 215 (1982): 934–43; John Priest, "Scientific Creationism: Structure and Sub-Structure," lecture in *Darwinism Reconsidered* series, Florida State University, November 30, 1982; Ruse, *Darwinism Defended*, pp. 303–29; George Ernest Webb, "The 'Baconian' Origins of Scientific Creationism," *National Forum* 62 (Spring 1983): 33–35; David B. Wilson, ed., *Did the Devil Make Darwin Do It? Modern Perspectives on the Creation-Evolution Controversy* (Ames: The Iowa State University Press, 1983).

39. The standard textbook for classroom use is John N. Moore and Harold S. Slusher, *Biology: A Search for Order in Complexity* (Grand Rapids, Mich.: Zondervan, 1974, rev. ed.); other popular expositions of the position can be found in Arthur C. Custance, *Creation or Evolution*, Vol. 4 of The Doorway Papers (Grand Rapids, Mich.: Zondervan, 1976); Bolton Davidheiser, *Evolution and Christian Faith* (Philadelphia: Presbyterian and Reformed Publishing Co., 1969); Norman Macbeth, *Darwin Retried: an appeal to reason* (Ipswich, Mass.: Gambit, 1971).

40. Henry M. Morris, ed., *Scientific Creationism* (San Diego: Creation-Life Publishers, 1974), p. 4.

41. Ibid., pp. 9–11.

42. Ibid., p. 12, emphasis is by Morris; cf. Duane T. Gish, *Evolution? The Fossils Say NO!* (San Diego: Creation-Life Publishers, 1978), pp. 39–42.

43. Morris, *Scientific Creationism*, p. 13.

44. Ibid., p. 20.

45. See A. David Kline, "Theories, Facts, and Gods: Philosophical Aspects of the Creation-Evolution Controversy," in *Did the Devil Make Darwin Do It?*, ed. D.B. Wilson, pp. 37-43.

46. Ibid., p. 39; Kitcher, *Abusing Science*, p. 46.

47. Henry M. Morris, *A Symposium on Creation* (Grand Rapids, Mich.: Baker Book House, 1968), p. 12-13.

48. See chapter 2 and David Hull, *Philosophy of Biology*, pp. 70-100; Kitcher, *Abusing Science*, pp. 33-36; Kline, "Theories, Facts, and Gods," p. 40.

49. Kitcher, *Abusing Science*, p. 39.

50. Karl Popper, "Autobiography," in *The Philosophy of Karl Popper*, Book 1, ed. P. Schlipp (LaSalle, Ill.: Open Court, 1974), p. 134.

51. Karl Popper, letter to the editor, *New Scientist* 87 (21 August, 1980): 611; cf. "Natural Selection and the Emergence of Mind," *Dialectica* 32 (1978): 339-55.

52. See Ruse's discussion in *Darwinism Defended*, pp. 135-40, 303-6.

53. Duane Gish, *Evolution?*, p. 40. Emphasis is his.

54. Morris, *Scientific Creationism*, pp. 37-45.

55. Ibid., pp. 51-69, 131-69. See discussion in Kitcher, *Abusing Science*, pp. 86-88.

56. Gish, *Evolution?*, pp. 62-174, provides the most extensive argument regarding the fossil evidence; cf. Morris, *Scientific Creationism*, pp. 91-130, 171-77.

57. See Priest, "Scientific Creationism: Structure and Substructure."

58. Morris, *Scientific Creationism*, p. 14.

59. Ibid., pp. 14-15; Henry M. Morris, *Evolution and the Modern Christian* (Grand Rapids, Mich.: Baker Book House, 1967, 1981), pp. 66-68; *The Twilight of Evolution* (Grand Rapids, Mich.: Baker Book House, 1963), pp. 14-23.

60. Jeremy Rifkin, *Algeny: A New Word—A New World*, in collaboration with Nicanor Perlas (New York: Penguin Books, 1983), p. 17.

61. Ibid., p. 72.

62. Ibid., p. 252.

63. Stanley L. Jaki, *The Road of Science and the Ways to God*, The Gifford Lectures, 1974-75 and 1975-76, (Chicago: The University of Chicago Press, 1978), p. vii.

64. Ibid., p. 286.

65. Ibid., p. 296.

66. Huston Smith, *Beyond the Post-Modern Mind* (New York: Crossroad, 1982), p. 134.

67. Huston Smith, "Evolution and Evolutionism," *The Christian Century* 99 (1982): 755-57; *Beyond the Post-Modern Mind*, pp. 162-76; *Forgotten Truth: The Primordial Tradition* (New York: Harper and Row, 1976), pp. 118-45.

Chapter 4

1. See the study of Michael Anthony Schuler, "Religious Humanism in Twentieth-Century American Thought," Ph.D. diss., Florida State University, 1982, pp. 141-48.

2. For example, see Barbour, *Issues*, pp. 108-11; an interesting study of other British figures has been provided by Frank Miller Turner, *Between Science and Religion: The Reaction to Scientific Naturalism in Late Victorian England* (New Haven, Conn.: Yale University Press, 1974).

3. See especially William R. Hutchison, *The Modernist Impulse in American Protestantism* (Cambridge, Mass.: Harvard University Press, 1976), pp. 12-40 and Stow Persons, *Free Religion: An American Faith* (New Haven, Conn.: Yale University Press, 1947); also Schuler, "Religious Humanism," pp. 118-40; a more descriptive work is found in Sidney Warren, M.A., *American Freethought, 1860-1914* (New York: Columbia University Press, 1943).

4. Hutchison, *Modernist Impulse*, pp. 26-27.

5. Persons, *Free Religion*, pp. 28-29, 42-44.

6. Octavius Brooks Frothingham, *The Religion of Humanity*, 2nd ed. (New York: Asa K. Butts, 1873), p. 7.

7. Ibid., p. 8.

8. Ibid., p. 40.

9. Ibid., p. 58.

10. Ibid., p. 169.

11. Ibid., p. 287.

12. Persons, *Free Religion*, pp. 31-35, 43-53.

13. Francis E. Abbot, "The Philosophy of Space and Time," *North American Review* 99 (1864): 64-116.

14. Francis E. Abbot, "The Conditioned and the Unconditioned," *North American Review* 99 (1864): 440-41.

15. Francis Ellingwood Abbot, Ph.D., *Organic Scientific Philosophy: SCIENTIFIC THEISM* (London: Macmillan and Co., 1885), p. ix.

16. Ibid., p. 40.

17. F.E. Abbot, "The God of Science," *The Index* 3 (1872): 57.

18. Abbot, *Scientific Theism*, pp. 150-51.

19. The attack on Darwin appears more explicitly in Abbot's review of Spencer's *The Principles of Biology*, in "Philosophical Biology," *North American Review* 107 (1868): 377-422.

20. Abbot, "God of Science," p. 59.

21. Abbot, *Scientific Theism*, p. 192.

22. Abbot, "God of Science," p. 59.

23. Abbot, *Scientific Theism*, p. 205.

24. Ibid., pp. 217–18.

25. David B. Anderson, *Robert Ingersoll* (New York: Twayne Publishers, Inc., 1972), pp. 21–83.

26. Robert G. Ingersoll, "The Gods," in *The Works of Robert G. Ingersoll*, Vol. 1 (New York: The Ingersoll Publishers, Inc., 1900), p. 8.

27. Ibid., p. 14.

28. Ibid., p. 49.

29. Ibid., p. 60; also, Robert G. Ingersoll, "Why I Am an Agnostic," in *Ingersoll's Greatest Lectures*, authorized ed. (New York: The Freethought Press Association, 1944), p. 52.

30. Ingersoll, "The Gods," p. 86.

31. Ingersoll, "What Is Religion?" in *Ingersoll's Greatest Lectures*, p. 500.

32. Persons, *Free Religion*, pp. 99–112.

33. Henry Nelson Wieman, "Intellectual Autobiography," in *The Empirical Theology of Henry Nelson Wieman*, ed. Robert Bretall (Carbondale: Southern Illinois University Press, 1969; reprint of 1963 edition), pp. 8–9; William S. Minor, *Creativity in Henry Nelson Wieman* (Metuchen, N.J.: Scarecrow Press, 1977), pp. 118–79.

34. Wieman, "Autobiography," p. 3.

35. Henry N. Wieman, *The Source of Human Good* (Carbondale: Southern Illinois University Press, 1946), p. 8.

36. Henry Nelson Wieman, *Religious Experience and Scientific Method* (New York: Macmillan Company, 1926), p. 23.

37. Wieman, *Religious Experience*, pp. 153–59; *The Wrestle of Religion with Truth* (New York: Macmillan Co., 1928), pp. 179–96; *Source of Human Good*, pp. 189–96.

38. Henry Nelson Wieman, "The Problem of Religious Inquiry," *Zygon* 1 (1966): 380–81.

39. Henry Nelson Wieman, "The Organization of Interests," Ph.D. diss., Harvard University, 1917, in *Seeking A Faith For A New Age*, ed. C.L. Hepler (Metuchen, N.J.: Scarecrow Press, 1975), p. 19.

40. Wieman, *Source of Human Good*, pp. 4–13; *Man's Ultimate Commitment* (Carbondale: Southern Illinois University Press, 1958), pp. 130–32.

41. Wieman, "Organization of Interests," pp. 25–29.

42. Wieman, *Source of Human Good*, pp. 273–74.

43. Wieman, "Problem of Religious Inquiry," p. 384.

44. Henry Nelson Wieman, "Science and a New Religious Reformation," *Zygon* 1 (1966): 131.

45. Henry Nelson Wieman, "Wrong Ways to Justify Religion," *The Christian Century* 46 (1929): 1571–73; "Co-Operative Functions of Science and Religion," *Zygon* 3 (1968): 32–58.

46. Wieman, "Problem of Religious Inquiry," p. 387.

47. Ibid., pp. 399–400; also Henry Nelson Wieman, *Religious Inquiry: Some Explorations* (Boston: Beacon Press, 1968), pp. 39–66.

48. See the discussion in chapter 1.

49. Julian Huxley, *Evolution in Action* (New York: Harper and Row, 1953), p. 132.

50. Julian Huxley, *Essays of a Biologist* (New York: Books for Libraries Press, 1970; reprint of 1923 edition), p. 4.

51. Ibid., p. 59.

52. Julian Huxley, *Religion without Revelation*, new and revised ed. (New York: Harper and Brothers, 1957), pp. 31–43.

53. Julian Huxley, *Man Stands Alone* (Freeport, N.Y.: Books for Libraries Press, 1970; reprint of 1941 edition), p. 260.

54. Ibid., p. 274.

55. Julian Huxley, *New Bottles for New Wine* (New York: Harper and Brothers, 1957), pp. 41–43; "The Evolutionary Vision," in *Issues in Evolution*, Vol. 3 of *Evolution After Darwin*, ed. Sol Tax and Charles Callender (Chicago: University of Chicago Press, 1960), pp. 249–50.

56. Huxley, "Evolutionary Humanism as a Developed Religion," in *Religion Without Revelation*, pp. 203–39; "Evolutionary Vision," pp. 257–60; *Essays of a Humanist* (New York: Harper and Row, 1964), pp. 73–109, 241–80.

57. The debate, with both of the Huxleys' articles, is found in T.H. Huxley and Julian Huxley, *Evolution and Ethics, 1893–1943* (London: The Pilot Press, 1947).

58. *Humanist Manifestos I and II* (Buffalo, N.Y.: Prometheus Books, 1973), p. 17.

59. For commentary on the Manifesto, see Schuler, "Religious Humanism," pp. 10–22.

60. *Zygon* 1 (1966): 1.

61. See Karl Peters, "The Image of God as a Model for Humanization," *Zygon* 9 (1973): 98–125; "Evolutionary Naturalism: Survival as a Value," *Zygon* 15 (1980): 213–22; "Religion and an Evolutionary Theory of Knowledge," *Zygon* 17 (1982): 385–415; "Modern Science and Religious Pluralism," *National Forum* 62 (Spring 1983): 15–16.

62. Several of Burhoe's articles have been collected in the book *Toward a Scientific Theology* (Belfast: Christian Journals Limited, 1981).

63. Ralph Wendell Burhoe, "Salvation in the Twentieth Century," in *Science Ponders Religion*, ed. Harlow Shapley, p. 67.

64. Ralph Wendell Burhoe, "Five Steps in the Evolution of Man's Knowledge of Good and Evil," *Zygon* 2 (1967): 77–87; also "The Human Prospect and the 'Lord of History'," *Zygon* 10 (1975): 318–33.

65. Burhoe, "Five Steps," pp. 87–94; "Values Via Science," *Zygon* 4 (1969): 65–99.

66. Ralph Wendell Burhoe, "Potentials for Religion from the Sciences," *Zygon* 5 (1970): 119–29; *Science and Human Values in the 21st Century* (Philadelphia: Westminster Press, 1971), pp. 21–31, 135–52.

67. Ralph Wendell Burhoe, "Religion's Role in Human Evolution: The Missing Link between Ape-Man's Selfish Genes and Civilized Altruism," *Zygon* 14 (1979): 150.

68. Burhoe, "The Human Prospect," pp. 328–29; *Science and Human Values*, pp. 171–73.

69. Ralph Wendell Burhoe, "Natural Selection and God," *Zygon* 7 (1972): 35.

70. Ibid., p. 56.

71. Ibid., p. 62; Burhoe, *Science and Human Values*, p. 19.

72. Burhoe, "The Human Prospect," pp. 342, 359–68, 373 n. 78; Ralph Wendell Burhoe, "The Concepts of God and Soul in a Scientific View of Human Purpose," *Zygon* 8 (1973): 412–42.

73. Edward O. Wilson, *On Human Nature* (Cambridge, Mass.: Harvard University Press, 1978; Bantam Books ed.), pp. 1–2.

74. Ibid., pp. 2–7.

75. See *Genes, Mind and Culture* (Cambridge, Mass.: Harvard University Press, 1981) and *Promethean Fire* (Cambridge, Mass.: Harvard University Press, 1983).

76. Wilson, *On Human Nature*, p. 192.

77. Ibid., p. 200.

78. Ibid, pp. 202–17; Edward O. Wilson, "The Relation of Science to Theology," *Zygon* 15 (1980): 425–34.

79. The shape of the debate can be found in Anthony Flew, *Evolutionary Ethics* (London: Macmillan, 1967); John C. Greene, "From Huxley to Huxley," in *Science, Ideology and World View*, pp. 159–88; Philip Hefner, "Is/Ought: A Risky Relationship Between Theology And Science," in *The Sciences and Theology in the Twentieth Century*, ed. A.R. Peacocke, pp. 58–78, and "Sociobiology, Ethics, and Theology," *Zygon* 19 (1984): 185–207.

Chapter 5

1. Moore, *Post-Darwinian Controversies*, pp. 217–51.

2. John Fiske, *Outlines of Cosmic Philosophy Based on the Doctrine of Evolution, with Criticisms on the Positive Philosophy*, 2 vols. (Boston: Houghton, Mifflin and Company, 1889), I: 71.

3. Ibid., I: 81.

4. Ibid., I: 312.

5. Ibid., II: 8.

6. John Fiske, *The Destiny of Man Viewed in the Light of His Origin* (Boston: Houghton, Mifflin and Company, 1885), p. 25.

7. This discussion is found in Fiske's *The Idea of God as Affected by Modern Knowledge* (Boston: Houghton, Mifflin and Company, 1885).

8. Fiske, *Cosmic Philosophy*, II: 428.

9. Fiske, *The Idea of God*, p. 149.

10. John Fiske, *Through Nature to God* (Boston: Houghton, Mifflin and Company, 1899), p. 113; cf. *Cosmic Philosophy*, II: 462.

11. Henry Ward Beecher, *Evolution and Religion*, part I (Boston: The Pilgrim Press, 1885), p. 115; James McCosh, *The Religious Aspect of Evolution*, The Bedell Lectures, 1887 (New York: G.P. Putnam's Sons, 1888), p. 58.

12. For a comparative study of Hodge and McCosh, see Joseph E. Illick, III, "The Reception of Darwinism at the Theological Seminary and the College at Princeton, New Jersey," *Journal of the Presbyterian Historical Society* 38 (1960): 152–65, 234–43; Gary S. Smith, "Calvinists and Evolution, 1870–1920," *Journal of Presbyterian History* 61 (1983): 335–52.

13. James McCosh, *The Method of Divine Government, Physical and Moral* (London: Macmillan, 1882), p. 136.

14. See the discussion in Moore, *Post-Darwinian Controversies*, p. 246.

15. Smith, "Calvinists and Evolution," p. 338.

16. McCosh, *Religious Aspect of Evolution*, p. 52.

17. Ibid., pp. 79–80.

18. Ibid., p. 7.

19. James McCosh, *Christianity and Positivism: A Series of Lectures to the Times on Natural Theology and Christian Apologetics* (New York: Robert Carter and Bros., 1871), p. 90.

20. A flavor of the debate is found in *The Central Presbyterian* of Richmond, Virginia, September 21, 1887, p. 2, which was discovered inside a copy of the book which this writer found at an old book sale.

21. Henry Drummond, *Natural Law in the Spiritual World* (New York: A.L. Burt Co., 1883), pp. 20–21.

22. Ibid., p. 46.

23. Ibid., p. 58.

24. Ibid., pp. 70–71.

25. Henry Drummond, *The Ascent of Man*, 3rd ed. (New York: John Pott and Co., 1894), p. 13.

26. Ibid., p. 208.

27. Ibid., p. 231.

28. Drummond, *Natural Law*, pp. 388–89.

29. Drummond, *Ascent*, pp. 335–44.

30. Ian Barbour has, as usual, provided good "maps" for the debate surrounding Teilhard. See *Issues*, pp. 399–408; "Five Ways of Reading Teilhard," *Soundings* 51 (1968): 115–45; "The Significance of Teilhard," *The Christian Century* 84 (1967): 1098–1102; "Teilhard's Process Metaphysics," *The Journal of Religion* 49 (1969): 136–59.

31. See Ernst Benz, *Evolution and Christian Hope*, pp. 143–220; Stephen Toulmin, "Pierre Teilhard de Chardin," in *The Return to Cosmology: Postmodern Science and the Theology of Nature* (Berkeley: University of California Press, 1982), pp. 113–26.

32. See J.A. Lyons, *The Cosmic Christ in Origen and Teilhard de Chardin* (London: Oxford University Press, 1982), pp. 147–81.

33. Teilhard de Chardin, *The Phenomenon of Man*, introd. Sir Julian Huxley, trans. Bernard Wall (New York: Harper Torchbook, 1965), p. 31.

34. Ibid., p. 56.

35. Ibid., pp. 64–65.

36. Ibid., p. 302.

37. Ibid., p. 149, n. 1.

38. Ibid., pp. 218–19.

39. Teilhard, "The God of Evolution," (1953), in *Christianity and Evolution*, trans. René Hague (New York: Harcourt Brace Jovanovich, 1971), p. 238.

40. See, for example, J.A. Lyons, *The Cosmic Christ*, pp. 147–219; Christopher Mooney, *Teilhard de Chardin and the Mystery of Christ* (New York: Harper and Row, 1966) and Claude Stewart, *Nature in Grace: A Study in the Theology of Nature* (Macon, Ga.: Mercer University Press, 1983), pp. 175–234.

41. Teilhard, "Christ the Evolver, or a Logical Development of the Idea of Redemption," (1942) in *Christianity and Evolution*, pp. 143–44.

42. John B. Cobb, Jr., "Is Christian Theology Still Possible?" in *God and the World* (Philadelphia: Westminster Press, 1969), pp. 117–38.

43. Ibid., pp. 131–32.

44. John B. Cobb, Jr., *Living Options in Protestant Theology* (Philadelphia: Westminster Press, 1962), p. 29.

45. John B. Cobb, Jr., "Natural Causality and Divine Action," *Idealistic Studies* 3 (1973): 218; cf. "God and the Scientific Worldview," in *Talking About God*, by David Tracy and John B. Cobb, Jr. (New York: Seabury Press, 1983), pp. 39–56.

46. Charles Birch, "What Does God Do in the World?" *Union Seminary Quarterly Review* 30 (1975): 76–84.

47. John B. Cobb, Jr. and David Ray Griffin, *Process Theology: an Introductory Exposition* (Philadelphia: Westminster Press, 1976), p. 26.

48. Cobb, *God and the World*, p. 52.

49. Charles Birch and John B. Cobb, Jr., *The Liberation of Life* (Cambridge: Cambridge University Press, 1981), p. 3.

50. Ibid., p. 29.

51. Charles Birch, "Chance, Necessity and Purpose," in *Studies in the Philosophy of Biology*, ed. F.J. Ayala and T. Dobzhansky, p. 227.

52. Birch and Cobb, *Liberation of Life*, p. 86.

53. Ibid., p. 106.

54. John B. Cobb, Jr., *Is It Too Late? A Theology of Ecology* (Beverly Hills, Calif.: Bruce Publishing Co., 1972), pp. 110–13; "Process Theology and Environmental Issues," *Journal of Religion* 60 (1980): 440–58.

55. Cobb and Griffin, *Process Theology*, pp. 8–10.

56. Ibid., pp. 67–68.

57. Birch and Cobb, *Liberation of Life*, p. 182.

58. Charles Birch, *Nature and God* (London: SCM Press, 1965), p. 110.

59. Birch and Cobb, *Liberation of Life*, p. 196.

60. Cobb, *God and the World*, p. 93.

61. Charles Birch, "Creation and the Creator," *Journal of Religion* 37 (1957): 93.

62. F.R. Tennant, *Philosophical Theology*, 2 vols. (Cambridge: Cambridge University Press, 1930), I: 33–69; cf. Peter Anthony Bertocci, *The Empirical Argument for God in Late British Thought*, foreword Frederick Robert Tennant (Cambridge, Mass.: Harvard University Press, 1938), pp. 192–202, to which this discussion is indebted.

63. Tennant, *Philosophical Theology*, I: 183.

64. Peter Anthony Bertocci, *Introduction to the Philosophy of Religion* (New York: Prentice-Hall, Inc., 1951), p. 9.

65. Ibid., p. 74–78.

66. Ibid., pp. 153–89.

67. Tennant, *Philosophical Theology*, II: 79.

68. Bertocci, *Philosophy of Religion*, p. 331.

69. For a summary of the arguments, see Bertocci, *Empirical Argument for God*, pp. 227–38.

70. Tennant, *Philosophical Theology*, II: 104.

71. Bertocci, *Philosophy of Religion*, p. 359.

72. Ibid., pp. 360–62, 395–441; *Empirical Argument for God*, pp. 256–82.

73. Michael Polanyi, *Personal Knowledge* (Chicago: University of Chicago Press, 1958, 1962), especially chapter 13.

74. A.R. Peacocke, *Creation and the World of Science*, The Bampton Lectures of 1978 (Oxford: Clarendon Press, 1979), pp. 1–22.

75. Arthur Peacocke, "Biological Evolution and Christian Theology Today," *Theology* 87 (1984): 39.

76. A.R. Peacocke, *Science and the Christian Experiment* (London: Oxford University Press, 1971), pp. vi, 5–28.

77. Peacocke, *Creation and the World of Science*, p. 106.

78. Ibid., pp. 112–27; A.R. Peacocke, "Reductionism," *Zygon* 11 (1976): 307–34.

79. Peacocke, *Science and the Christian Experiment*, pp. 84–88.

80. Arthur Peacocke, "Sociobiology and Its Theological Implications," *Zygon* 19 (1984): 178–79.

81. Birch and Cobb, *Liberation of Life*, p. 310. Examples of the feminist studies may be found in *Discovering Reality: Feminist Perspectives on Epistemology, Metaphysics, Methodology, and Philosophy of Science*, ed. Sandra Harding and Merrill B. Hintikka (Dordrecht: D. Reidel Publishing Company, 1983) and *Reflections on Gender and Science* by Evelyn Fox Keller (New Haven: Yale University Press, 1985).

82. Rosemary Radford Ruether, "A Feminist Perspective on Religion and Science," p. 57; Elizabeth Dodson Gray, *Green Paradise Lost*, formerly "Why the Green Nigger?" (Wellesley, Mass.: Roundtable Press, 1979, 1981), p. 6.

83. Rosemary Radford Ruether, *Sexism and God-Talk* (Boston: Beacon Press, 1983), pp. 85-92; cf. *New Woman/New Earth* (New York: Seabury Press, 1975), pp. 186-211.

84. Gray, *Green Paradise Lost*, p. 73.

Chapter 6

1. See Asa Gray, *Natural Science and Religion* (New York: Charles Scribner's Sons, 1880), pp. 8-9.

2. A. Hunter Dupree, *Asa Gray, 1810-1888* (Cambridge, Mass.: The Belknap Press of Harvard University Press, 1959), pp. 20-22, 44-47, 135-48, 217-31.

3. For the first group, see Barbour, *Issues*, pp. 90-91, 99, and Gillespie, *Darwin and the Problem of Creation*, pp. 111-17; for the second, Dupree, *Asa Gray*, pp. 269-378, and Moore, *Post-Darwinian Controversies*, pp. 269-80.

4. May 25, 1868, in *The Letters of Asa Gray*, ed. Jane Loring Gray, 2 vols. (Boston: Houghton, Mifflin and Co., 1893), II: 562.

5. Asa Gray, *Darwiniana*, ed. A. Hunter Dupree (Cambridge, Mass.: The Belknap Press of Harvard University Press, 1963), p. 11.

6. Ibid., p. 119.

7. Gray, *Natural Science and Religion*, pp. 5-9, 60-66.

8. Gray, *Darwiniana*, pp. 88-89.

9. Ibid., p. 107; cf. Gray, *Natural Science and Religion*, pp. 68-73.

10. Gray, *Darwiniana*, p. 44.

11. Gray, *Natural Science and Religion*, pp. 66-69.

12. Gray, *Darwiniana*, p. 46.

13. Gray, *Darwiniana*, pp. 121-22.

14. Ibid., pp. 316-17.

15. Philip P. Wiener, *Evolution and the Founders of Pragmatism* (Cambridge, Mass.: Harvard University Press, 1949), pp. 1-69, 208-11; Dupree, *Asa Gray*, pp. 289-92.

16. "Living according to Nature," in *Letters of Chauncey Wright*, ed. J.B. Thayer (Cambridge, Mass., 1878), p. 328.

17. Letter to Mrs. Lesley, Feb. 12, 1860, in *Letters*, p. 43.

18. Letter to Abbot, Aug. 13, 1867, in *Letters*, p. 113.

19. Chauncey Wright, *Philosophical Discussions* (New York: Henry Holt and Co., 1877), p. 131.

20. See Moore, *Post-Darwinian Controversies*, pp. 280-98.

21. G. Frederick Wright, *The Logic of Christian Evidences*, 4th ed. (Andover, Mass.: Warren F. Draper, 1883), pp. 4-5.

22. G. Frederick Wright, *Studies in Science and Religion* (Andover, Mass.: Warren F. Draper, 1882), pp. 7-8.

23. Wright, *Logic*, pp. 9–17, 64–73; *Studies*, pp. 9–18.

24. Wright, *Logic*, pp. 42, 78–88.

25. Wright, *Studies*, p. 74.

26. Ibid., pp. 75, 89.

27. Ibid., pp. 212–55.

28. Ibid., p. 368.

29. Ibid., pp. 196–211.

30. G. Frederick Wright, *Scientific Aspects of Christian Evidences* (New York: D. Appleton and Company, 1898), p. 80.

31. Francis John McConnell, *Borden Parker Bowne: His Life and His Philosophy* (New York: Abingdon Press, 1929), chapters 1–2.

32. Ibid., p. 51.

33. Borden P. Bowne, *Metaphysics* (New York: American Book Company, 1882, 1898), p. iii.

34. Ibid., p. 8.

35. Borden P. Bowne, *Theism* (New York: American Book Company, 1887, 1902), p. 127; cf. *Metaphysics*, pp. 31–32, and Borden P. Bowne, *Personalism* (Boston: Houghton, Mifflin and Company, 1908), pp. 40–49.

36. Bowne, *Personalism*, p. 44.

37. Bowne, *Metaphysics*, pp. 60–70.

38. Bowne, *Theism*, p. 57.

39. Borden P. Bowne, *The Immanence of God* (Boston: Houghton, Mifflin and Company, 1905), p. 15.

40. Bowne, *Theism*, p. 103; cf. *Metaphysics*, pp. 271–72.

41. Bowne, *Metaphysics*, p. 273.

42. Ibid., p. 274.

43. Bowne, *Personalism*, p. 249; cf. *Theism*, p. 105.

44. Bowne, *Immanence of God*, pp. 22–23; *Metaphysics*, p. 280.

45. Bowne, *Theism*, pp, 106–107; *Personalism*, pp. 254–66.

46. See Karl Barth, *Church Dogmatics*, Vol. 3, Parts 1 and 3, trans. T.F. Torrance et al. (Edinburgh: T. and T. Clark, 1958); and Barbour's discussion in *Issues*, pp. 116–18, 422–25.

47. The two were published as *Natural Theology*, trans. Peter Fraenkel with an introd. by John Baillie (London: Geoffrey Bles, The Centenary Press, 1946).

48. Ibid., pp. 24–25.

49. Emil Brunner, *Revelation and Reason*, trans. O. Wyon (Philadelphia: Westminster Press, 1946), p. 23.

50. Emil Brunner, *The Christian Doctrine of Creation and Redemption*, trans. O. Wyon (Philadelphia: Westminster Press, 1952), p. 27.

51. Ibid., pp. 21–22.

52. Ibid., p. 35.

53. Ibid., p. 40.

54. Reinhold Niebuhr, *The Nature and Destiny of Man*, 2 vols. (New York: Charles Scribner's Sons, 1964), I: 164–82.

55. Reinhold Niebuhr, "Coherence, Incoherence, and Christian Faith," in *Christian Realism and Political Problems* (New York: Charles Scribner's Sons, 1953), p. 176.

56. Reinhold Niebuhr, "The Truth in Myths," in *The Nature of Religious Experience* (New York: Harper and Bros., 1937), p. 119.

57. Reinhold Niebuhr, "The Tyranny of Science," *Theology Today* 10 (1954): 466.

58. Niebuhr, "Truth in Myths," p. 129.

59. Niebuhr, *Nature and Destiny of Man*, I: 132–34.

60. Reinhold Niebuhr, *Faith and History* (New York: Charles Scribner's Sons, 1949), p. 33; cf. "Intellectual Autobiography," in *Reinhold Niebuhr: His Religious, Social, and Political Thought*, ed. C.W. Kegley and R.W. Bretall (New York: Macmillan Co., 1956), p. 21.

61. Reinhold Niebuhr, *Beyond Tragedy* (New York: Charles Scribner's Sons, 1937), p. 7.

62. Niebuhr, *Faith and History*, pp. 48–49.

63. Reinhold Niebuhr, "Christianity and Darwin's Revolution," in *A Book That Shook the World*, ed. Ralph Buchsbaum (Pittsburgh: University of Pittsburgh Press, 1958), p. 30.

64. Ibid., p. 32.

65. Reinhold Niebuhr, *The Self and the Dramas of History* (New York: Charles Scribner's Sons, 1955), p. 109.

66. Niebuhr, *Christian Realism and Political Problems*, pp. 199–200.

67. This discussion is indebted to those in Zoltan Alszeghy, "Development in the Doctrinal Formulation of the Church concerning the Theory of Evolution," in *The Evolving World and Theology*, ed. J. Metz, *Concilium* 26 (New York: Paulist Press, 1967); John Rickard Betts, "Darwinism, Evolution, and American Catholic Thought"; John L. Morrison, "A History of American Catholic Opinion on the Theory of Evolution, 1859–1950"; Karl Rahner, *Hominisation: The Evolutionary Origin of Man as a Theological Problem*, trans. W.J. O'Hara (New York: Herder and Herder, 1965).

68. See the exposition of this Thomistic position in Karl Rahner, *Spirit in the World*, trans. W. Dych (New York: Herder and Herder, 1968).

69. Alszeghy, "Development in Doctrinal Formulation," p. 26.

70. J.A. Zahm, *Evolution and Dogma* (Chicago: D.H. McBride and Co., 1896), p. 424, 134–36 and *Scientific Theory and Catholic Doctrine* (Chicago: D.H. McBride and Co., 1896), pp. 125–68.

71. Pius XII, *Humani Generis* (1950), trans. R.A. Knox, paragraph 36.

72. Rahner, *Hominisation*, p. 16.

73. Philip G. Fothergill, *Evolution and Christians* (London: Longmans, Green and Co., 1961), p. 3.

74. Paul VI, *Gaudium et Spes*, paragraph 36, in *The Documents of Vatican II*, ed. Walter M. Abbott (Chicago: Follett Publishing Company, 1966), p. 234.

75. Vawter's argument is presented in "Creationism: Creative Misuse of the Bible," in *Is God A Creationist?*, ed. Roland M. Frye (New York: Charles Scribner's Sons, 1983), pp. 71-82. Though no longer considered an official teacher in the Roman Catholic Church, Hans Küng argues a position similar to that of Pope John Paul II. See Hans Küng, *Does God Exist?*, trans. E. Quinn (Garden City, N.Y.: Doubleday and Company, 1980), pp. 101-24, 170-76, 344-49, 643-59; also speeches by Pope John Paul II, *The Pope Speaks* 26 (1981): 209-13, 350-52; 27 (1982): 365-68; esp. 28 (1983): 245-49.

76. Langdon Gilkey, *Maker of Heaven and Earth* (Garden City, NY: Anchor Books, 1965), p. 16.

77. Ibid., p. 151.

78. Ibid., p. 351.

79. Langdon Gilkey, "Cosmology, Ontology, and the Travail of Biblical Language," *Journal of Religion* 41 (1961): 194-205 and "The Concept of Providence in Contemporary Theology," *Journal of Religion* 43 (1963): 171-92.

80. Langdon Gilkey, *Naming the Whirlwind: The Renewal of God-Language* (Indianapolis, Ind.: Bobbs-Merrill Publishing, 1969), pp. 3-106, 247-305.

81. Langdon Gilkey, "Darwin and Christian Thought," in *Science and Religion*, ed. I. Barbour (New York: Harper and Row, 1968), p. 164-65. Reprint of 1960 *Christian Century* article.

82. Gilkey addressed the American Association for the Advancement of Science in January 1982, and adaptations of that speech have appeared as "Creationism: The Roots of the Conflict," *Christianity & Crisis* 42 (1982): 108-15; by the same title in *Is God a Creationist?*, pp. 56-67; "The Creationist Controversy: The Interrelation of Inquiry and Belief," *Science, Technology, and Human Values* 7 (Summer 1982): 67-71; "The Creationist Issue: A Theologian's View," in *Cosmology and Theology*, ed. D. Tracy and N. Lash, *Concilium* 166 (New York: Seabury Press, 1983), pp. 55-69.

83. Gilkey, "Creationism," *Christianity and Crisis* 42 (1982): 111.

84. Langdon Gilkey, "Evolutionary Science and the Dilemma of Freedom and Determinism," *Christian Century* 84 (1967): 339-43.

85. Langdon Gilkey, *Religion and the Scientific Future* (New York: Harper and Row, 1970), p. 22.

86. Langdon Gilkey, "Biblical Symbols in a Scientific Culture," in *Science and Human Values*, ed. R.W. Burhoe, p. 76.

87. Gilkey, *Religion and the Scientific Future*, p. 132; cf. *Society and the Sacred* (New York: Crossroad Publishing Co., 1981), pp. 104-19.

88. Gilkey, *Religion and the Scientific Future*, pp. 40-62; *Society and the Sacred*, pp. 75-89.

89. See the discussions in Langdon Gilkey, *Reaping the Whirlwind* (New York: Seabury Press, 1976), chapter 3 and *Message and Existence* (New York: Seabury Press, 1980), chapter 5.

Chapter 7

1. See his 1929 American lectures in Werner Heisenberg, *The Physical Principles of the Quantum Theory* (Chicago: Dover Publications, 1930); at a more popular level, *Physics and Philosophy* (New York: Harper and Row, 1958).

2. Albert Einstein, *The World as I See It* (New York: The Wisdom Library, n.d.), p. 29.

3. Arthur H. Compton, *The Freedom of Man* (New York: Greenword Press, 1935).

4. Charles Hartshorne, *Beyond Humanism* (Lincoln: University of Nebraska Press, 1937, 1968).

5. William G. Pollard, *Chance and Providence* (New York: Charles Scribner's Sons, 1958).

6. The scientific side of this argument is presented well in Douglas R. Hofstadter, "Metamagical Themas," *Scientific American,* July 1981, pp. 18ff.

7. William Temple, *Nature, Man and God* (London: Macmillan, 1934, 1949), pp. 228ff.

8. This summary has been drawn from H. Richard Niebuhr, *Christ and Culture*, pp. 190–256.

9. James M. Gustafson, *Ethics from a Theocentric Perspective.* Vol. 1: *Theology and Ethics* (Chicago: University of Chicago Press, 1981), pp. 235–79.

10. See the discussions in Barbour, *Issues in Science and Religion*, pp. 452–63; *Myths, Models, and Paradigms*, especially pp. 165–170.

11. Arthur Peacocke, *Intimations of Reality: Critical Realism in Science and Religion,* The Mendenhall Lectures 1983 (Notre Dame, Ind.: University of Notre Dame Press, 1984), pp. 11–53.

12. Niebuhr himself began to sketch what such a sociological study of the scientific community and its values might look like in his *Radical Monotheism and Western Culture* (New York: Harper Torchbooks, 1970), pp. 78–89.

13. As this analysis was being revised for this publication, it was discovered that similar comments have been made about Peacocke's proposal in the Spring 1985 volume of *Religion and Intellectual Life*, which includes a shorter version of Peacocke's lecture and critical responses by Philip Hefner, Ernan McMullin, Robert John Russell, and Robert P. Scharlemann. Thanks must be given to Professor Hefner for pointing me to this volume. In Professor Russell's response, a reference is made to an article by Nancey Murphy to appear in the Spring 1985 volume of the *Pacific Theological Review* which would also develop a Niebuhrian analysis of the relationship between science and religion. It was not possible to include that article in this project.

Bibliography

This bibliography has been divided into two sections for ease of use. Though the distinctions are artificial at times, the first section includes those works most directly related to the analysis of responses to Darwinism.

Primary Sources

Abbot, Francis Ellingwood. "The Conditioned and Unconditioned." *North American Review* 99(1864): 402–48.

_____. "The Development Theory." *Index* 3(1872): 113–15.

_____. "The God of Science." *Index* 3(1872): 37–60.

_____. "Philosophical Biology." *North American Review* 107(1968): 337–422.

_____. "The Philosophy of Space and Time." *North American Review* 99(1864): 64–116.

_____. *Organic Scientific Philosophy: SCIENTIFIC THEISM.* London: The Macmillan Company, 1885.

Abbott, Lyman. *The Evolution of Christianity.* Boston: Houghton, Mifflin and Company, 1892.

_____. *The Theology of an Evolutionist.* Boston: Houghton, Mifflin and Company, 1897.

Alexander, Samuel. *Space, Time and Deity.* New York: The Macmillan Company, 1920.

Alves, Rubem A. "On the Eating Habits of Science." In *Faith and Science in an Unjust World,* Vol. 1. Ed. Roger Shinn. Philadelphia: Fortress Press, 1980, pp. 41–43.

_____. "What Does It Mean to Say the Truth." In *The Sciences and Theology in the Twentieth Century.* Ed. A.R. Peacocke. Notre Dame, Ind.: Notre Dame University Press, 1981, pp. 163–81.

Anderson, Bernhard. "The Earth is the Lord's." In *Is God A Creationist?* Ed. Roland M. Frye. New York: Charles Scribner's Sons, 1983, pp. 176–96.

Baillie, John. *Natural Science and the Spiritual Life.* New York: Charles Scribner's Sons, 1952.

_____, ed. *Natural Theology.* Trans. Peter Fraenkel. London: Geoffrey Bles, Centenary Press, 1946.

Barbour, Ian. *Issues in Science and Religion.* New York: Harper Torchbooks, 1971.

_____. "The Methods of Science and Religion." In *Science Ponders Religion.* Ed. Harlow Shapley. New York: Appleton-Century-Crofts, 1960, pp. 196–215.

_____. *Myths, Models, and Paradigms.* New York: Harper and Row, 1974.

Barth, Karl. *Church Dogmatics,* 4 vols. Trans. and eds. G.W. Bromiley et al. Edinburgh: T. and T.Clark, 1936–69.

Beecher, Henry Ward. *Evolution and Religion.* Part I: Eight Sermons Discussing the Bearings of Evolutionary Philosophy on Fundamental Doctrines of Evangelical Christianity. Boston: The Pilgrim Press, 1885.

———. *Henry Ward Beecher in England, 1886.* London: James Clark and Company, n.d.

Bergson, Henri. *Creative Evolution.* Trans. Arthur Mitchell. New York: Modern Library, 1944.

Bertocci, Peter Anthony. *The Empirical Argument for God in Late British Thought,* Foreword by Frederick Robert Tennant. Cambridge, Mass.: Harvard University Press, 1938.

———. *Introduction to the Philosophy of Religion.* New York: Prentice-Hall Inc., 1951.

Birch, Charles. "A Biological Basis of Human Purpose." *Zygon* 8(1973): 244–60.

———. "Can Evolution Be Accounted for Solely in Terms of Mechanical Causation?" In *Mind in Nature.* Ed. John B. Cobb and David Ray Griffin. Washington, D.C.: University Press of America, 1977, pp. 13–18.

———. "Chance, Necessity and Purpose." In *Studies in the Philosophy of Biology.* Eds. Francisco J. Ayala and T. Dobzhansky. Berkeley: University of California Press, 1974.

———. "Creation and the Creator." *Journal of Religion* 37(1957): 85–98.

———. *Nature and God.* London: SCM Press, 1965.

———. "Nature, Humanity and God in an Ecological Perspective." In *Faith and Science in an Unjust World,* Vol. 1. Ed. Roger Shinn. Philadelphia: Fortress Press, 1980, pp. 62–73.

———. "Participatory Evolution." *Journal of the American Academy of Religion* 40(1972): 141–63.

———. "What Does God Do in the World?" *Union Seminary Quarterly Review* 30(1975): 76–84.

Birch, Charles and Cobb, John B., Jr. *The Liberation of Life.* Cambridge: Cambridge University Press, 1981.

Bowne, Borden Parker. *The Immanence of God.* Boston: Houghton, Mifflin and Company, 1905.

———. *Metaphysics.* New York: American Book Company, 1882, 1898.

———. *Personalism.* Boston: Houghton, Mifflin and Company, 1908.

———. *Theism.* New York: American Book Company, 1887.

Brownson, Henry F., ed. *The Works of Orestes A. Brownson,* Vol. 9. Detroit: Thorndike Nourse, 1884.

Brunner, Emil. *Christian Doctrine of Creation and Redemption.* Trans. Olive Wyon. Philadelphia: Westminster Press, 1952.

———. *Revelation and Reason.* Trans. Olive Wyon. Philadelphia: Westminster Press, 1946.

Burhoe, Ralph Wendell. "The Concepts of God and Soul in a Scientific View of Human Purpose." *Zygon* 8(1973): 412–42.

———. "Five Steps in the Evolution of Man's Knowledge of Good and Evil." *Zygon* 2(1967): 77–87.

———. "The Human Prospect and the 'Lord of History'." *Zygon* 10(1975): 299–375.

———. "Natural Selection and God." *Zygon* 7(1972): 30–63.

———. "The Phenomenon of Religion Seen Scientifically." In *Changing Perspectives in the Study of Religion.* Ed. Allan W. Eister. New York: Wiley-Interscience, 1974, pp. 15–39.

———. "Potentials for Religion from the Sciences." *Zygon* 5(1970): 110–29.

———. "Religion's Role in Human Evolution." *Zygon* 14(1979): 135–62.

———. "Salvation in the Twentieth Century." In *Science Ponders Religion.* Ed. Harlow Shapley. New York: Appleton-Century-Crofts, Inc., 1960, pp. 65–86.

———. "The Source of Civilization in the Natural Selection of Coadapted Information in Genes and Culture." *Zygon* 11(1976): 263–303.

———. *Toward a Scientific Theology.* Belfast: Christian Journals Limited, 1981.

———. "What Does Determine Human Destiny?" *Zygon* 12(1977): 336–89.

———, ed. *Science and Human Values in the Twenty-First Century.* Philadelphia: Westminster Press, 1972.

Bushnell, Horace. *Nature and the Supernatural as Together Constituting the One System of God,* 3rd ed. New York: Charles Scribner, 1858.

_____. "Science and Religion." *Putnam's Magazine* 1(1868): 265–75.

Capra, Fritjof. *The Tao of Physics.* New York: Bantam, 1975.

Cobb, John B., Jr. *Christ in a Pluralistic Age.* Philadelphia: Westminster Press, 1975.

_____. *A Christian Natural Theology: Based on the Thought of Alfred North Whitehead.* Philadelphia: Westminster Press, 1965.

_____. *God and the World.* Philadelphia: Westminster Press, 1969.

_____. *Is It Too Late? A Theology of Ecology.* Beverly Hills, Calif.: Bruce Publishing Company, 1972.

_____. *Liberal Christianity at the Crossroads.* Philadelphia: Fortress Press, 1973.

_____. *Living Options in Protestant Theology.* Philadelphia: Westminster Press, 1960.

_____. "Natural Causality and Divine Action." *Idealistic Studies* 3(1973): 207–22.

_____. "Process Thought and Environmental Issues." *Journal of Religion* 60(1980): 440–58.

_____. *The Structure of Christian Existence.* Philadelphia: Westminster Press, 1967.

Cobb, John B., Jr. and Griffin, David Ray. *Mind in Nature.* Washington, D.C.: University Press of America, 1977.

_____. *Process Theology: An Introductory Exposition.* Philadelphia: Westminster Press, 1976.

Cobb, John B., Jr. and Tracy, David. *Talking About God.* New York: Seabury Press, 1983.

Compton, Arthur H. *The Freedom of Man.* New York: Greenword Press, 1935.

Custance, Arthur C. *Creation or Evolution.* The Doorway Papers, Vol. 4. Grand Rapids, Mich: Zondervan, 1976.

Darwin, Charles. *The Autobiography of Charles Darwin.* Ed. Nora Barlow. New York: W.W. Norton and Co., 1969.

_____. *The Descent of Man, and Selection in Relation to Sex.* Intro. by John T. Bonner and Robert M. May. Princeton: Princeton University Press, 1969.

_____. *The Origin of Species,* 6th ed. Intro. by Julian Huxley. New York: Mentor Books, 1959.

_____. *The Variation of Plants and Animals under Domestication.* 2 vols. 2nd ed. rev. London: John Murray, 1874.

Darwin, Francis, ed. *The Life and Letters of Charles Darwin.* 3 vols. London: John Murray, 1887.

Davies, Paul. *God and the New Physics.* New York: Simon and Schuster, 1983.

Ditfurth, Hoimar von *The Origins of Life: Evolution as Creation.* Trans. Peter Heinegy. New York: Harper and Row, 1982.

Dobzhansky, Theodosius. *Biological Basis of Human Freedom.* New York: Columbia University Press, 1956.

_____. *Biology of Ultimate Concern.* New York: World Publishing Company, 1966, 1969.

_____. *Mankind Evolving.* New Haven, Conn.: Yale University Press, 1962.

_____. "Teilhard de Chardin and the Orientation of Evolution." *Zygon* 3(1968): 242–58.

Drummond, Henry. *The Ascent of Man,* 3rd ed. New York: John Pott and Company, 1894.

_____. *Natural Law in the Spiritual World.* New York: Burt and Company, 1883.

DuNouy, Lecomte. *Human Destiny.* New York: Longman's Green and Company, 1947.

Einstein, Albert. *The World as I See It.* New York: The Wisdom Library, n.d.

Fiske, John. *Darwinism and Other Essays.* Boston: Houghton, Mifflin and Company, 1879, 1885.

_____. *The Destiny of Man Viewed in the Light of His Origin.* Boston: Houghton, Mifflin and Company, 1885.

_____. *The Idea of God as Affected by Modern Knowledge.* Boston: Houghton, Mifflin and Company, 1885, 1900.

_____. *Outlines of Cosmic Philosophy Based on the Doctrine of Evolution, with Criticisms on the Positive Philosophy.* 2 vols. Boston: Houghton, Mifflin and Company, 1874, 1889.

_____. *Through Nature to God.* Boston: Houghton, Mifflin and Company, 1899.

Fothergill, Philip G. *Evolution and Christians.* London: Longmans, Green and Company, Ltd., 1961.

Frothingham, Octavius B. *The Religion of Humanity.* Hicksville, N.Y.: Regina Press, 1975. Reprint of 1883 ed.

Frye, Roland Mushat. "The Two Books of God." *Theology Today* 39(1982): 260–66.

———, ed. *Is God A Creationist?* New York: Charles Scribner's Sons, 1983.

Gilkey, Langdon. "Biblical Symbols in a Scientific Culture." In *Science and Human Values in the Twenty-First Century.* Ed. R.W. Burhoe. Philadelphia: Westminster Press, 1972.

———. "The Concept of Providence in Contemporary Theology." *Journal of Religion* 43(1963): 171–92.

———. "Cosmology, Ontology, and the Travail of Biblical Language." *Journal of Religion* 41(1961): 194–205.

———. "Creationism: The Roots of the Conflict." *Christianity and Crisis* 42(1982): 108–15.

———. "The Creationist Controversy: The Interrelation of Inquiry and Belief." *Science, Technology and Human Values* 7(Summer 1982): 67–71.

———. "The Creationist Issue." In *Cosmology and Theology.* Eds. David Tracy and Nicholas Lash. Concilium 166. New York: Seabury Press, 1983, pp. 55–69.

———. "Darwin and Christian Thought." In *Science and Religion.* Ed. Ian Barbour. New York: Harper and Row, 1968, pp. 159–72. Reprint of 1960 article.

———. "Evolutionary Science and the Dilemma of Freedom and Determinism." *Christian Century* 84(1967):339–43.

———. *Maker of Heaven and Earth: A Study in the Christian Doctrine of Creation.* Garden City, N.Y.: Doubleday Anchor Books, 1959, 1965.

———. *Message and Existence.* New York: Seabury Press, 1980.

———. *Naming the Whirlwind: The Renewal of God-Language.* Indianapolis, Ind.: Bobbs-Merrill Company, 1969.

———. *Reaping the Whirlwind: A Christian Interpretation of History.* New York: Seabury Press, 1976.

———. *Religion and the Scientific Future.* New York: Harper and Row, 1970.

———. "Religious Dimensions of Scientific Inquiry." *Journal of Religion* 50(1970): 245–67.

———. "Robert Heilbroner's Vision of History." *Zygon* 10(1975): 215–33.

———. *Society and the Sacred.* New York: Crossroad, 1981.

Gish, Duane T. *Evolution? The Fossils Say NO!* San Diego: Creation-Life Publishers, 1978.

Gray, Asa. *Darwiniana: Essays and Reviews Pertaining to Darwinism.* Ed. A. Hunter Dupree. Cambridge, Mass.: Harvard University Press, 1963.

———. *The Letters of Asa Gray.* Ed. Jane Loring Gray. 2 vols. Boston: Houghton, Mifflin and Company, 1893.

———. *Natural Science and Religion.* New York: Charles Scribner's Sons, 1880.

Gray, Elizabeth Dodson. *Green Paradise Lost.* Wellesley, Mass.: Roundtable Press, 1979, 1981.

Gustafson, James M. *Ethics from a Theocentric Position.* Vol. 1: *Theology and Ethics.* Chicago: University of Chicago Press, 1981.

Haeckel, Ernst. *The Riddle of the Universe.* Trans. Joseph McCabe. New York: Harper and Brothers, 1900.

Hardin, Garrett J. *Nature and Man's Fate.* New York: Mentor Books, 1959.

Hardy, Alistair. *The Biology of God.* New York: Taplinger Publishing Company, 1976.

Harris, C. Leon, ed. *Evolution: Genesis and Revelations.* Albany, N.Y.: S.U.N.Y. Press, 1981.

Hartshorne, Charles. *Beyond Humanism.* Lincoln: University of Nebraska Press, 1937, 1968.

———. *The Divine Relativity: A Social Conception of God.* New Haven, Conn.: Yale University Press, 1948.

———. *A Natural Theology for Our Time.* LaSalle, Ill: Open Court Publishing Company, 1967.

Haselden, Kyle and Hefner, Philip, eds. *Changing Man.* Garden City, N.Y.: Doubleday and Company, 1968.

Hayward, Alan. *God Is.* Nashville, Tenn.: Thomas Nelson, 1978.

Heim, Karl. *Christian Faith and Natural Science.* Trans. Neville Horton Smith. London: SCM Press, 1953.

———. *The Transfiguration of the Scientific World View.* Trans. W.A. Whitehouse. London: SCM Press, 1953.

Heisenberg, Werner. *The Physical Principles of the Quantum Theory.* Chicago: Dover Publications, 1930.

———. *Physics and Philosophy.* New York: Harper and Row, 1958.

Hendry, George S. *Theology of Nature.* Philadelphia: Westminster Press, 1980.

Hocking, William Ernest. *Science and the Idea of God.* Chapel Hill, N.C.: University of North Carolina Press, 1944.

Hodge, Charles. *Systematic Theology.* 3 vols. New York: Scribner, Armstrong, and Company, 1877.

———. *What Is Darwinism?* New York: Scribner, Armstrong and Company, 1874.

Hofstadter, Douglas R. "Metamagical Themes." *Scientific American,* July 1981, pp. 18ff.

Humanist Manifestos I and II. Buffalo, N.Y.: Prometheus Books, 1933, 1973.

Huxley, Julian. *Essays of a Biologist.* Freeport, N.Y.: Books for Libraries Press, 1970. Reprint of 1923 edition.

———. *Essays of a Humanist.* New York: Harper and Brothers, 1964.

———. *Evolution in Action.* New York: Harper and Brothers, 1953.

———. *Evolution: The Modern Synthesis.* 2nd ed. New York: Wiley and Sons, 1964.

———. "The Evolutionary Vision." In *Issues in Evolution.* Ed. Sol Tax and Charles Callender. Chicago: University of Chicago Press, 1960, pp. 249–61.

———. *The Humanist Frame.* New York: Harper and Row, 1961.

———. *New Bottles for New Wine.* New York: Harper and Brothers, 1957.

———. *Religion without Revelation.* New and revised ed. New York: Harper and Brothers, 1957.

Huxley, Julian and Huxley, Thomas H. *Evolution and Ethics 1893–1943.* London: The Pilot Press, 1947.

Huxley, Thomas H. *Science and the Christian Tradition.* New York: D. Appleton and Company, 1898.

Ingersoll, Robert G. *Complete Lectures.* Chicago: M.A. Donohue and Company, 1910.

———. *Ingersoll: Immortal Infidel.* Ed. R. Greely. Buffalo, N.Y.: Prometheus Books, 1977.

———. *Ingersoll's Greatest Lectures.* New York: Free Thought Press, 1944.

———. *The Works of Robert G. Ingersoll.* New York: The Ingersoll Publishers, Inc., 1900.

Jaki, Stanley. *The Road of Science and the Ways to God.* The Gifford Lectures 1974–75 and 1975–76. Chicago: University of Chicago Press, 1978.

———. "Science and Christian Theism." *Scottish Journal of Theology* 32(1979): 563–70.

———. *Science and Creation: From Eternal Cycles to an Oscillating Universe.* New York: Science History Publication, 1974.

John Paul II. "Science and Christianity." In *Is God A Creationist?* Ed. Roland M. Frye. New York: Charles Scribner's Sons, 1983, pp. 141–54.

———. *The Pope Speaks* 26(1981): 209–13, 350–52.

———. *The Pope Speaks* 28(1983): 245–49.

Koestler, Arthur. *The Ghost in the Machine.* New York: Macmillan, 1967.

———. *Janus: A Summing Up.* London: Hutchison Co., 1978.

Küng, Hans. *Does God Exist?* Trans. Edward Quinn. Garden City, N.Y.: Doubleday and Company, 1980.

LeConte, Joseph. *Evolution: Its Nature, Its Evidences, and Its Relation to Religious Thought.* New York: D. Appleton and Company, 1888, 1897.

————. *Religion and Science.* New York: D. Appleton and Company, 1873.

McCosh, James. *Christianity and Positivism.* New York: Robert Carter and Brothers, 1871.

————. *The Development Hypothesis.* New York: Robert Carter and Brothers, 1876.

————. *Intuitions of the Mind Inductively Investigated.* New York: Robert Carter and Brothers, 1867.

————. *The Method of the Divine Government, Physical and Moral.* 12th ed. London: Macmillan, 1850, 1882.

————. *Realistic Philosophy Defended in a Philosophic Series.* New York: Charles Scribner's Sons, 1887.

————. *The Religious Aspect of Evolution.* The Bedell Lectures, 1887. New York: G.P. Putnam's Sons, 1888.

McLean v. Arkansas Board of Education, 529 F. Supp. 1255 (E.D. Arkansas, 1982). Reprinted in *Science* 215(1982): 934–43.

Macquarrie, John. "The Idea of a Theology of Nature." *Union Seminary Quarterly Review* 30(1975): 69–75.

Metz, Johannes, ed. *The Evolving World and Theology.* Concilium 26. New York: Paulist Press, 1967.

Miller, Perry, ed. *American Thought: Civil War to World War I.* New York: Holt, Rinehart, Winston, 1954

Moltmann, Jürgen. *The Future of Creation.* Trans. Margaret Kohl. Philadelphia: Fortress Press, 1979.

————. *The Trinity and the Kingdom.* Trans. Margaret Kohl. Philadelphia: Fortress Press, 1981.

Monod, Jacques. *Chance and Necessity.* Trans. Austyn Wainhause. New York: Vintage Books, 1972.

Montefiore, Hugh, ed. *Man and Nature.* London: William Collins Sons and Company, 1975.

Moore, John N. and Slusher, Harold S. *Biology: A Search for Order in Complexity.* Rev. ed. Grand Rapids, Mich.: Zondervan, 1974.

Morgan, C. Lloyd. *Emergent Evolution.* London: William and Norgate, 1923.

Morris, Henry M. *Evolution and the Modern Christian.* Grand Rapids, Mich.: Baker Book House, 1967.

————. *Scientific Creationism.* San Diego: Creation-Life Publishers, 1974.

————. *A Symposium on Creation.* Grand Rapids, Mich.: Baker Book House, 1968.

————. *The Twilight of Evolution.* Grand Rapids, Mich.: Baker Book House, 1963.

Niebuhr, H. Richard. *Christ and Culture.* New York: Harper Torchbooks, 1956.

————. *Radical Monotheism and Western Culture.* New York: Harper Torchbooks, 1970.

Niebuhr, Reinhold. *Beyond Tragedy.* New York: Charles Scribner's Sons, 1939.

————. *Christian Realism and Political Problems.* New York: Charles Scribner's Sons, 1953.

————. "Christianity and Darwin's Revolution." In *A Book That Shook the World.* Ed. Ralph Buchsbaum. Pittsburgh: University of Pittsburgh Press, 1958.

————. *Faith and History.* New York: Charles Scribner's Sons, 1949.

————. "Intellectual Autobiography." In *Reinhold Niebuhr: His Religious, Social, and Political Thought.* Ed. C.W. Kegley and R.W. Bretall. New York: Macmillan, 1956.

————. *The Nature and Destiny of Man.* 2 vols. New York: Charles Scribner's Sons, 1964.

————. *The Self and the Dramas of History.* New York: Charles Scribner's Sons, 1955.

————. "The Truth in Myths." In *The Nature of Religious Experience.* Ed. J.S. Dixler. New York: Harper and Brothers, 1937.

————. "The Tyranny of Science." *Theology Today* 10 (1954): 464–73.

O'Brien, John A. *Evolution and Religion.* New York: Century Press, 1932.

O'Connor, Daniel and Oakley, Francis. *Creation: The Impact of an Idea.* New York: Scribner's Sons, 1969.

Osborn, Robert T. "A Christian View of Creation for a Scientific Age." In *New Theology No. 10*. Ed. Martin Marty and Dean Peerman. New York: Macmillan, 1973.

Otto, Rudolf. *Naturalism and Religion*. Trans. J.A. Thomson, ed. W.D. Morrison. London: William and Norgate, 1907.

Pannenberg, Wolfhart. "The Doctrine of the Spirit and the Task of a Theology of Nature." In *New Theology No. 10*. Ed. Martin Marty and Dean Peerman. New York: Macmillan, 1973, pp. 17–37.

———. "The Nature of a Theological Statement." *Zygon* 7(1972): 6–19.

———. "Theological Questions to Scientists." In *The Sciences and Theology in the Twentieth Century*. Ed. A.R. Peacocke. Notre Dame, Ind.: University of Notre Dame Press, 1981, pp. 3–16.

———. *Theology and the Philosophy of Science*. Trans. F. McDonagh. Philadelphia: Westminster Press, 1976.

Paul VI. *Gaudium et Spes*. In *The Documents of Vatican II*. Ed. W.M. Abbott. Chicago: Follett Publishing Co., 1966.

Peacocke, Arthur R. "Biological Evolution and Christian Theology Today." *Theology* 87(1984): 34–39.

———. *Creation and the World of Science*. The Bampton Lectures, 1978. Oxford: Clarendon Press, 1978.

———. *Intimations of Reality: Critical Realism in Science and Religion*. The Mendenhall Lectures, 1983. Notre Dame, Ind.: University of Notre Dame Press, 1984.

———. "The Nature and Purpose of Man in Science and Christian Theology." *Zygon* 8(1973): 373–94.

———. "Reductionism." *Zygon* 11(1976): 307–34.

———. "A Sacramental View of Nature." In *Man and Nature*. Ed. Hugh Montefiore. London: William Collins Sons and Company, 1975, pp. 132–42.

———. *Science and the Christian Experiment*. London: Oxford University Press, 1971.

———. "Sociobiology and Its Theological Implications." *Zygon* 19(1984): 171–84.

———, ed. *The Sciences and Theology in the Twentieth Century*. Notre Dame, Ind.: University Of Notre Dame Press, 1981.

Peters, Karl. "Evolutionary Naturalism: Survival as a Value." *Zygon* 15(1980): 213–22.

———. "The Image of God as a Model for Humanization." *Zygon* 9(1974): 98–125.

———. "Modern Science and Religious Pluralism." *National Forum* 62(Spring 1983): 15–16.

———. "Religion and an Evolutionary Theory of Knowledge." *Zygon* 17(1982): 98–125.

Pius XII. *Modern Science and God*. Ed. and trans. P.J. McLaughlin. New York: Philosophical Library, 1954.

Polanyi, Michael. *Personal Knowledge*. Chicago: University of Chicago Press, 1958, 1962.

———. *Faith, Science and Society*. Chicago: University of Chicago Press, 1946, 1964.

Pollard, William G. *Chance and Providence*. New York: Charles Scribner's Sons, 1958.

Popper, Karl. "Autobiography." In *The Philosophy of Karl Popper*, Book 1. Ed. P. Schlipp. LaSalle, Ill.: Open Court, 1974.

———. Letter to the editor. *New Scientist* 87(1980): 611.

———. "Natural Selection and the Emergence of Mind." *Dialectica* 32(1978): 339–55.

Presbyterian Church in the United States. *The Dialogue between Science and Theology*. Atlanta: P.C.U.S., 1982.

Rabut, Olivier A. *God in an Evolving Universe*. Trans. W. Springer. New York: Herder and Herder, 1966.

Rahner, Karl. "Christology within an Evolutionary View of the World." In *Theological Investigations, V*. Trans. Karl-H. Kruger. Baltimore: Helicon Press, 1966, pp. 157–92.

———. *Hominisation: The Evolutionary Origin of Man as a Theological Problem*. Trans. W.J.

O'Hara. New York: Herder and Herder, 1965.

―――. "On the Relationship between Theology and the Contemporary Sciences." In *Theological Investigations, XIII*. Trans. David Bourke. New York: Seabury Press, 1975, pp. 94–102.

―――. *Science, évolution et pensée chrétienne*. Paris: Desclee, 1967.

―――. *Spirit in the World*. Trans. William Dych. New York: Herder and Herder, 1968.

―――. "Theology Engaged in an Interdisciplinary Dialogue with the Sciences." In *Theological Investigations, XIII*. Trans. David Bourke. New York: Seabury Press, 1975, pp. 80–93.

―――. "The Unity of Spirit and Matter in the Christian Understanding." In *Theological Investigations, VI*. Trans. Karl-H. and Boniface Kruger. New York: Seabury Press, 1969, 1974, pp. 153–77.

Rifkin, Jeremy. *Algeny: A New Word—A New World*. New York: The Viking Press, 1983.

Ruether, Rosemary Radford. "A Feminist Perspective on Religion and Science." In *Faith and Science in an Unjust World*, Vol. 1. Ed. Roger Shinn. Philadelphia: Fortress Press, 1980, pp. 55–58.

―――. *New Woman, New Earth*. New York: Seabury Press, 1975.

―――. *Sexism and God-Talk: Toward a Feminist Theology*. Boston: Beacon Press, 1983.

Russell, Alan and Gerhart, Mary. *Metaphoric Process: The Creation of Scientific and Religious Understanding*. Fort Worth: Texas Christian University Press, 1984.

Sandon, Leo, Jr. "Darwinism and Religious Thought in America." Lecture in *Darwinism Reconsidered* series, Florida State University, October 19, 1982.

Savage, Minot Judson. *The Irrepressible Conflict between Two World-Theories*. Boston: Arena Publishing Co., 1892.

―――. *The Religion of Evolution*. Boston: Lockwood, Brooks and Co., 1876.

Schilling, Harold K. *The New Consciousness in Science and Religion*. Philadelphia: Pilgrim Press, 1973.

―――. *Science and Religion*. New York: Charles Scribner's Sons, 1962.

Schurman, Jacob G. *The Ethical Import of Darwinism*. New York: Charles Scribner's Sons, 1893.

Shapley, Harlow, ed. *Science Ponders Religion*. New York: Appleton-Century-Crofts, 1960.

Shinn, Roger L., ed. *Faith and Science in an Unjust World*. Report of the World Council of Churches' Conference on Faith, Science, and the Future, M.I.T., Cambridge, USA, 12–24 July 1979. Volume 1: Plenary Presentations. Philadelphia: Fortress Press, 1980.

Shipley, Maynard. *The War on Modern Science*. New York: A. A. Knopf, 1927.

Smith, Huston. *Beyond the Post-Modern Mind*. New York: Crossroad, 1982.

―――. "Evolution and Evolutionism." *Christian Century* 99(1982): 755–57.

―――. *Forgotten Truth: The Primordial Tradition*. New York: Harper and Row, 1976.

―――. "Science and Theology: The Unstable Detente." *Anglican Theological Review* 63(1981): 367–79.

―――. "Scientism in Sole Command." *Christianity and Crisis* 42(1982): 197–98.

Smuts, Jan. *Holism and Evolution*. New York: Macmillan, 1926.

Tax, Sol and Callender, Charles. *Issues in Evolution*. Volume 3 of *Evolution After Darwin*. Chicago: University of Chicago Press, 1960.

Teilhard de Chardin, Pierre. *Christianity and Evolution*. Trans. René Hague. New York: Harper and Row, 1968.

―――. *The Divine Milieu*. New York: Harper and Row Torchbook, 1968.

―――. *The Future of Man*. Trans. Norman Denny. New York: Harper Colophon Books, 1964.

―――. *Hymn of the Universe*. Trans. Gerald Vann. New York: Harper Torchbook, 1969.

―――. *The Phenomenon of Man*. Trans. Bernard Wall and introd. Julian Huxley. New York: Harper Torchbook, 1965.

———. *Science and Christ.* Trans. René Hague. New York: Harper and Row, 1968.

———. *Toward the Future.* Trans. René Hague. New York: Harcourt Brace Jovanovich, 1975.

Temple, Frederick. *The Relations Between Religion and Science.* London: Macmillan, 1885.

Temple, William. *Nature, Man and God.* London: Macmillan, 1949.

Tennant, Frederick Robert. "The Influence of Darwin upon Theology." *Quarterly Review* 211(1909): 418–40.

———. *Philosophical Theology.* 2 vols. Cambridge: Cambridge University Press, 1930.

———. *Philosophy of the Sciences.* Cambridge, Mass.: Harvard University Press, 1932. Archon Books reprint, 1973.

Tillich, Paul. *Dynamics of Faith.* New York: Harper Torchbook, 1958.

———. *Systematic Theology.* 3 vols. Chicago: University of Chicago Press, 1951–1963.

———. *Theology of Culture.* Ed. Robert C. Kimball. New York: Oxford University Press, 1959.

Tracy, David and Lash, Nicholas. *Cosmology and Theology.* Concilium 166. New York: Seabury Press, 1983.

Vawter, Bruce. "Creationism: Creative Misuse of the Bible." In *Is God A Creationist?* Ed. Roland M. Frye. New York: Charles Scribner's Sons, 1983, pp. 71–82.

Whitehead, Alfred North. *The Concept of Nature.* Cambridge: Cambridge University Press, 1920.

———. *Process and Reality.* Corrected ed., eds. David Ray Griffin and Donald W. Sherburne. New York: The Free Press, 1929, 1978.

———. *Religion in the Making.* New York: Meridian Books, 1926.

———. *Science and the Modern World.* New York: The Free Press, 1925, 1967.

Wieman, Henry Nelson. "Cooperative Functions of Science and Religion." *Zygon* 3(1968): 32–58.

———. *The Directive in History.* Boston: Beacon Press, 1949.

———. "Intellectual Autobiography." In *The Empirical Theology of Henry Nelson Wieman.* Ed. Robert Bretall. Carbondale: Southern Illinois University Press, 1963.

———. *Intellectual Foundation of Faith.* New York: Philosophical Library, 1961.

———. *The Issues of Life.* New York: Abingdon, 1930.

———. *Man's Ultimate Commitment.* Carbondale: Southern Illinois University Press, 1958.

———. "The Problem of Religious Inquiry." *Zygon* 1(1966): 373–400.

———. *Religious Experience and Scientific Method.* New York: Macmillan, 1926.

———. *Religious Inquiry: Some Explorations.* Boston: Beacon Press, 1968.

———. *Seeking a Faith for a New Age.* Ed. C.L. Hepler. Metuchen, N.J.: Scarecrow Press, 1975.

———. "Science and a New Religious Reformation." *Zygon* 1(1966): 125–39.

———. *The Source of Human Good.* Carbondale: Southern Illinois University Press, 1946.

———. *The Wrestle of Religion with Truth.* Chicago: University of Chicago Press, 1928.

———. "Wrong Ways to Justify Religion." *Christian Century* 46(1929): 1571–73.

Wilson, Edward O. *On Human Nature.* New York: Bantam, 1978.

———. "The Relation of Science to Theology." *Zygon* 15(1980): 425–34.

———. *Sociobiology: The New Synthesis.* Cambridge, Mass.: Harvard University Press, 1975.

Wilson, Edward O. and Lumsden, C.J. *Genes, Mind and Culture.* Cambridge, Mass.: Harvard University Press, 1981.

———. *Promethean Fire.* Cambridge, Mass.: Harvard University Press, 1983.

Woodrow, James. *Dr. James Woodrow.* Ed. Marion W. Woodrow. Columbia, S.C.: R.L. Bryan and Co., 1909.

Wright, Chauncey. *Letters of Chauncey Wright.* Ed. J.B. Thayer. Cambridge, Mass.: 1878.

———. *Philosophical Discussions.* New York: Henry Holt and Company, 1877.

Wright, G. Frederick. "Calvinism and Darwinism." *Bibliotheca Sacra* 66(1909): 685–91.

———. *The Logic of Christian Evidences,* 4th ed. Andover, Mass.: Warren F. Draper, 1897.

_____. *Scientific Aspects of Christian Evidences.* New York: D. Appleton and Company, 1898.
_____. *Studies in Science and Religion.* Andover, Mass.: Warren F. Draper, 1882.
Zahm, John A. *Evolution and Dogma.* Chicago: D.H. McBride and Co., 1896.
_____. *Scientific Theory and Catholic Dogma.* Chicago: D.H. McBride and Co., 1896.

Secondary Sources

Abelé, Jean. *Christianity and Science.* Trans. R.F. Trevett. New York: Hawthorne Books, 1961.
Abrecht, Paul, ed. *Faith and Science in an Unjust World.* Report of the World Council of Churches' Conference on Faith, Science, and the Future, M.I.T., Cambridge, Mass., USA. 12–24 July 1979. Volume 2: Reports and Recommendations. Philadelphia: Fortress Press, 1980.
_____, ed. *Faith, Science, and the Future.* Philadelphia: Fortress Press, 1978.
Ahlstrom, Sidney. *A Religious History of the American People.* 2 vols. Garden City, N.Y.: Image Books, 1975.
_____. "The Scottish Philosophy and American Theology." *Church History* 24(1955): 257–72.
_____. *Theology in America.* Indianapolis, Ind.: Bobbs-Merrill, 1967.
Albright, John R. "A Physicist's View of Evolution." Lecture in *Darwinism Reconsidered* series, Florida State University, September 7, 1982.
Alszeghy, Zoltan. "Development in the Doctrinal Formulation of the Church Concerning the Theory of Evolution," in *The Evolving World and Theology.* Ed. J. Metz. Concilium 26. New York: Paulist Press, 1967, pp. 25–33.
Altner, Günter. "The Evolutionary Shift in Cosmology and Theology." In *Cosmology and Theology.* Eds. David Tracy and N. Lash. Concilium 166. New York: Seabury Press, 1983, pp. 21–26.
_____. *Schöpfungsglaube und Entwicklungsglaube in der protestantischen Theologie zwischen Ernst Haeckel und Teilhard de Chardin.* Zurich: EVZ-Verlag, 1965.
Anderson, David B. *Robert Ingersoll.* New York: Twayne Publishers, Inc., 1972.
Appleman, Philip, ed. *Darwin: A Norton Critical Edition.* 2nd ed. New York: W.W. Norton, 1979.
Arnold, Anthony. "The Emergence of Hierarchical Structure in Evolutionary Theory: Implications for Darwinism." Lecture in *Darwinism Reconsidered* series, Florida State University, September 21, 1982.
Attfield, Robin. "Science and Creation." *Journal of Religion* 58(1978): 37–47.
Aubrey, Edwin Ewart. "Religious Bearings of the Modern Scientific Movement." In *Environmental Factors in Christian History.* Eds. J. T. McNeill et al. Chicago: University of Chicago Press, 1939.
Austin, William H. *The Relevance of Natural Science to Theology.* New York: Barnes and Noble, 1976.
Ayala, Francisco J. and Dobzhansky, Theodosius. *Studies in the Philosophy of Biology.* Berkeley: University of California Press, 1974.
Bakan, David. *The Duality of Human Existence.* Boston: Beacon Press, 1966.
Barbour, Ian. *Christianity and the Scientist.* New York: Association Press, 1960.
_____. "Five Ways of Reading Teilhard." *Soundings* 51(1968): 115–45.
_____. *Science and Secularity.* New York: Harper and Row, 1970.
_____. "The Significance of Teilhard." *Christian Century* 84(1967): 1098–1102.
_____. *Technology, Environment, and Human Values.* New York: Praeger, 1980.
_____. "Teilhard's Process Metaphysic." *Journal of Religion* 49(1969): 136–59.
_____, ed. *Earth Might Be Fair.* Englewood Cliffs, N.J.: Prentice-Hall, 1972.
_____, ed. *Science and Religion: New Perspectives on the Dialogue.* New York: Harper and Row, 1968.

_____, ed. *Western Man and Environmental Ethics.* Reading, Mass.: Addison-Wesley, 1973.

Barker, Eileen. "Science as Theology: The Theological Function of Western Science." In *The Sciences and Theology in the Twentieth Century.* Ed. A.R. Peacocke. Notre Dame, Ind.: Notre Dame University Press, 1981, pp. 262–80.

Barnes, Michael. "Faith and Imagination in Science and Religion." *Theology Today* 40(1983): 15–24.

Bedau, Hugo Adam. "Complementarity and the Relation between Science and Religion." *Zygon* 9(1974): 202–24.

Benz, Ernst. *Evolution and Christian Hope.* Trans. Heinz G. Frank. Garden City, N.Y.: Doubleday and Co., 1966.

Berry, Richard W. "The Beginning." *Theology Today* 39(1982): 249–58.

Betts, John Rickard. "Darwinism, Evolution, and American Catholic Thought, 1860–1900." *Catholic Historical Review* 45(1959): 161–85.

Black, Max. *Models and Metaphors.* Ithaca, N.Y.: Cornell University Press, 1962.

Blinderman, Charles. "Unnatural Selection: Creationism and Evolutionism." *Journal of Church and State* 24(Winter 1982): 73–86.

Bollier, Paul F. *American Thought in Transition: The Impact of Evolutionary Naturalism.* Chicago: Rand McNally and Co., 1969.

Bowden, Henry W. *Church History in the Age of Science.* Chapel Hill: University of North Carolina Press, 1971.

Bowker, J.W. "The Aeolian Harp." *Zygon* 15(1980): 307–33.

_____. "Did God Create this Universe?" In *The Sciences and Theology in the Twentieth Century.* Ed. A.R. Peacocke. Notre Dame, Ind.: University of Notre Dame Press, 1981, pp. 98–126.

Bowler, Peter J. "Darwinism and the Argument from Design." *Journal of the History of Biology* 10(1977): 29–43.

_____. *Evolution: The History of an Idea.* Berkeley: University of California Press, 1984.

Bozeman, Theodore Dwight. *Protestants in an Age of Science.* Chapel Hill: University of North Carolina Press, 1977.

Brown, Harold I. *Perception, Theory, and Commitment.* Chicago: University of Chicago Press, 1977.

Brown, Robert Hanbury. "The Nature of Science." In *Faith and Science in an Unjust World,* Vol. I. Ed. Roger Shinn. Philadelphia: Fortress Press, 1980, pp. 31–40.

Brush, Stephen G. "Creationism/Evolution: The Case AGAINST 'Equal Time'." *The Science Teacher,* April 1981, pp. 29–33.

_____. "Ghosts from the Nineteenth Century." In *Scientists Confront Creationism.* Ed. Laurie Godfrey. New York: W.W. Norton, 1983, pp. 49–84.

Bube, Richard H. *The Encounter between Christianity and Science.* Grand Rapids, Mich.: Eerdmans, 1968.

Bunch, Richard Alan. "Evolution and Contemporary Religious Sensibility." Ph.D. dissertation, Vanderbilt University, 1971.

Caldin, Edward Francis. *Science and Christian Apologetic.* Oxford: Blackfriars, 1951.

Campbell, Dennis M. *Authority and the Renewal of American Theology.* Philadelphia: Pilgrim Press, 1976.

Campbell, John Angus. "Nature, Religion, and Emotional Response." *Victorian Studies* 18(1974): 159–74.

_____. "A Rhetorical Analysis of *The Origin of Species* and of American Christianity's Response to Darwinism." Ph.D. dissertation, University of Pittsburgh, 1968.

Carter, Paul A. "Science and the Death of God." *American Scholar* 42(1973): 406–21.

_____. *The Spiritual Crisis of the Gilded Age.* DeKalb, Ill.: Northern Illinois University Press, 1971.

Cauthen, Kenneth. *The Impact of American Religious Liberalism,* 2nd ed. Washington, D.C.: University Press of America, 1983.

———. *Science, Secularization, and God.* Nashville, Tenn.: Abingdon Press, 1969.

Chadwick, Owen. *The Secularization of the European Mind in the Nineteenth Century.* Cambridge: Cambridge University Press, 1975.

———. *The Victorian Church.* 2 vols. London: A. and C. Black, 1966.

Chauchard, Paul. *Science and Religion.* Trans. S.J. Lester. New York: Hawthorne Books, 1962.

Cherfas, Jeremy and Gribbin, John. *The Monkey Puzzle.* New York: McGraw-Hill Book Co., 1982.

———. "Updating Man's Ancestry." *The New York Times Magazine,* August 29, 1982, pp. 22–25, 55.

Cherry, Conrad. *Nature and Religious Imagination.* Philadelphia: Fortress Press, 1980.

Cole, John R. "Scopes and Beyond: Antievolutionism and American Culture." In *Scientists Confront Creationism.* Ed. Laurie Godfrey. New York: W.W. Norton, 1983.

Collingwood, R.G. *The Idea of Nature.* New York: Oxford University Press, 1945, 1981.

Collins, James. "Darwin's Impact on Philosophy." In *Darwin's Vision and Christian Perspectives.* Ed. Walter Ong. New York: Macmillan, 1960, pp. 33–103.

Commager, Henry Steele. *The American Mind.* New Haven, Conn.: Yale University Press, 1950.

Conklin, Paul K. *American Christianity in Crisis.* The First Charles Edmondson Historical Lectures. Waco, Texas: Baylor University Press, 1978.

Cooper, R.M. "Religion, Theology and Science." *Anglican Theological Review.* 62(1980): 171–76.

Cornell, John F. "From Creation to Evolution." *Journal of the History of Biology* 16(1983): 137–70.

Coulson, Charles A. *Science and Christian Belief.* Chapel Hill: University of North Carolina Press, 1955.

Cracraft, Joel. "The Scientific Response to Creationism." *Science, Technology, and Human Values* 7(Summer 1982): 79–85.

Cupitt, Don. "Darwinism and English Religious Thought." *Theology* 78(1975): 125–31.

———. *The Worlds of Science and Religion.* New York: Hawthorne Books, 1976.

Daniels, George, ed. *Darwinism Comes to America.* Waltham, Mass.: Blaisdell Publishing Company, 1968.

D'Aquila, Eugene G. "Senses of Reality in Science and Religion." *Zygon* 17(1982): 361–84.

Davis, Dennis Royal. "Presbyterian Attitudes toward Science and the Coming of Darwinism in America." Ph.D. dissertation, University of Illinois, 1980.

Dawkins, Richard. *The Selfish Gene.* New York: Oxford University Press, 1976.

Dean, William. "An American Theology." *Process Studies* 12(1982): 111–28.

Deely, John N. "Philosophical Dimensions of the *Origin of Species*." *The Thomist* 33(1969): 75–149, 251–335.

Deely, John N. and Nogar, Raymond J., eds. *The Problem of Evolution.* New York: Appleton-Century-Crofts, 1973.

DeNicola, Daniel R. "Sociobiology and Religion." *Zygon* 15(1980): 407–23.

Dillenberger, John. *Protestant Thought and Natural Science.* Garden City, N.Y.: Doubleday and Co., 1960.

———. "Science and Religion Today." *Christian Century* 76(1959): 72–74.

Draper, John William. *History of the Conflict between Religion and Science.* New ed. London: Pioneer Press, 1902, 1923.

Dupree, A. Hunter. *Asa Gray, 1810–1888.* Cambridge, Mass.: The Belknap Press of Harvard University Press, 1959.

Eccles, John C. *The Human Mystery.* The Gifford Lectures, University of Edinburgh 1977–78. London: Routledge and Kegan Paul, 1979.

Eisely, Loren. *Darwin's Century: Evolution and the Men Who Discovered It.* Garden City, NY: Anchor Books, 1961.

Eldredge, Niles. *The Monkey Business.* New York: Washington Square Press, 1982.

_____. and Tattersall, Ian. *The Myths of Human Evolution.* New York: Columbia University Press, 1982.

Ellegard, Alvar. *Darwin and the General Reader: The Reception of Darwin's Theory of Evolution in the British Periodical Press, 1859-1872.* Goteberg: Elanders Boktryckeri Aktiebolag, 1958.

Ellis, William E. "Evolution, Fundamentalism, and the Historians." *The Historian* 44(1981): 15–35.

Ferré, Frederick. "Faith, Science, and Creation." *National Forum* 62(Spring 1983): 12–14.

_____. *Language, Logic and God.* New York: Harper and Row, 1961.

_____. "Mapping the Logic of Models in Science and Theology." *Christian Scholar* 46(1963): 9–39.

_____. "Metaphors, Models, and Religion." *Soundings* 51(1968): 327–45.

_____. "Religious World Modeling and Postmodern Science." *Journal of Religion* 62(1982): 261–71.

Fisch, Max. "Evolution in American Philosophy." *Philosophical Review* 56(1947): 357–73.

Foster, Frank Hugh. *The Modernist Movement in American Theology.* Freeport, N.Y.: Books for Libraries Press, 1939.

Foster, Michael B. "The Christian Doctrine of Creation and the Rise of Modern Science." *Mind* ns 43(1934): 446–68; 44(1935): 439–66; 45(1936): 1–27.

Foxe, Arthur N. *The Common Sense from Heraclitus to Peirce.* New York: The Turnbridge Press, 1962.

Freske, Stanley. "Creationist Misunderstanding, Misrepresentation, and Misuse of the Second Law of Thermodynamics." *Creation/Evolution* 4(1981): 8–16.

Futuyama, Douglas J. *Science on Trial.* New York: Pantheon Press, 1984.

Gale, Barry G. *Evolution without Evidence.* Albuquerque: University of New Mexico Press, 1982.

Ghiselin, Michael. "The Individual in the Darwinian Revolution." *New Literary History* 3(1979): 113–34.

_____. *The Triumph of the Darwinian Method.* Berkeley: University of California Press, 1969.

Gillespie, Neal C. *Charles Darwin and the Problem of Creation.* Chicago: University of Chicago Press, 1979.

Gillispie, Charles Coulston. *Genesis and Geology.* Cambridge, Mass.: Harvard University Press, 1951.

Goatley, James L. and Graham, W. Fred. "Natural Theology and the Natural Sciences." *Religion in Life* 47(1978): 23–32.

Godfrey, Laurie R., ed. *Scientists Confront Creationism.* New York: W.W. Norton and Co., 1983.

Goodman, Lenn E. and Goodman, Madeleine J. "Creation and Evolution: Another Round in an Ancient Struggle." *Zygon* 18(1983): 3–43.

Gould, Stephen Jay. "Darwin's Untimely Burial—Again!" In *Scientists Confront Creationism.* Ed. Laurie Godfrey. New York: W.W. Norton and Co., 1983, pp. 139–46. Reprint of 1976 *Natural History* article.

_____. "Darwinism and the Expansion of Evolutionary Theory." *Science* 216(1982): 80–87.

_____. *Ever Since Darwin: Reflections in Natural History.* New York: W.W. Norton and Co., 1977.

_____. *Hen's Teeth and Horse's Toes.* New York: W.W. Norton and Co., 1983.

Graham, W. Fred and Goatley, James L. "Issues in Science and Religion." *Religion in Life* 49(1980): 157–68.

Greene, John C. *Darwin and the Modern World View.* Baton Rouge: Louisiana State University Press, 1961.

——. "Darwin and Religion." In *Science Ponders Religion.* Ed. Harlow Shapley. New York: Appleton-Century-Crofts, 1960, pp. 254–76.

——. *The Death of Adam: Evolution and Its Impact on Western Thought.* Ames, Iowa: Iowa State University Press, 1959.

——. *Science, Ideology, and World View.* Berkeley: University of California Press, 1981.

Gregorios, Paulus. "Science and Faith: Complementary or Contradictory?" In *Faith and Science in an Unjust World,* Vol. 1. Ed. Roger Shinn. Philadelphia: Fortress Press, 1980, pp. 46–55.

Gruber, Howard E. and Barrett, Paul K. *Darwin on Man.* London: Wildwood House, 1974.

Gruner, Rolf. "Science, Nature and Christianity." *Journal of Theological Studies* 26(1975): 55–81.

Haught, John F. *Nature and Purpose.* Washington, D.C.: University Press of America, 1980.

——. *The Cosmic Adventure.* New York: Paulist Press, 1984.

Hefner, Philip. "Is/Ought: A Risky Relationship between Theology and Science." In *The Sciences and Theology in the Twentieth Century.* Ed. A.R. Peacocke. Notre Dame, Ind.: University of Notre Dame Press, 1981, pp. 58–78.

——. "Science and Religion: Athens and Jerusalem in Dialogue about Athens' Salvation." *Zygon* 14(1979): 217–28.

——. "Sociobiology, Ethics, and Theology." *Zygon* 19(1984): 185–207.

——. "To What Extent Can Science Replace Metaphysics?" *Zygon* 12(1977): 88–104.

Hesse, Mary B. "Cosmology as Myth." In *Cosmology and Theology.* Eds. David Tracy and Nicholas Lash. Concilium 166. New York: Seabury Press, 1983.

——. "On the Alleged Incompatibility between Christianity and Science." In *Man and Nature.* Ed. Hugh Montefiore. London: William Collins Sons and Co., 1975.

——. *Models and Analogies in Science.* Notre Dame, Ind.: University of Notre Dame Press, 1966.

——. *Science and the Human Imagination.* London: SCM Press, 1954.

Himmelfarb, Gertrude. *Darwin and the Darwinian Revolution.* New York: W.W. Norton and Co., 1959, 1962.

Hodge, M.J.S. "England." In *The Comparative Reception of Darwinism.* Ed. T.F. Glick. Austin: University of Texas Press, 1974, pp. 168–205.

Hoeveler, J. David. *James McCosh and the Scottish Intellectual Tradition.* Princeton, N.J.: Princeton University Press, 1981.

Hofstadter, Richard. *Social Darwinism in American Thought.* rev. ed. Boston: Beacon Press, 1944, 1955.

Holifield, E. Brooks. *The Gentlemen Theologians.* Durham, N.C.: Duke University Press, 1978.

Hooykaas, Reijer. *Natural Law and Divine Miracle.* Leiden: E.J. Brill, 1962.

——. *Religion and the Rise of Modern Science.* Grand Rapids, Mich.: Eerdman's, 1972.

Horton, Walter Marshall. *Theism and the Scientific Spirit.* New York: Harper and Brothers, 1933.

Hovenkamp, Herbert. *Science and Religion in America, 1800–1860.* Philadelphia: University of Pennsylvania Press, 1978.

Howe, Daniel Walker, ed. *Victorian America.* Philadelphia: University of Pennsylvania Press, 1976.

Hubner, Jürgen. "Schöpfungsglaube und Theologie der Natur." *Evangelische Theologie* 37(1977): 49–68.

Hull, David L. "Charles Darwin and Nineteenth-Century Philosophies of Science." In *Foundations of Scientific Method: The Nineteenth Century.* Ed. Ronald N. Giere and Richard S. Westfall. Bloomington: Indiana University Press, 1973, pp. 115–32.

_____. *Darwin and His Critics.* Cambridge, Mass.: Harvard University Press, 1973.

_____. "The Metaphysics of Evolution." *The British Journal for the History of Science.* 3(1967): 309–37.

_____. *Philosophy of Biological Science.* Englewood Cliffs, N.J.: Prentice-Hall, Inc., 1974.

Hulsbosch, Ansfried. *God in Creation and Evolution.* Trans. M. Versfeld. New York: Sheed and Ward, 1965.

Hutchison, William R. *The Modernist Impulse in American Protestantism.* Cambridge, Mass.: Harvard University Press, 1976.

Hyers, Conrad. "Biblical Literalism: Constricting the Cosmic Dance." *Christian Century* 99(1982): 823–27.

Illick, Joseph E. "The Reception of Darwinism at the Theological Seminary and College at Princeton." *Journal of the Presbyterian Historical Society* 38(1960): 152–65, 234–41.

James, Frances C. "On Nature Vs. Nurture: The Redwing Experiment." *Florida State University Bulletin Research in Review* 77(June 1984): 3–5, 10.

Johnson, Daryl Freeman. "The Attitudes of Princeton Theologians Toward Darwinism and Evolution from 1859–1929." Ph.D. dissertation, University of Iowa, 1968.

Jonas, Hans. *The Phenomenon of Life: Toward a Philosophy of Biology.* New York: Harper and Row, 1966.

Jones, James W. *The Texture of Knowledge.* Washington, D.C.: University Press of America, 1981.

Jukes, Thomas H. "Molecular Evidence for Evolution." In *Scientists Confront Creationism.* Ed. Laurie Godfrey. New York: W.W. Norton and Co., 1983, pp. 117–38.

Kaufman, Gordon D. *God the Problem.* Cambridge, Mass.: Harvard University Press, 1972.

_____. *The Theological Imagination.* Philadelphia: Westminster Press, 1981.

Kehoe, Alice B. "The Word Of God." In *Scientists Confront Creationism.* Ed. Laurie Godfrey. New York: W.W. Norton and Co., 1983, pp. 1–12.

Keller, Evelyn Fox. *A Feeling for the Organism: The Life and Work of Barbara McClintock.* New York: W.H. Freeman and Co., 1983.

Kelly, Alfred. *The Descent of Darwin: The Popularity of Darwin in Germany.* Chapel Hill: University of North Carolina Press, 1981.

Kennedy, Gail, ed. *Evolution and Religion.* Lexington, Mass.: D.C. Heath and Company, 1957.

Kent, John. *From Darwin to Blatchford: The Role of Darwinism in Christian Apologetic.* London: Dr. Williams' Trust, 1966.

King, Ursula. "Modern Cosmology and Eastern Thought." In *Cosmology and Theology.* Eds. David Tracy and Nicholas Lash. Concilium 166. New York: Seabury Press, 1983.

Kitcher, Philip. *Abusing Science: The Case against Creationism.* Cambridge, Mass.: M.I.T. Press, 1982.

_____. "Darwin, The Bogeyman." *National Forum* 62(Spring 1983): 28–29.

Klaaren, Eugene M. *Religious Origins of Modern Science.* Grand Rapids, Mich.: Eerdmans, 1972.

Kline, A. David. "Theories, Facts, and Gods: Philosophical Aspects of the Creation—Evolution Controversy." In *Did the Devil Make Darwin Do It?* Ed. D.B. Wilson. Ames: Iowa State University Press, 1983, pp. 37–43.

Kuhn, Thomas S. *The Structure of Scientific Revolutions,* 2nd ed., enlarged. Chicago: University of Chicago Press, 1970.

Kurtz, Paul. "Humanism, Science, and Religion." *National Forum* 62(Spring 1983): 17–20.

_____, ed. *The Humanist Alternative.* Buffalo, N.Y.: Prometheus Books, 1973.

Lack, David. *Evolutionary Theory and Christian Belief: The Unresolved Conflict.* London: Methuen and Co., 1957.

Larson, Arlin T. "Evolution and Creation." *Christian Century* 99(1982): 932.

Laudan, Larry. *Progress and Its Problems.* Berkeley: University of California Press, 1977.

Lewin, Roger. "Creationism on the Defensive in Arkansas." *Science* 215(1982): 33–34.

———. "Creationism Goes on Trial in Arkansas." *Science* 214(1981): 1101–1102, 1104.

———. "Judge's Ruling Hits Hard at Creationism." *Science* 215(1982): 381–83, 384.

———. "Where is the Science in Creation Science." *Science* 215(1982): 142–46.

Lewis, John, ed. *Beyond Chance and Necessity.* London: Garnstone Press, 1974.

———. "Where is the Science in Creation Science." *Science* 215 (1982): 142–46.

Lewis, Ralph W. "Why Scientific Creationism Fails to Meet the Criteria of Science." *Creation/Evolution* 5(1981): 7–11.

Lewontin, R.C. "Darwin's Revolution." *The New York Review,* June 16, 1983, pp. 21–27.

Light, Robley. "Chemistry and Evolution: A New Modern Synthesis?" Lecture in *Darwinism Reconsidered* series, Florida State University, September 14, 1982.

Livingstone, David N. "Evolution as Metaphor and Myth." *Christian Scholar's Review* 12(1983): 111–25.

Livingstone, James C. "Darwin, Darwinism and Theology: Recent Studies." *Religious Studies Review* 8(1982): 105–16.

Loewenberg, Bert James. "The Controversy over Evolution in New England, 1859–1873." *New England Quarterly* 8(1935): 232–57.

———. *Darwinism Comes to America, 1859–1900.* Philadelphia: Fortress Press, 1969. Reprint of 1941 ed.

———. "The Mosaic of Darwinian Thought." *Victorian Studies* 3(1959): 3–18.

———. "The Reaction of American Scientists to Darwinism." *American Historical Review* 38(1933): 687–701.

Lovejoy, Arthur O. *The Great Chain of Being.* Cambridge, Mass.: Harvard University Press, 1936.

Lyons, J.A. *The Cosmic Christ in Origen and Teilhard de Chardin.* London: Oxford University Press, 1982.

McConnell, Francis John. *Borden Parker Bowne: His Life and His Philosophy.* New York: Abingdon, 1929.

MacCormac, Earl R. *Metaphor and Myth in Science and Religion.* Durham, N.C.: Duke University Press, 1976.

———. "Religious Metaphors: Mediators Between Biological and Cultural Evolution that Generate Transcendent Meaning." *Zygon* 18(1983): 45–65.

McFague, Sallie. *Metaphorical Theology.* Philadelphia: Fortress Press, 1983.

MacIntyre, Alasdair, ed. *Metaphysical Beliefs.* London: SCM Press, 1957.

MacKay, Donald M. "Complementarity in Scientific and Theological Thinking." *Zygon* 9(1974): 225–44.

McPherson, Thomas. *The Argument from Design.* London: St. Martin's Press, 1972.

Macquarrie, John. *Twentieth Century Religious Thought: The Frontiers of Philosophy and Theology, 1900–1980.* rev. ed. New York: Charles Scribner's, 1981.

Macy, Christopher. *Science, Reason and Religion.* Buffalo, N.Y.: Prometheus Books, 1974.

Manier, Edward. *The Young Darwin and His Cultural Circle.* Dordrecht: D. Reidel Publishing Co., 1978.

Marsden, George M. *Fundamentalism in American Culture.* New York: Oxford University Press, 1978.

———. "Understanding Fundamentalist Views of Science." In *Science and Creationism.* Ed. Ashley Montagu. New York: Oxford University Press, 1984, pp. 95–116.

Marty, Martin E. "Science Versus Religion: The Old Squabble Simmers Down." *Saturday Review,* December 10, 1977, pp. 29–35.

Mascall, Eric L. *Christian Theology and Natural Science.* New York: The Ronald Press, 1956.
———. *The Openness of Being.* Philadelphia: Westminster Press, 1971.
Mathews, Shailer. *Contributions of Science to Religion.* New York: D. Appleton and Co., 1924.
Mayr, Ernst. "The Nature of the Darwinian Revolution." *Science* 176(1972): 981–89.
Mead, Sidney E. *The Lively Experiment: The Shaping of Christianity in America.* New York: Harper and Row, 1963.
Meland, Bernard E. *The Realities of Faith: The Revolution in Cultural Forms.* New York: Oxford University Press, 1962.
———, ed. *The Future of Empirical Theology.* Chicago: University of Chicago Press, 1969.
Melsen, Andrew G. van. *Evolution and Philosophy.* Duquesne Studies Philosophical Series 19. Pittsburgh: Duquesne University Press, 1965.
Merton, Robert K. *Science, Technology and Society in Seventeenth-Century England.* New York: Harper and Row, 1970. Reprint from *Osiris* 4(1938): 360–632, with new introduction.
———. *Social Theory and Social Structure.* Glencoe, Ill.: The Free Press, 1957.
Meyer, D.H. "American Intellectuals and the Victorian Crisis of Faith," in *Victorian America.* Ed. Daniel Walker. Philadelphia: University of Pennsylvania Press, 1976, pp. 59–77.
Miles, John A., Jr. "Burhoe, Barbour, Mythology, and Sociobiology." *Zygon* 12(1977): 42–71.
Miller, Kenneth. "Answers to Standard Creationist Arguments." *Creation/Evolution* 7(1982): 1–13.
Miller, Randolph Crump. *The American Spirit in Theology.* Philadelphia: The Pilgrim Press, 1974.
Minor, William Sherman. *Creativity in Henry Nelson Wieman.* Metuchen, N.J.: Scarecrow Press, 1977.
Montagu, Ashley, ed. *Science and Creationism.* New York: Oxford University Press, 1984.
Moore, James R. "Evolutionary Theory and Christian Faith." *Christian Scholar's Review* 4(1975): 211–30.
———. *The Post-Darwinian Controversies: A Study of the Protestant Struggle to Come to Terms with Darwin in Great Britain and America, 1870–1900.* Cambridge: Cambridge University Press, 1979.
Moore, John A. "Evolution and Public Education." *Bio-Science* 32(1982): 606–10.
Morin, Alexander J. "Sociobiology and Religion: Conciliation or Confrontation." *Zygon* 15(1980): 397–405.
Morrison, John L. "A History of American Catholic Opinion on the Theory of Evolution, 1859–1950." Ph.D. dissertation, University of Missouri, 1951.
Muelder, Walter G. "The New Debate on Faith, Science, and the Future." *Andover Newton Quarterly* 20(1980): 199–207.
Musser, Donald M. "Two Types of Scientific Theology: Burhoe and Barbour." *Zygon* 12(1977): 72–87.
Nebelsick, Harold P. *Theology and Science in Mutual Modification.* New York: Oxford University Press, 1981.
Neel, Samuel Regester, Jr. "The Reaction of Certain Exponents of American Religious Thought to Darwin's Theory of Evolution." Ph.D. dissertation, Duke University, 1942.
Nelkin, Dorothy. *The Creation Controversy: Science or Scripture in the Schools.* New York: W.W. Norton and Co., 1982.
Nelson, J. Robert. *Science and Our Troubled Conscience.* Philadelphia: Fortress Press, 1980.
———. "A Theologian's Response to Wilson's *On Human Nature.*" *Zygon* 15(1980): 397–405.
Nelson, Kenneth. "Evolution and the Argument from Design." *Religious Studies* 14(1978): 423–43.
Neville, Robert C. *Creativity and God.* New York: Seabury Press, 1980.
Nogar, Raymond J. *The Wisdom of Evolution.* New York: Doubleday and Company, 1963.

Numbers, Ronald L. "Creationism in Twentieth-Century America." *Science* 218(1982): 538–44.

Oakley, Francis. "Christian Theology and the Newtonian Science: The Rise of the Concept of the Laws of Nature." *Church History* 30(1961): 433–57.

Oldroyd, D.R. *Darwinian Impacts: and introduction to the Darwinian Revolution.* Atlantic Highlands, N.J.: Humanities Press, 1980.

Olshewsky, Thomas M. "Between Science and Religion." *Journal of Religion* 62(1982): 242–60.

Ong, Walter J., ed. *Darwin's Vision and Christian Perspectives.* New York: Macmillan, 1960.

Ospovat, Dov. "God and Natural Selection: The Darwinian Idea of Design." *Journal of the History of Biology* 13(1980): 169–94.

Overman, Richard H. *Evolution and the Christian Doctrine of Creation: A Whiteheadian Interpretation.* Philadelphia: Westminster Press, 1967.

Pannill, H. Burnell. *The Religious Faith of John Fiske.* Durham, N.C.: Duke University Press, 1957.

Passmore, John. *A Hundred Years of Philosophy.* New York: Penguin Books, 1957, 1966.

Paul, Harry W. *The Edge of Contingency.* Gainesville: University of Florida Press, 1979.

_____. "Religion and Darwinism: Varieties of Catholic Reactions." In *The Comparative Reception of Darwinism.* Ed. T.F. Glick. Austin: University of Texas Press, 1974, pp. 403–36.

Peckham, Morse. "Darwinism and Darwinisticism." In *The Triumph of Romanticism.* Columbia: University of South Carolina Press, 1970, pp. 176–201.

Pelikan, Jaroslav. *The Christian Intellectual.* New York: Harper and Row, 1965.

_____. "Creation and Causality in the History of Christian Thought." In *Issues in Evolution.* Ed. Sol Tax and Charles Callender. Chicago: University of Chicago Press, 1960, pp. 29–40.

Persons, Stow. "Evolution and Theology in America." In *Evolutionary Thought in America.* New Haven: Yale University Press, 1950, pp. 422–51.

_____. *Free Religion: An American Faith.* New Haven, Conn.: Yale University Press, 1947.

_____. "Religion and Modernity, 1865–1914." In *The Shaping of American Religion.* Eds. James W. Smith and A.L. Jamison. Princeton: Princeton University Press, 1961, pp. 369–84.

Pfeifer, Edward J. "The Genesis of American Neo-Lamarckianism." *Isis* 56(1965): 156–67.

_____. "United States." In *The Comparative Reception of Darwinism.* Ed. T.F. Glick. Austin: University of Texas Press, 1974, pp. 173–205.

Phipps, William E. "Darwin, The Scientific Creationist." *Christian Century* 100(1983): 809–11.

Priest, John. "Scientific Creationism: Structure and Sub-Structure." Lecture in *Darwinism Reconsidered* series, Florida State University, November 30, 1982.

Ramsey, Ian T. *Religion and Science, Conflict and Synthesis.* London: S.P.C.K., 1964.

Raschke, Carl. "From God to Infinity, or How Science Raided Religion's Patent on Mystery." *Zygon* 17(1982): 227–42.

Ratner, Sidney. "Evolution and the Rise of the Scientific Spirit in America." *Philosophy of Science* 3(1936): 104–22.

Raven, Charles Earle. *Natural Religion and Christian Theology.* Cambridge: Cambridge University Press, 1953

_____. *Science, Religion and the Future.* Cambridge: Cambridge University Press, 1943.

Ravin, Arnold W. "On Natural and Human Selection, or Saving Religion." *Zygon* 12(1977): 27–41.

Richardson, Alan. *The Bible in an Age of Science.* Philadelphia: Westminster Press, 1961.

_____. *Science and Existence: Two Ways of Knowledge.* London: SCM Press, 1957.

Roberts, Jon Harlan. "The Impact of Darwinism on American Protestant Theology." Ph.D. dissertation, Harvard University, 1980.

Roberts, Windsor Hall. "The Reaction of American Protestant Churches to the Darwinian Philosophy, 1860–1900." Ph.D. dissertation, University of Chicago, 1936.

Rolston, Holmes, III. "Methods in Scientific and Religious Inquiry." *Zygon* 16(1981): 29–63.

Roy, Rustum. *Experimenting with Truth.* The Hibbert Lectures for 1979. New York: Pergamum Press, 1981.

Rudwick, Martin. "Senses of the Natural World and Senses of God." In *The Sciences and Theology in the Twentieth Century.* Ed. A.R. Peacocke. Notre Dame, Ind.: University of Notre Dame Press, 1981, pp. 241–61.

Ruse, Michael. "Creation Science is Not Science." *Science, Technology, and Human Values* 7(Summer 1982): 72–78.

———. "Darwin's Debt to Philosophy." *Studies in the History of Philosophy and Science* 6(1975): 159–81.

———. *The Darwinian Revolution.* Chicago: University of Chicago Press, 1979.

———. *Darwinism Defended.* Reading, Mass.: Addison-Wesley Publishing Company, 1982.

———. "Philosophical Aspects of the Darwinian Revolution." In *Pragmatism and Purpose.* Eds. L.W. Summer et al. Toronto: University of Toronto Press, 1981, pp. 220–35.

———. "The Relationship between Science and Religion in Britian, 1830–1870." *Church History* 44(1975): 505–22

———. "The Revolution in Biology." *Theoria* 36(1970): 1–22.

———. "Two Biological Revolutions." *Dialectica* 25(1971): 17–38.

Rushdoony, Rousas John. *The Mythology of Science.* Natley, N.J.: Craig Press, 1967.

Russell, Bertrand. *Religion and Science.* London: Oxford University Press, 1935.

Russell, Colin A., ed. *Science and Religious Belief.* London: University of London Press, 1973.

Russett, Cynthia Eagle. *Darwin in America: The Intellectual Response, 1865–1912.* San Francisco: W.H. Freeman Co., 1976.

Rust, Eric C. *Evolutionary Philosophies and Contemporary Faith.* Philadelphia: Westminster Press, 1969.

———. *Nature—Garden or Desert?* Waco, Texas: Word Books, 1971.

———. *Science and Faith: Towards a Theology of Nature.* New York: Oxford University Press, 1967.

Schlegel, Richard. "Is Science the Only Way to Truth?" *Zygon* 17(1982): 343–59.

Schlesinger, Arthur M. *A Critical Period in American Religion, 1875–1900.* Philadelphia: Fortress Press, 1967.

Schlesinger, George. *Religion and Scientific Method.* Dordrecht: D. Reidel Co., 1977.

Schneider, Herbert W. *A History of American Philosophy,* 2nd ed. New York: Columbia University Press, 1963.

———. "The Influence of Darwin and Spencer on American Philosophical Theology." *Journal of the History of Ideas* 6(1945): 3–18.

Schuler, Michael Anthony. "Religious Humanism in Twentieth-Century American Thought." Ph.D. dissertation, Florida State University, 1982.

Schwarz, Hans. "Darwinism between Kant and Haeckel." *Journal of the American Academy of Religion* 48(1980): 581–602.

———. *Our Cosmic Journey.* Minneapolis, Minn.: Augsburg Publishing House, 1977.

———. "The Significance of Evolutionary Thought for American Protestant Theology: Late 19th-Century Resolutions and 20th-Century Problems." *Zygon* 16(1981): 261–84.

Simberloff, Daniel S. "Is All Biology Just a Footnote to Darwin?" Lecture in *Darwinism Reconsidered* series, Florida State University, September 28, 1982.

Simpson, George Gaylord. *The Meaning of Evolution.* rev. ed. New Haven, Conn.: Yale University Press, 1967.

———. *This View of Life: The World of an Evolutionist.* New York: Harcourt Brace and World, 1964.

Singer, Peter. *The Expanding Circle: Ethics and Sociobiology.* New York: Farrar, Straus and Giroux, 1981.

Smart, Ninian. "Religious Vision and Scientific Method." *National Forum* 62(Spring 1983): 3–5.

Smethurst, Arthur F. *Modern Science and Christian Beliefs.* Nashville, Tenn.: Abingdon, 1955, 1957.

Smith, David L. *Symbolism and Growth: The Religious Thought of Horace Bushnell.* Chico, Calif.: Scholar's Press, 1981.

Smith, Gary S. "Calvinists and Evolution, 1870–1920." *Journal of Presbyterian History* 61(1983): 335–52.

Smith, James Ward. "Religion and Science in American Philosophy." In *The Shaping of American Religion.* Eds. J.W. Smith and A.L. Jamison. Princeton, N.J.: Princeton University Press, 1961, pp. 402–42.

Spilsbury, Richard. *Providence Lost: A Critique of Darwinism.* London: Oxford University Press, 1974.

Stebbins, G. Ledyard. *Darwin to DNA, Molecules to Humanity.* San Francisco: W.H. Freeman and Co., 1982.

Stewart, Claude Y. *Nature in Grace: A Study in the Theology of Nature.* Macon, Ga.: Mercer University Press, 1983.

Street, T. Watson. "The Evolution Controversy in the Southern Presbyterian Church." *Journal of the Presbyterian Historical Society* 37(1959): 232–50.

Szasz, Ferenc Morton. *The Divided Mind of Protestant America, 1880–1930.* University, Ala.: University of Alabama Press, 1982.

Templeton, John N. *The Humble Approach: Scientists Discover God.* New York: Seabury Press, 1981.

Thwaites, William and Awbrey, Frank. "Biological Evolution and the Second Law." *Creation/Evolution* 4(1981): 5–7.

Torrance, Thomas F. *Christian Theology and Scientific Culture.* New York: Oxford University Press, 1981.

———. *Divine and Contingent Order.* Oxford: Oxford University Press, 1981.

———. *The Ground and Grammar of Theology.* Charlottesville: University of Virginia Press, 1980.

———. *Space, Time and Incarnation.* New York: Oxford University Press, 1969.

———. *Theological Science.* New York: Oxford University Press, 1969.

Toulmin, Stephen. "Contemporary Scientific Mythology." In *Metaphysical Beliefs.* Ed. Alasdair MacIntyre. London: SCM Press, 1957, pp. 13–81.

———. *The Return to Cosmology: Postmodern Science and the Theology of Nature.* Berkeley: University of California Press, 1982.

Trachtenberg, Alan. "The Darwinian Metaphor in America." Lecture in *Darwinism Reconsidered* series, Florida State University, October 5, 1982.

Tracy, David. *Blessed Rage for Order: The New Pluralism in Theology.* New York: Seabury Press, 1975.

Turner, Frank Miller. *Between Science and Religion.* New Haven: Yale University Press, 1974.

Warren, Sidney. *American Freethought, 1860–1914.* New York: Columbia University Press, 1943.

Waters, F. William. *The Way In and The Way Out: Science and Religion Reconciled.* Toronto: Oxford University Press, 1967.

Wavel, Bruce B. "Scientific and Religious Universes of Discourse." *Zygon* 17(1982): 327–42.

Webb, George Ernest. "The 'Baconian' Origins of Scientific Creationism." *National Forum* 62(Spring 1983): 33–35.

Wells, Albert N. *The Christian Message in a Scientific Age.* Richmond: John Knox Press, 1962.

Werkmeister, W.H. *A History of Philosophical Ideas in America.* New York: The Ronald Press, 1949.

White, Andrew Dickson. *A History of the Warfare of Science with Theology in Christendom.* New York: D. Appleton and Co., 1896.

White, Edward A. *Science and Religion in American Thought: The Impact of Naturalism.* Stanford, Calif.: Stanford University Press, 1952.

White, Morton. *Science and Sentiment in America.* New York: Oxford University Press, 1972.

Whitehouse, Walter A. *Christian Faith and the Scientific Attitude.* Edinburgh: Oliver, 1952.

_____. *Creation, Science and Theology: Essays in Response to Karl Barth.* Grand Rapids, Mich.: Eerdman's, 1981.

Wiener, Philip P. *Evolution and the Founders of Pragmatism.* Cambridge, Mass.: Harvard University Press, 1949.

Wildiers, N. Max. *The Theologian and His Universe.* Trans. Paul Dunphy. New York: Seabury Press, 1982.

Williams, Daniel Day. *The Andover Liberals.* New York: Octagon Books Reprint, 1941, 1970.

Wilson, David B., ed. *Did the Devil Make Darwin Do It? Modern Perspectives on the Creation—Evolution Controversy.* Ames: The Iowa State University Press, 1983.

Wilson, John B. "Darwin and the Transcendentalists." *Journal of the History of Ideas* 26(1965): 286–90.

Wood, John K. *The Nature of the Conflicts between Science and Religion.* Logan: Utah State University, 1962.

Young, Norman. *Creator, Creation, and Faith.* Philadelphia: Westminster Press, 1976.

Young, Robert M. "Darwin's Metaphor: Does Nature Select?" *Monist* 55(1971): 442–503.

_____. "The Historiographic and Ideological Contexts of the Nineteenth-Century Debate on Man's Place in Nature." In *Changing Perspectives in the History of Science.* Eds. Mikulas Teich and Robert Young. London: Heinemann Educational Books, 1973, pp. 344–438.

_____. "The Impact of Darwin on Conventional Thought." In *The Victorian Crisis of Faith.* Ed. Anthony Symondson. London: S.P.C.K., 1970, pp. 13–36.

Index